L2 Writing in the Global Context:
Represented, Underrepresented, and Unrepresented Voices

全球视野下的二语写作研究：
已知与待知

主 编
（美）Tony Silva 王俊菊 张 聪 （美）Joshua M. Paiz

外语教学与研究出版社
FOREIGN LANGUAGE TEACHING AND RESEARCH PRESS
北京 BEIJING

图书在版编目（CIP）数据

全球视野下的二语写作研究：已知与待知：英文 ／（美）托尼·席尔瓦
(Tony Silva) 等主编. -- 北京：外语教学与研究出版社，2016.9（2016.9 重印）
ISBN 978-7-5135-8059-5

I. ①全… II. ①托… III. ①第二语言－写作－研究－英文 IV.
①H05

中国版本图书馆 CIP 数据核字（2016）第 222750 号

出 版 人　蔡剑峰
责任编辑　巢小倩　　付分钗
封面设计　高　蕾
出版发行　外语教学与研究出版社
社　　址　北京市西三环北路 19 号（100089）
网　　址　http://www.fltrp.com
印　　刷　北京九州迅驰传媒文化有限公司
开　　本　650×980　1/16
印　　张　19.75
版　　次　2016 年 9 月第 1 版 2016 年 9 月第 2 次印刷
书　　号　ISBN 978-7-5135-8059-5
定　　价　59.90 元

购书咨询：（010）88819926　电子邮箱：club@fltrp.com
外研书店：https://waiyants.tmall.com
凡印刷、装订质量问题，请联系我社印制部
联系电话：（010）61207896　电子邮箱：zhijian@fltrp.com
凡侵权、盗版书籍线索，请联系我社法律事务部
举报电话：（010）88817519　电子邮箱：banquan@fltrp.com
法律顾问：立方律师事务所　刘旭东律师
　　　　　中咨律师事务所　殷　斌律师
物料号：280590001

Introduction

The purpose of this book is to take a broad look at the field of second language (L2) writing studies as we continue through the second decade of the 21st century. To achieve this purpose, thirteen authors explore the status of second language writing and writing instruction in a number of national or regional contexts—some well represented, some underrepresented, and some largely unrepresented in the currently published scholarship on second language writing. It is hoped that this book will help to broaden the scope of second language writing studies, especially by recognizing what is being done and what contributions are being made by scholars working in areas that are typically neglected by the field and, consequently, move the field toward a more truly global perspective.

In the opening chapter, Neomy Storch notes that Australia is a multicultural nation with a linguistically diverse population and that the recent influx of international students into the Australian higher education system has greatly added to the system's diversity. She adds that this diversity has been the impetus for a strong interest in research on second language learning and teaching. The chapter begins with a brief socio-political snapshot of Australia—outlining important policy decisions at the macro (government) and micro level (Australian Applied Linguistics Association). This snapshot contextualizes the review of the research that follows and helps to explain its focus. The review of research on L2 writing conducted by Australian scholars shows a focus on three main areas: (a) writing assessment and writing development, (b) the nature of academic writing based predominantly on analysis of academic and professional texts, and (c) issues related to writing pedagogy and feedback. This chapter concludes with a discussion of the main trends in the reviewed research and its contributions to L2 writing scholarship.

In Chapter 2, Alister Cumming describes the development of research on writing in second languages in Canada from the 1980s to the present. He chronicles how three generations of researchers have addressed issues arising from Canada's social policies for bilingualism, immigrant settlement, and international education, particularly in the culturally diverse cities of Montreal, Toronto, and Vancouver and from within graduate programs at major universities in those and other cities. It is noted that (a) the first generation in the 1980s applied perspectives on cognitive processes and rhetorical characteristics of writing in English as a mother tongue to investigations of second language writing in English among adults at universities and young children in schools; (b) in the 1990s a second generation of Canadian scholars established programs of research focused on composing processes, writing for academic purposes, assessment, and establishing innovative educational programs; and (c) by the mid-2010s, a third generation of Canadian and Canadian-educated scholars have established themselves as researchers of second language writing at universities across Canada and around the world. In these positions, Canadian researchers have addressed such issues as biliteracy and identity, development and transfer of academic multiliteracies, sociocultural perspectives on literacy development, applications of systemic-functional linguistics, writing assessment practices to promote learning, writing in workplaces, the functional value of the first language in second language writing, textual borrowing practices, multimedia innovations, critical and community-based literacy, teacher development, design based research, and systematic syntheses of specific aspects of second language writing research.

In the third chapter, Junju Wang describes a study that explores the ecology of a number of previous studies on L2 writing in the Chinese context. For this study, a total of 11,889 articles published in 1,417 journals between 1962 and 2015 were collected and analyzed for categorical features concerning development pattern and level of scholarship, as well as the subject matter and focal areas of these studies. Her results indicate that the number of studies on L2 writing in China are increasing and can be divided into three phases of development: the "early period", the "developmental period", and the "flourishing period". Wang notes that while most papers are non-empirical studies published in humanities journals, they have undergraduate L2 writing as their primary subject matter and are mostly focused on the teaching and learning of L2 writing. Therefore, she suggests that a disproportionate and off-balance phenomena are the characteristics of the L2 writing field in China. Wang concludes that L2 writing in China is a young, active, and promising area of studies, and she asserts that to improve the ecology of studies in this field, efforts should be made to develop its own theories, diversify its methodology, balance its focal areas, and promote the quality and level of studies.

In Chapter 4, Icy Lee examines the teaching, learning, and assessment of EFL writing in Hong Kong schools, with a specific focus on the "best practices" advice that has informed the writing curriculum vis-à-vis teachers' actual practices in local classrooms. Her review uncovers a number of areas in which teachers' practices are at odds with the "best practices". For example, she notes that although teachers are advised to avoid a primarily error-focused approach to feedback in the writing classroom, the majority of teachers spend a great deal of time responding to errors in student writing. This is despite the fact that a process pedagogy has been advocated to complement a text-based approach that sensitizes students to issues of genre in writing. Hong Kong writing classrooms are largely dominated by a product-oriented approach that values the timed impromptu writing model. Lee discusses the disconnects between the suggested principles and teachers' actual practices and concludes with recommendations to bridge the idealism-realism gap.

In the fifth chapter, Miyuki Sasaki examines links between goals, teaching practices, and student achievement in the third (and final) year of English writing instruction in Japanese senior high schools. She explains that the final year was judged to represent the end-product of six years of formal English education in Japan because over 95% of 18-year-olds complete their education up to this level compared to the nearly 50% who proceed on to tertiary education. Drawing on Gaddis' (2002) historical-ecological approach, Sasaki compares the goals set by the most recent Course of Study [1] with the results of a nationwide survey of the writing abilities of third-year senior high school students and of their teachers' classroom practices related to English writing. Her findings reveal a discrepancy between curricular goals, pedagogical activities, and students' abilities—suggesting that the goal of cultivating the students' ability to write coherent texts was neither practiced nor acquired in classrooms. She compares the results of two nationwide achievement tests administered in 2002 and 2005, and affected by the particular Course of Study in effect at the time, and analyzes the high-stakes nationwide university entrance exams taken by many of those who took the 2005 test. Based on this analysis, she suggests that students' underwhelming performance on these exams was crucially related to the discrepancy between governmental goals and classroom practices. Based on these findings, Sasaki discusses directions for future English writing instruction that could better empower Japanese students to survive in a rapidly globalizing world.

In the sixth chapter, Yeon Hee Choi provides a review of master's and doctoral theses and research articles on L2 writing published in South Korea from 1965 to 2012 in order to explore historical development and emerging trends. She also discusses the interconnected relationships of L2 writing studies with various institutional and pedagogical contexts (including the influence of South Korean government policies), as well as the influence of international L2 writing theories, practices, and research trends. She focuses her review on studies of adults, including university students, due to the lack of L2 writing instruction in the secondary school context; the institutional context of authors who are university academics; and the influence of the international field of L2 writing, which has focused on academic writing in tertiary education. The author suggests that the review reveals that writing instruction has been a dominant research topic from the beginning of L2 writing studies and that a

---

1 These are the curricular standards issued by the Japanese Ministry of Education, Culture, Sports, Science, and Technology (MEXT).

variety of topics including genre, academic writing, and writers' affective and/or cognitive factors are currently trending in the literature. She also points out that the assessment-dominant educational culture and the minimal role of L2 writing in South Korea have created a vicious cycle—one that leads to a lack of research infrastructure. Yet, the author notes that the growing number of theses and articles on L2 writing represents the emergence of the field. Finally, Choi addresses the unique features of the Korean EFL writing research context and its issues and challenges, including a lack of research networks and collaboration. She ends with a discussion on future directions and development of South Korea-based L2 writing studies.

In Chapter 7, Fatima Esseili presents findings from research on second language writing in Lebanon. Her study is based on a synthesis of 72 sources originating from three major universities in the country: the Lebanese American University, Balamand University, and the American University of Beirut. She begins by describing the Lebanese context and the infrastructure that supports the teaching and learning of writing in English and proceeds to a discussion of Lebanese writers' characteristics and their writing processes. Her discussion of student-writers' characteristics and processes focuses on L2 writing difficulties, attitudes, students' motivation, textual borrowing, transfer, and translation. Esseili also addresses research on types of written corrective feedback, highlighting studies on teachers and students' feedback preferences, peer-review, and error correction. Writing assessment and WAC/WID initiatives are other areas discussed in this synthesis. Esseili concludes by offering possible future directions for research on EFL writing in Lebanon.

In the eighth chapter, John Bitchener notes that, despite the limited number of teachers and researchers working in the field of L2 writing in New Zealand, the contribution from this national context is relatively extensive and that many of the prominent areas of international L2 writing research are ones that have been contributed to by New Zealand researchers. His chapter backgrounds the contexts in which L2 writing is taught and researched, outlines some of the main areas of L2 writing research that have been addressed and that are currently being researched and published by New Zealand researchers (including doctoral students), and assesses the contribution of this work to the field as a whole.

In Chapter 9, Łukasz Salski argues that EFL writing instruction in Poland has been influenced by two opposing traditions. He notes that, on the one hand, in spite of Poland's rich literary heritage, Polish schools pay relatively little attention to teaching writing in Polish as a native language; and conversely, since writing is highly valued in the English-language context, writing permeates instruction in English as a foreign language. Salski asserts that this tendency has been reinforced by the popularity of English language examinations—the UCLES exams, TOEFL, or IELTS, all of which include a writing test and are prepared for by many Polish students. He says that, as a result, many Polish EFL learners admit that their EFL writing instruction has been more systematic and more effective than the Polish L1 writing practice they have done at school and that this paradoxical imbalance can be observed in the context of writing research—noting that although writing studies is far from being a discipline commonly recognized in Poland, a number of Polish researchers have studied writing in English as a foreign language. Salski begins his chapter by characterizing writing instruction in Poland in general and then sketches out the Polish EFL writing context and outlines EFL writing research done in Poland, referring both to studies carried out by renowned scholars and to those done by a younger generation of researchers, often within the general field of EFL studies. Finally, he presents what appear to be the prospects of the field of EFL writing in Poland and mentions initiatives aiming at establishing a united community of foreign language writing specialists in Poland and Eastern Europe.

In the tenth chapter, Diane Pecorari explains that the tradition of second language writing studies is less well developed in Sweden than in some other countries. She explores some of the reasons for this phenomenon and identifies two main factors. She states that several sociolinguistic factors (including the absence of a liberal arts tradition in Swedish universities and a belief that Swedish university students have, or should have, sufficient skills in English) have contributed to research interest in applied linguistics being channeled into other directions. She suggests that this has resulted in a situation in which Swedish scholars are somewhat underrepresented in second language writing studies. She notes that, nonetheless, there is an active body of scholarship in Sweden exploring questions of considerable relevance for second language writing, although it frequently appears outside of the dominant channels for scholarly communication (such as the *Journal of Second Language Writing,* or the Symposium on Second Language Writing) most closely associated with the discipline. Pecorari believes that it is therefore relevant to ask why this is the case. One possible explanation, she asserts, lies in the fact that the field has traditionally placed strong emphasis on English, rather than other second languages; on adult rather than younger learners; and on academic writing as opposed to other genres. The author concludes that this rather narrow focus in the field may well cause scholars to perceive that their work does not fit neatly into the area of second language writing, and in turn to cause the field to lose potentially important diversity.

In Chapter 11, Tatyana Yakhontova, suggests that foreign language writing has attracted little attention in Ukraine in the recent past, mostly due to specific cultural assumptions and sociopolitical circumstances. She notes that, in Ukrainian culture, writing is generally treated as a gift, and emphasis has traditionally been laid upon the so-called "culture of the word," which reflects a striving towards grammatically and stylistically correct written texts. Yakhontova adds that, in Ukrainian foreign language education, writing has traditionally been viewed as one of four language skills and that this may have contributed to disconnects between how writing is viewed and taught in primary and secondary education versus how it is approached in tertiary settings. A growing interest in L2 writing in Ukraine has led to the formation of the Center for English Academic Writing at the Ivan Franko National University of L'viv, which is tasked with increasing awareness of L2 writing issues. She concludes that, though publications on researching and teaching writing are scarce in Ukraine, more and more papers devoted to theoretical and applied aspects of writing in foreign languages (primarily English) have started to appear in Ukrainian journals and that it can be anticipated that the field of L2 writing in Ukraine will further develop based on Western approaches with the simultaneous preservation of the traditional, for this part of the world, focus on linguistic and stylistic aspects of writing.

In Chapter 12, Tony Silva addresses the current status of second language writing studies primarily in institutions of higher education in the United States, focusing specifically on (a) the rapid and ongoing expansion of interest in and work on second language writing and some of the reasons for it; (b) the steadily increasing development of disciplinary infrastructure in terms of scholarly journals, book series, authored and edited books, academic units, doctoral programs, dissertations, professional organizations, professional conferences, special interest groups and committees, and resources for research; and (c) trends in disciplinary influences, ideology, inquiry paradigms, research methodology, and instruction as well as a strong move toward internationalization.

In the final chapter, Melinda Reichelt explains that many factors have influenced the development of L2 writing instruction and research in Western Europe, including the following: the lack of a long-standing tradition of explicit writing instruction in higher education; the multilingualism of Western Europe; the significant role of English in that context; and the fact that much L2 writing undertaken in Europe is FL writing. She notes that L2 writing specialists in Western Europe have developed pedagogical and research approaches that are suitable to the unique circumstances in which they work and that they have also created local organizations and journals that foster connections among themselves and the worldwide community of L2 writing specialists. Reichelt delineates how local factors impact approaches to teaching L2 writing in Western Europe and describes Western European organizations, affiliated conferences, and academic journals devoted to L2 writing. She also overviews the following key lines of research regarding L2 writing instruction in Western Europe: text analysis; writers' processes and strategies; language learning and errors in relation to L2 writing; assessment; publishing in English; and computer-assisted language learning (CALL).

About the Authors

John Bitchener is Professor of Applied Linguistics at AUT University, Auckland, New Zealand. His teaching and research interests include the theoretical and empirical contribution of written corrective feedback for second language (L2) development, the role of individual and contextual factors in L2 learning, and supervisor feedback on doctoral students' thesis/dissertation writing. His research has been published in a wide range of leading international journals like *Applied Linguistics, TESOL Quarterly, Modern Language Journal,* and the *Journal of Second Language Writing.* His recent books include *Written Corrective Feedback in Second Language Acquisition and Writing* (Routledge, 2012), *Written Corrective Feedback for L2 Development* (Multilingual Matters, 2016), and *Writing an Applied Linguistics Thesis or Dissertation: A Guide to Presenting Empirical Research, 2009* (Palgrave Macmillan). *An Approach to Overcoming the L2 Writing Issues of Doctoral Students* (Routledge, 2016) is likely to be popular with both supervisors and students.

Yeon Hee Choi is Professor of English Education at Ewha Womans University in Seoul, South Korea, and currently president of the Korea Association of Teachers of English (KATE). She earned her M.A. in TESOL and Ph.D. in Applied Linguistics at the University of Illinois, Urbana-Champaign. She was Secretary General of Asia TEFL. She has been involved in diverse government projects, including the development of the national English curriculum and national English ability test (NEAT). She has presented her papers at international conferences including TESOL, AAAL, and SSLW and has published books and research articles on L2/EFL reading, writing, assessment, and written discourse analysis.

Alister Cumming is Professor in the Centre for Educational Research on Languages and Literacies (CERLL, formerly the Modern Language Centre) at the Ontario Institute for Studies in Education, University of Toronto, where he has been employed since 1991, following briefer periods at the University of British Columbia, McGill University, Carleton University, and Concordia University. From 2013 to 2016 Professor Cumming is also a Changjiang Scholar in the National Research Centre for Foreign Language Education at Beijing Foreign Studies University. His research and teaching focus on writing in second languages, language assessment, language program evaluation and policies, and research methods.

Fatima Esseili received her Ph.D. in Second Language Studies/ESL from Purdue University. She is currently Assistant Professor of English/TESOL at the University of Dayton. Her research focuses on second language writing and world Englishes with a particular focus on the Middle East. Recent publications include a coauthored study on international students in the US composition course (2015) and a discussion of English language teaching in Lebanese schools (2014). In addition to teaching at various US universities, Dr. Esseili has wide experience teaching EFL in international contexts such as China, Lebanon, the UAE, and Mexico.

Icy Lee is Professor in the Faculty of Education at The Chinese University of Hong Kong, where she is currently serving as Chair of the Department of Curriculum and Instruction. Her research interests are in second language writing and second language teacher education. Her works have appeared in international journals such as *Journal of Second Language Writing, TESOL Quarterly, Language Teaching, Language Teaching Research, ELT Journal,* and *System.*

Diane Pecorari is Professor of English Linguistics at Linnaeus University in southern Sweden. Her research interests include English for academic purposes and educational linguistics. She is currently investigating the outcomes of English-medium instruction in European higher education. Her recent publications include *Teaching to Avoid Plagiarism* (Open University Press) and *Introducing English for Academic Purposes* (Routledge; with Maggie Charles).

Melinda Reichelt is Professor of English at the University of Toledo, where she directs the ESL writing program and teaches courses in TESOL and linguistics. She is also a member of the editorial board of the *Journal of Second*

Language Writing. She has published many articles on second language writing and has co-edited, with Tony Cimasko, of a collection on foreign language writing entitled, *Foreign Language Writing: Principles and Practices* (Parlor Press, 2011).

Łukasz Salski is Assistant Professor at the Institute of English, University of Łódź, where he is a pre-service teacher trainer and English language writing instructor. His academic interests include writing studies and second/foreign language acquisition and learning. He coordinates the Institute's writing courses and writing center, the first initiative of this kind in the country. He is the organizer of an international conference on foreign language writing practice and theory FLOW (Foreign Language Opportunities in Writing). He also serves on the board of the European Writing Centers Association.

Miyuki Sasaki is Professor in the Graduate School of Humanities and Social Sciences at Nagoya City University, where she teaches courses in teacher education and applied linguistics. She has contributed chapters to books published by Multilingual Matters, Kluwer Academic, and Blackwell. Her articles have appeared in *Language Learning, Language Testing, Journal of Second Language Writing, Journal of Pragmatics, International Review of Applied Linguistics,* and *Word*. Her current research interests include the longitudinal development of L1 and L2 writing ability, effects on ratings of the value and belief systems of Japanese L1 and English L2 composition raters, and effects of the environment on L2 learning motivation.

Tony Silva directs the Graduate Program in Second Language Studies/ESL in the Department of English at Purdue University, where he teaches graduate courses for Ph.D., M.A., and Certificate students and writing support courses for graduate and undergraduate international students. With Ilona Leki, he founded and edited the *Journal of Second Language Writing* from 1992-2007, and with Paul Kei Matsuda he founded and hosted the (now annual and international) Symposium on Second Language Writing from 1998-2013. He has co-edited or co-authored eight books and has published articles in numerous journals. He is an active member of the TESOL International Association, where he is currently a member of the Board of Directors; he has also served the Conference on College Composition and Communication as a member of the Executive Board.

Neomy Storch is a senior lecturer in the School of Languages & Linguistics, at the University of Melbourne. She lectures on a range of ESL and Applied Linguistics subjects and convenes the ESL program. Her research interests focus on issues related to L2 pedagogy and in particular the teaching of L2 writing. These issues include collaborative writing, writing development, and feedback on writing. Her publications include two books, one entitled *Collaborative Writing in L2 Classrooms* (2013) and another book co-authored with John Bitchener, entitled *Written Corrective Feedback for L2 Development* (2016).

Junju Wang is Professor of Applied Linguistics and Dean of the School of Foreign Languages at Shandong University. She holds her B.A. in English, M.A. in bilingual translation, and Ph.D. in applied English linguistics. Her research interests include second language writing, EFL teaching and learning, teacher development, and language testing and assessment. Professor Wang is the author of *From Ideas to Text: A Cognitive Study of English Writing Processes* and the co-author of *Introduction to Academic English Writing*. She is also the editor of several books, and her published articles appear in both domestic and international journals.

Tatyana Yakhontova is Professor of English for Specific Purposes at the Ivan Franko National University of L'viv. Her current research interests lie within the fields of genre and discourse analysis, contrastive rhetoric, and stylistics. Professor Yakhontova has published more than 140 papers in Ukrainian and international volumes and journals, the first textbook in Ukraine on English academic writing, and a monograph on genres of research communication. Together with her colleagues, she founded the Center for English Academic Writing—the first in Ukraine and one of the first writing support structures in Eastern Europe. She has given plenary and panel presentations at more than 60 international conferences, was awarded grants from several international scientific and educational foundations, and participated in a number of international research projects.

Table of Contents

Chapter 1

L2 Writing Research in Australia: Assessing, Analyzing and Teaching L2 Writing

Neomy Storch

The University of Melbourne

Introduction

This paper aims to showcase research conducted by Australian scholars on topics related to second language (L2) writing. In reviewing this research I drew on research published mainly in the past 10 years or so as well as forthcoming publications. I have also attempted to include the work of established and less known scholars, published in international journals as well as in Australian journals which may not be as well known to an international audience (e.g., *The Australian Review of Applied Linguistics, Prospect, The University of Sydney papers in TESOL, TESOL in Context*).

In order to contextualize the review I begin with a brief snapshot of Australia's linguistically diverse population, a diversity augmented more recently by the internationalization of the education sector. I then present a chronology of significant government policies as well as milestones in the history of applied linguistics in Australia. Research on L2 writing in Australia shows a focus on the following three broad areas: writing assessment and development, the nature of academic writing, and writing pedagogy. I discuss these areas of research in terms of key findings and the contributions of this research to L2 writing scholarship.

A Snapshot of Australia: A Linguistically Diverse Population

Australia is the sixth largest nation in the world (in terms of land area), but a relatively small country in terms of its population. Its current population is just over 23 million and is predicted to grow by about a million every year. The main driver of population growth is and has been net migration (contributing to 60% of the population growth). People born overseas currently make up about one quarter of the total population (About Australia, 2013).

In total, over seven million people from 200 countries have migrated to Australia since 1945 (Department of Immigration and Citizenship, n.d.). Whereas post war migrants came predominantly from Europe (e.g., Greece, Italy, East European countries), later waves have come predominantly from Asia, from China, India, and Vietnam. Among more recent migrant groups, there are also refugees from Africa.

Although English is the national language of Australia, more than 300 different languages are spoken at home (Department of Immigration and Citizenship, n.d.). These languages include about 60 indigenous languages (Walsh & Yallop, 2005). Chinese is now the most widely spoken language after English (Orton, 2008).

This linguistically diverse population has been the impetus for a strong interest in research on second language learning and teaching. Another factor that helps explain perhaps why certain issues have received more research attention than others, and how the research agenda in Australia differs to that in other major English speaking countries is successive government policies. In the following section I outline some of these policies in a chronological order.

Key Dates and Developments

Although migrants came to Australia in fairly large numbers directly after WWII, the initial government policy was that of assimilation and monolingualism (English). In 1973, however, the government introduced a policy of multiculturalism, a policy which finally recognized the value that diverse languages and cultures bring to Australian society. Language diversity began to be celebrated, and a number of languages beyond the traditional foreign languages (French, German, and, of course, Latin) began to be offered at schools and universities.

In 1976, the Applied Linguistics Association of Australia (ALAA) was established. McNamara (2001) notes that unlike the USA and UK, where applied linguistics had its roots in the English language teaching of international students, in Australia the association had its roots in foreign language teaching (particularly in the university sector) and research on language maintenance in migrant communities. The first graduate programs in applied linguistics were established in 1980 in Melbourne and Sydney.

In the early 1980s, the government recognized the need to provide migrants with English language tuition for successful settlement and the Adult Migrant English Program (AMEP) was established (for more details, see Moore & Hargreaves, 2009). AMEP also provided a site for research into ESL teaching and assessment scales. Furthermore, in 1987 a new national policy on languages was announced which funded the establishment of a number of research centers. Many of the research projects in these centers focused on developing language tests and assessment scales.

In the late 1980s we see two further important changes: the arrival of international students and a burgeoning industry offering English language intensive courses for overseas students (ELICOS). The research emphasis shifted from teaching ESL to migrants to the teaching of English for Academic Purposes (EAP) to prepare international students for undergraduate and graduate programs.

Recent migration trends and the strengthening trade links with Asia have led Australia to increasingly see itself as part of the Asian Pacific region. In 1995, the Australian government began prioritizing the learning of Asian languages (Chinese, Japanese, Indonesian and Korean) (see Lo Bianco, 2012). Public investment in these four languages has been extensive.[1] Research has focused on how achievement in these Asian languages should be measured, whether a generic framework is appropriate, and how learners' first language affects performance in the foreign languages studied.

From the mid-1990s until today, there has been a big growth in international students, particularly in the university sector. In 2012 international students formed 28% of the 1.2 million higher education students in Australia compared to just over 21% in 2010 (Australian Education International, 2012). The majority of international students are from non-English speaking backgrounds (NESB), particularly from Asian countries, with China being the largest source country of international students in Australia. The influx of international students has added to the diversity of learners across the Australian education system, but particularly in the higher education sector. This diverse student population has raised issues of linguistic and cultural adjustments.

Let me now turn to the discussion of the three main areas of research related to L2 writing that have been conducted in Australia.

Writing Assessment: Assessing Performance and Development

Assessment has featured prominently in L2 writing research in Australia. This focus can be partially attributed to the establishment of research centers and their focus on language testing as noted above. This body of research can

---

1 Despite the investment, the initial increase in enrolments, particularly in Japanese and Indonesian (Lo Bianco & Slaugher, 2009) has not been sustained. It is clear from both expert and media reports (e.g., Tovey, 2013) that enrolments in Asian languages (with the exception of Chinese) are dropping, reflecting similar trends for all language enrolments in the senior school.

be further subdivided into two large sub-areas: writing assessment tasks and the impact of learners' L1 background on L2 writing performance. Each sub-area has focused on a different L2 population. Thus, whereas the former has focused on ESL learners, initially migrants and then international students entering Australian universities, the latter has focused on foreign language learners, and mainly in the school sector.

Assessing Writing Performance: Tasks

Following the establishment of AMEP, tests and assessment scales were developed in order to place migrants into level-appropriate ESL classes (see discussion of the development of the Australian Second Language Proficiency Scales by Ingram and Wylie in Moore, 2007). Subsequent research focused on the development and implementation of assessment tasks (e.g., Brindley, 2000; Moore & Hargreaves, 2009), including writing tasks that can be used with low/pre-literacy adult ESL learners, as is the case with refugees coming from African countries (Moore, 2007).

Writing tasks used by IELTS and TOEFL have also been investigated by Australian researchers. Both testing authorities have funded a number of studies in Australia, especially IELTS. The use of IELTS is more widespread in Australia, not only for assessing proficiency for university entrance purposes but also for migration and for some professional registration purposes.

A number of these funded studies have considered the tasks used in the writing tests. For example, Moore, and Morton (2005) analyzed and compared IELTS Writing Task 2 (argumentative essay) and a large number (n = 155) of assessment tasks in undergraduate and graduate courses for the kind of language and content they require of learners. The researchers found that university tasks are based on research whereas responses to IELTS Task 2 tend to rely on prior knowledge. Furthermore, university tasks require the use of a wider range of rhetorical functions (e.g., summarizing and synthesizing) than those in IELTS Writing Task 2. Moore and Morton concluded that Writing Task

2 seems to share more characteristics with non-academic genres (e.g., letters to the editor) than with authentic academic writing tasks. These findings have implications for the predictive validity of IELTS writing assessment tasks.

Two studies, also funded by IELTS, are currently investigating whether IELTS writing tasks reflect the writing needs of the professions. One study, led by Moore and Morton, is examining the demands made by the writing tasks on the IELTS General Training (GT) version and surveying members of a range of professions about their perspectives on these tasks. Another project led by Knoch, and in which I am involved, aims to analyze IELTS writing tasks (on both the GT and academic versions of the test) and university written assessment tasks, and compare them to the writing tasks in the professions. This study focuses on two professions (accounting and engineering) and plans to gather information (interviews and analysis of writing samples) from a range of stakeholders (university lecturers, students, employers).

Another research project led by Knoch (Knoch, Macqueen & O'Hagan, forthcoming) has compared the discourse produced by students on two TOEFL iBT writing tasks: the independent task and the integrated task. This work extends on the earlier work of Cumming, Kantor, Baba, Erdosy, Eouanzoui and James (2005). The study also sought to identify what features of writing are typical of different score levels of the TOEFL iBT. The study used a large number of discourse analytical measures, including new measures specifically designed for this study (e.g., density patterns). Preliminary findings suggest that the two tasks elicit significantly different language from the test takers and that the discourse at the various score levels is different.

Assessing Writing Performance: Learner Background

Learners' language background and its impact on L2 achievement, including writing achievement, has received scant research attention in Australia until fairly recently. This is quite surprising given Australia's history of migration and hence the linguistically diverse profile of learners in any foreign language class. Unlike the body of research on tasks and writing assessment, the studies on this topic have been conducted with foreign language learners, and predominantly with school aged children.

The first scholars to investigate the issue of learner background in Australian schools were Elder (1996) and Clyne, Fernandez, Chen, and Summo-O'Connell (1997). These studies compared the performance of background and non-background learners on commonly taught European languages (e.g., German, Italian) and on Chinese and demonstrated the complexity of categorizing background learners because of the learners' varying degrees of linguistic and cultural association with the target language.[1]

With the growth in migrants from Asia, the prioritization and investment by the Australian government in Asian languages, and the influx of international students from Asia, interest in the impact of learner language background on achievement has been reignited. The focus of this research has been predominantly on background learners in Asian language classes in Australian schools. A large scale research project entitled *Student Achievement in Asian Languages Education* (SAALE) was conducted by a team of Australian language policy and testing experts and led by Scarino (see Scarino, Elder, Iwashita, Kim, Kohler & Scrimgeour, 2011)

SAALE is the first study in Australia to systematically investigate and develop baseline descriptions of student achievements for diverse learner groups learning Asian languages (Chinese, Indonesian, Japanese and Korean) in schools from kindergarten through to the final year of school (K–12). These languages are perceived as posing a distinct challenge in the Australian context because of the linguistic and cultural distance from English. The research

---

1 In Australia the distinction between background and non-background learners is not uniform across the states (see discussion in Elder et al., 2012; Scarino, 2012). For example, in some states learners are allocated to different streams in language classes in the upper secondary school (Years 11-12), based on their self-reported exposure to the target language. In other states, allocation is based on a set of eligibility criteria. However, the curriculum and text books used in the different streams may in fact be the same. Furthermore, some states use complex scaling procedures to adjust for learners' background in the final year language grade (final year grades are important as they determine university offers). The scales aim to provide an incentive to non-background learners and deal with the perceived advantage of background learners.

project considered achievement in speaking and writing and the impact of two factors—length of language instruction and the learner's linguistic background relative to the target language (TL) as well as the interaction of these two factors. However, my discussion here is limited to studies that considered the impact of learner background on L2 writing achievement. The project required students to complete two writing tasks: a self introduction (formal register) and a response to a blog about visiting Australia (informal register). I summarise here three of the studies from the projects which dealt with performance on L2 writing.

Scrimgeour (2012) investigated the writing performance of learners of Chinese in Year 10 by comparing the performance of two groups: background learners ($n = 40$) who spoke Mandarin or Cantonese at home and non-background learners ($n = 70$) on the two writing tasks. A comparison of the writing scores confirmed that background learners performed at a significantly higher level than the non-background learners. However, a number of distinctive features characterized high level achievement in both groups. For example, whereas the writing produced by high achievers from non-background learners displayed the use of a limited range of structures, but with few orthographic errors; the texts produced by high achiever background learners showed the use of a wider range of grammatical structure, but with errors attributable to the transfer of a colloquial style derived from everyday speech.

Korean classes in Australia continue to suffer from low enrolments. Thus Kim's (2012) study investigating the performance of Korean learners was small scale. The study compared five non-background and four background learners and focused mainly on their use of forms/structures (morpho-syntactic elements considered salient in Korean, e.g., case markers, particles) and discourse (use of cohesive devices at the sentence and text level awareness of genre, e.g., use of appropriate honorifics). Kim found that the two groups performed differently on the two tasks. The non-background learners tended to use similar sentence structures in both tasks. These seemed to be well-rehearsed structures and, although quite accurate, were overly formal, particularly in Task

2 (blog). In contrast, the background speakers used a wider repertoire of forms/ structures and discourse devices, but tended to overuse speech-like (informal) forms in both tasks.

Iwashita (2012) looked at learners' performance in Japanese. Compared to Chinese, the number of background learners in Japanese classes is much smaller because of the composition of migration to Australia. Nevertheless, Japanese has attracted students from backgrounds in other Asian languages, such as Chinese and Korean. Iwashita's study compared the performance of two learner groups on writing (and speaking): learners from related language backgrounds (i.e., Chinese and Korean) ($n = 39$) and unrelated language background (English or other language backgrounds) ($n = 70$).

The study found that Japanese learners from the related language backgrounds received higher overall scores on writing (and speaking) than the other group. Furthermore, writing produced by the related language learners was richer in terms of content development, displayed a wider variety of forms (although some were used incorrectly due to L1 transfer) and more complex sentences than the writing produced by the unrelated language learners. This was a surprising finding given that the grammatical systems of Chinese and Korean are dissimilar to Japanese. Iwashita suggests that what seemed to affect the writing of related language learners was their positive disposition to Japanese and Japanese culture. These learners tended to seek more opportunities for TL input (e.g., by visiting Japanese websites and reading Japanese comic books).

In another study (not part of the SAALE project), Iwashita and Sekiguchi (2008) investigated how two factors: the nature of prior target language instruction (school or intensive first-year course at university) and first language background (character based or non-character based) impact on the writing skills in Japanese as a second language (JSL) in a university setting. The writing samples were analyzed for fluency (length), grammatical complexity and use of kanji (Chinese characters), and vocabulary. The study found that, in general, learners who started studying Japanese at university outperformed post-secondary students regardless of their L1 language background, but mainly on the use of kanji. Learners whose L1 was character-based and were educated in that L1 did best on kanji scores. Language learning background did not advantage learners on other aspects of writing.

What this research shows is that the impact of language background on L2 may be unpredictable and language specific. It also suggests the need to develop a context-sensitive approach in assessing L2 writing achievement rather than a generic standards-based framework that currently dominates the field of language education in Australia and elsewhere. As Scarino (2012) argues, the problem with standardized and generic assessment frameworks, which are not language specific, is that they assume that the language learning trajectory in all languages is the same.

Assessing Writing Development

A related issue to assessing writing achievement is the assessment of progress in L2 writing over time. To date, very few studies in Australia have examined what features of writing develop over time. This issue seems particularly relevant in the case of international students who presumably come to Australia not only to gain a degree but also to improve their English language skills. We assume that for these students studying in an L2 medium university will lead to improvement in their L2 because the immersion experience provides them with rich exposure to the L2 and opportunities to use and produce the L2.

However, a number of experimental studies (e.g., Elder & O'Loughlin, 2003; Storch, 2007, 2009; Storch & Hill, 2008) which investigated whether there is improvement in ESL proficiency, and particularly writing, following one semester of study (10-12 weeks) reported mixed results. Using a test-retest design, these studies compared students' writing in terms of band scores, and some also employed a range of discourse measures of grammatical and lexical complexity, accuracy, and fluency, referred to in the literature as CAF. In some studies, students were also interviewed about their language learning and language writing experience.

In terms of band scores, the studies reported that the learners showed improvement after one semester of study. However, the level of improvement was greatest for those with lower scores on the pre-test (Elder & O'Loughlin, 2003; Storch & Hill, 2008) than for those with higher scores. Perhaps students with lower writing scores at the outset have more room to improve. Furthermore, Elder and O'Loughlin (2003) found that compared to reading and listening, writing scores showed the smallest improvement. In terms of CAF measures, the studies found no improvement in the students' fluency over time (counted generally in terms of words produced in a given time) or in grammatical complexity (see Storch, 2007a, 2009; Storch & Hill, 2008). The only study that found improvement in accuracy and linguistic complexity (e.g., proportion of academic words used) was the study I conducted with Tapper (Storch & Tapper, 2009), and involved students who had completed an EAP subject concurrently with their degree course.

Students' interview data indicated that learners felt a greater confidence in their overall writing abilities, but not necessarily in their grammatical accuracy (Storch & Hill, 2008). The students also reported that the assessment tasks they complete are often group assignments, where they each individually write very little, or short-answer exams. Furthermore, they receive minimal feedback from their instructors on the quality of their written assignments. In my 2009 paper (Storch, 2009) I suggested that it is the absence of feedback that may explain lack of progress in accuracy over time. This argument was validated in the Storch and Tapper (2009) study, where the students felt that their accuracy had improved (as the relevant measures showed) and attributed this improvement to the feedback they received in their EAP subject.

The study by O'Loughlin and Arkoudis (2009) was one of the few studies that examined development beyond one semester. The authors examined writing development of undergraduates and graduates (n = 66) at a large Australian university. The researchers compared the participants' reported

IELTS score used for entry to the university and the score they received on an IELTS test toward the end of their final semester (between 1.5 to 3 years later, depending on their program). The results showed that writing showed the least improvement among the language skills. Again those participants with a lower writing score at the outset showed greatest improvement.

A research project which investigated development in writing over one year (Knoch, Roushad & Storch, 2014) and over three years (Knoch, Roushad, Oon & Storch, 2015) found that students' writing showed no improvement on the band scores or on any of the discourse measures, with the exception of fluency. One reason for the findings may be the relative high proficiency of the participants at the outset. All were university students who had met the university's entry requirement of an IELTS score of 6.5 (or equivalent score on other accepted pathways). However another reason, and one that I believe has not received sufficient attention in research on writing development using a test-retest design (including my own research), is the students' orientation to the re-test. I wonder whether students' are as highly motivated to perform to the best of their ability on re-tests which they complete for research purposes compared to the initial tests which are generally of higher stakes. The initial tests are completed for diagnostic purposes (e.g., Elder & O'Loughlin, 2003; Knoch, Macqueen & O'Hagan, in preparation; Knoch et al., 2014, 2015) or for admission purposes (e.g., O'Loughlin & Arkoudis, 2009).

An alternative research design, and one that I believe is more ecologically valid, is to consider students' writing on successive authentic tasks. This is the research design adopted by Benevento in her minor thesis (see Benevento & Storch, 2011). Benevento's study was conducted in an ongoing French class (final year of high school), and the writing (three different tasks) was completed in-class for assessment purposes. Thus all three tasks were high stakes tasks. The students' writing scripts were analyzed for global quality as well as for grammatical accuracy and syntactic complexity using several measures. The small scale study ($n = 15$) found no statistically significant improvement in grammatical accuracy over the duration of the study (six month), with certain typical errors persisting. However, there were improvements in the overall quality of the writing and in linguistic complexity. Furthermore, the study found that although the learners continued to rely on prefabricated chunks learned in class, the ability to use such chunks creatively improved over time.

Another way to investigate development is to use longitudinal case studies. For example, Macqueen (2012) used a longitudinal study and employed an analytical method called lexical trail analysis. This analysis involved detailed tracing of single words in the texts written by ESL learners for their courses (as well as writing tasks completed for the purposes of the research project). Macqueen also interviewed her case study learners about the histories of particular word combinations. The qualitative methodology enabled the researcher to capture how certain collocations became part of the L2 writers' linguistic repertoire which they drew upon in their writing. The analysis shows that internalization of new words and their use in combination with others depends not only on cognitive resources such as memory and attention but also the L2 learner's ability to imitate and adapt linguistic resources to suit their perceived writing needs.

In a longitudinal (over one year) study we conducted with 13 case study informants over a year, we investigated development in ESL students' selection and use of sources over time (Thompson, Morton & Storch, 2013). We found that initially students selected sources (mainly Internet sources) on the basis of accessibility and ease of understanding. Towards the end of the year, selection and use of sources were informed by a greater understanding of the role of the assessment task, argumentation and writer authority.

In terms of L2 writing scholarship, these studies suggest a need for a broader understanding of L2 writing development. They also suggest the need to carefully design such studies, and consider conducting studies in situ, with authentic writing tasks and different measures of development. The studies also suggest the need for universities to consider how to best facilitate L2 writing development. Dunworth (2010), for example, argues that universities need to embed the teaching of writing in regular subjects and reconsider the nature of assessment tasks. I would argue that universities need to rethink available language support options for ESL students and to encourage students to undertake concurrent ESL credit bearing subjects where they are more likely to engage in substantial writing and to receive feedback on their writing.

Academic (and Professional) Writing: Text Analysis

Our understanding of what constitutes appropriate academic or professional writing is based largely on the work of scholars who have analyzed prototypical but valued academic genres (e.g., the research article) for salient features, as well as features which can distinguish writing in different disciplines. Three different approaches to discourse analysis can be discerned in research conducted by Australian scholars.

The first approach, a genre analysis, builds on the work of Swales (1990, 2004) and has focused on academic genres, such as the thesis (e.g., Paltridge, 2002; Starfield & Ravelli, 2006) or professional genres (e.g., Jones, 2009). It is interesting to note that the approach Paltridge has used in his genre analysis has evolved over time. Whereas early work (Paltridge, 2002) focused on analyzing text structures, in his later work, Paltridge used textographies (2004, 2008). A textography is an approach to genre analysis which combines elements of text analysis with elements of ethnography (e.g., interviews, observations). In his most recent work, Paltridge (2013a, b) uses narrative inquiry in analyzing academic and professional genres. The aim is to go beyond how texts are structured to an examination of why texts are written the way they are. The ultimate purpose of this work is to advise instructors in designing and delivering appropriate writing instruction (e.g., see Paltridge & Woodrow, 2012).

The second approach to discourse analysis is one which focuses on lexico-grammatical choices that the writer makes and the impact these choices have on the reader. This approach is informed by Systemic Functional Linguistics (SFL), which originated from the work of Halliday (1978) and other educational linguists based mainly at Sydney University (see overview in Martin, 2000). For example, Hood (2006) investigated how writers use linguistic markers of attitude to establish a research niche. What distinguishes this analysis is that Hood considered the cumulative effect attained by multiple instances of these markers, across clauses and longer phases of the discourse (which she terms prosody), as well as levels of gradation. The analysis shows how writers draw on linguistic resources of attitude and gradation depending on the kind of arguments they are constructing, and these in turn vary in terms of their strength and persuasive impact. She concludes that this kind of analysis can be employed with L2 writers' to raise their awareness to the patterning of evaluative stances in academic discourse.

The third approach is informed by the work of scholars such as Hyland (2005) on the use of interpersonal markers (e.g., hedges, emphatics, personal pronouns) and that of Ivanič (1998) on the writer's representation of self in academic discourse. For example, Sheldon (2009) compared how writers in English and in Castilian Spanish articles (in the field of applied linguistics and language teaching) represent themselves to readers. Sheldon found similarities as well as some interesting differences between the two groups. Although both groups of writers used the first person pronoun most frequently in advanced organizers to guide the reader through the article, there were differences in the use of first person pronouns in describing how the research was conducted. The English writers frequently used the first person pronouns in the role of conductor of research as a means to promote their expertise as a researcher. The Spanish writers used first person pronouns in this role very sparingly, and when they did it was to demonstrate their competence in overcoming methodological problems. Sheldon suggests some disciplinary conventions may be language specific, and thus of relevance when instructing advanced L2 learners who may wish to publish in the L2.

As I noted in the discussion above, most of the authors concluded their articles with teaching implications, particularly for EAP instructors teaching L2 writing to advanced L2 learners in graduate programs. Instructors need to make explicit the linguistic expectations of the specific discipline in which the learner's research is located so that the novice researcher is accepted as a "legitimate" member of that discourse community. However, what this advice implicitly communicates to L2 writers is that their non-English literacy—ways of knowing and expressing that knowledge—is not valued. The ultimate outcome is that of silencing the voice of novice L2 writers. With a growing number of international students in the Australian education system, this issue of writer voice and representation has come to the fore in recent works of Australian scholars.

A poignant insider's perspective is offered in the writings of Phan Le Ha. Ha completed her graduate qualifications at Monash University in Melbourne and was subsequently a lecturer at the same university in the Education Faculty. Her writing includes her perspectives as a PhD student (Viete & Ha, 2007), as a supervisor of a Vietnamese MA student (Ha, 2009), and more recently a report on the perspectives of a number of students in her case study research (Ha, 2011) published in a book she co-edited. These papers show very clearly how writing is both a social act, influenced by a variety of linguistic, cognitive and interpersonal factors, but also a personal act of identity.

The 2007 paper was co-authored with her supervisor, Rosemary Viete. The paper is based on retrospective and introspective reflections and explores the two authors' at times differing perspectives on writing and how they negotiated to reach a resolution that enabled Ha to adopt a style that she felt provided a true representation of herself, as a bilingual writer, in her thesis.

In the 2009 paper, Ha begins by reflecting on her own journey as a writer and then presents that of the MA student she supervised. Reflecting on her own trajectory, she describes her resistance to being colonized by a discourse which alienated her writing from herself (e.g., rejection of personal anecdotes as evidence). She admits that what she learnt was not to reject all disciplinary norms and practices but to maneuver within these existing norms and write in her own voice. In her role as a supervisor, she tried to negotiate and help her student express his identity as a writer while accommodating to the demands of the university. The student's trajectory as a writer was quite different from Ha's. Initially, he did not want to resist the conventions but wanted to learn how to comply with them. He had concerns about expressing his own opinions because he thought that only "experts" could exert their voice (a view transmitted by EAP courses he attended). However, over time, the student began to value and employ his own unique writing style; which ironically Ha, in her role as his supervisor, at times had to temper.

In her 2011 chapter, Ha presents a contrastive analysis of Vietnamese and English essays and then the findings of a study which explored the writing experiences of four Vietnamese graduate students enrolled in Australian universities. The students were asked about the structure of essays they had to complete in Vietnam in their undergraduate degrees and the essays they had to complete in their current graduate degree courses in Australia. The study showed the differences in style of essays in both countries, and that writing is a social practice influenced by culture and social norms and by what is considered "valued" in the society. Thus, for example, whereas in Vietnam, the use of flowery language and long introductions are seen as reflecting the writer's ability to use language and to draw on knowledge of different disciplines, in Australia, what is valued is directness. Ha argues that these differences should be respected rather than be viewed as deficits; and that students should be made aware and encouraged to make use of their prior knowledge whilst writing in their L2.

Another researcher who has dealt with the notion of authorial voice is Thompson. Thompson has approached this topic by investigating students' incorporation of source materials in academic assignments, particularly in view of the mounting concerns over plagiarism. In a co-authored paper, Chandrasoma, Thompson, and Pennycook (2004), argue that rather than focusing on how to detect plagiarism, we should be focusing on why it may be occurring in the first place (see also Pennycook, 1996). Drawing on a range of data collected as part of the first two authors' PhDs, the authors show that incorporation of sources (intertextuality) relates to questions of writing development and that borrowings may be a strategy used particularly in assignments on topics where students have no personal investment, that is, an absence of authorial selves. They conclude that textual borrowings cannot be dealt with adequately by using sophisticated detection systems, university policies, or teaching correct citations practices and paraphrasing skills (the focus of many EAP courses).

Thompson (2011) elaborates on her stance on intertextuality. Using texts and interviews with case study informants (one being a bilingual speaker born in Australia to Chinese parents and the other student from Hong Kong SAR) and their lecturers she shows that borrowing from the text is done for a variety of purposes. These purposes include coping with a difficult and unfamiliar assignment as well as confusion about the boundaries of what constitutes common knowledge in different discourse communities. Furthermore, what appears at first glance as heavy borrowing, a closer analysis shows that both students managed to imprint their own unique voice on the material borrowed from the sources. This was also noted by their respective lecturers.

A number of Australian researchers (Cadman, 1997, 2002; Viete & Ha, 2007) now call for L2 writing pedagogies that do more than make expectations and text structures, like the PhD proposal or the literature review, explicit. They argue that these EAP pedagogies aim at reproduction of the status quo (a form of "vulgar pragmatism" to use Pennycook's 1997 terms). Rather, what they call for are critical EAP courses which promote transformation. Critical EAP requires a greater respect for L2 writers, encouraging them to develop agency in their texts. If we accept that writing is an expression of self—then the role of EAP is to enable L2 writers to write in a style which reverberates not only for the reader but also for the writer. In the case of graduate students, the role of the supervisor is to help L2 novice researchers not only to become acceptable users of English but also to raise their awareness of how they can express their own voice uniquely, in a meaningful third space (Kramsch, 2001).

L2 Writing Instruction & Feedback

The third large body of research on L2 writing conducted by Australian scholars is concerned with the teaching of L2 writing at the macro level (course design) and micro level (classroom). At the macro level, a number of authors have described and evaluated L2 writing courses which they had designed and implemented. Most of these have focused on the teaching of graduate ESL/EFL students (e.g., Paltridge & Woodrow, 2012) in Australia or workshops delivered off shore (e.g., Cargill & O'Connor, 2006).

Others adopt action research and report why and how they redesigned their approaches to L2 writing instruction (e.g., Cadman, 2002, 2005; Dovey, 2010). For example, Cadman (2002, 2005) described how the genre-based curriculum that was used to teach international graduate students at her university (Adelaide) to write research proposals, was redesigned to include a greater focus on writer identity. The impetus for the change was surveys and interviews she conducted with a number of research supervisors on what they considered successful research proposals which highlighted the importance of students positioning themselves in their proposals. The new course, rather than focusing only on the linguistic and rhetorical features of the research proposal genre, now includes a focus on how to express authorial stance and self-representation.

Dovey (2010) describes the evolution of an EAP writing subject teaching Information Technology graduate students how to write a literature-based report. The evolution was spurred by observations and reflections. Dovey observed that exposing learners to model texts and engaging them in discourse analysis did not reveal to the students the complex processes and skills needed to write from sources. Thus, she redesigned the course, adopting a hybrid genre-process approach, to better address the reading-writing needs of her students.

My own main area of research on L2 writing pedagogy, and that of a number of graduate students that I have supervised, has been on the use of collaborative writing in L2 classrooms. Collaborative writing is an activity in which students co-author a text, and are involved in all stages of the composition process: brainstorming ideas, composing, and revising/editing. My rationale for using collaborative writing in L2 writing classes is that it combines learner interaction and writing. It thus exposes L2 writers to different ideas and ways of expressing different ideas, encourages them to focus and deliberate about language choice, and provides them with opportunities to pool their linguistic resources in these deliberations (see Storch, 2013 for a more in-depth discussion of the rationale for collaborative writing).

I have investigated a number of aspects of collaborative writing, including the kind of tasks that may be best for encouraging learners to focus on language choice and accuracy (e.g., Storch, 1998a, 1999, 2001a, 2003a); what aspects of language learners focus on, how do they resolve difficulties or uncertainties they encounter about language use, and whether the resolutions reached are correct (e.g., Storch, 1997, 1998b). I have also investigated the nature of learners' deliberations in these resolutions, noting whether more extensive engagement leads to longer term retention of the items discussed (Storch, 2008).

Another aspect that I have investigated is the nature of the pair dynamics; that is, the kind of relationships learners form when co-authoring (Storch, 2001b, 2002, 2004). As I have mentioned in a number of my publications, simply assigning learners to co-author a text does not necessarily mean that they will collaborate. In my investigations into the relationships learners form during pair writing, I identified four distinct patterns based on the equality of their control over and contributions to the composition process and the level of engagement with each other's contributions.

One other important issue investigated is comparing texts produced by learners writing in pairs to those produced by learners writing individually. My own small scale classroom based studies (e.g., Storch, 2005, 2007) and subsequent larger scale empirical studies with my colleague Wigglesworth have shown that texts produced collaboratively are better in terms of quality and grammatical accuracy than those produced individually (see Storch &

Wigglesworth, 2007; Wigglesworth & Storch, 2009).

My graduate students have extended this line of research on collaborative L2 writing by investigating this activity in different contexts (e.g., foreign language rather than ESL classes), and more recently by comparing face to face collaborative writing with computer mediated collaborative writing. For example, Aldosari's PhD investigated collaborative writing in an EFL context in Saudi Arabia. Aldosari compared the interaction of learners who were paired according to their L2 proficiency when completing a range of writing tasks (see Storch & Aldosari, 2010, 2013). He found (see Storch & Aldosari, 2013) that pairs composed of similar L2 proficiency (high-high or low-low) were more likely to collaborate; those composed of learners of mixed proficiency were more likely to form asymmetrical relationships, where the higher proficiency learner dominates the interaction and the lower proficiency learner remains fairly passive. My previous research (Storch, 2002, 2013) suggests that dominant/passive relationships are not conducive to language learning.

Another student, Liana Tan, compared face to face and computer mediated (using *MSN Messenger*) collaborative writing activities completed by Australian students studying Chinese at the university. The study (Tan, Wigglesworth & Storch, 2010) found that in the face to face mode pairs were more likely to collaborate, whereas in the computer mediated mode they were more likely to cooperate. When cooperating the learners contributed to the task but did not necessarily engage with each other's contribution.

In a more recent study Rouhshad, another of my PhD students, also compared face to face and computer mediated collaborative writing, but used Google Docs as the computer platform. His results (Rouhshad & Storch, forthcoming) confirm those reported by Tan et al. (2010) that computer mediated writing is more likely to encourage cooperation rather than collaboration. However, the form of cooperation in *Google Docs* was one of a division of labor: one student took on the role of the scribe, the other dictated the text. Furthermore, in both studies, the computer mediated mode encouraged fewer deliberations about language than the face to face mode.

Another area of investigation related to L2 writing instruction is that of the impact of corrective feedback on writing. In a large-scale project,[1] Wigglesworth and I investigated the efficacy of direct (reformulation) and indirect feedback on the writing of high intermediate and advanced ESL writers. Our research on feedback was unique in the sense that we had students writing and subsequently processing the feedback they received in pairs. The pair talk during this processing session enabled us to determine some of the factors which may explain the impact of feedback on writing.

In our study we found somewhat unexpected results. For example, we found that although indirect feedback elicited more elaborate attention to language than reformulations and led to more uptake in the revised version (Storch & Wigglesworth, 2010a), reformulations seemed to be more enduring in the longer term (three weeks after the feedback was given) (Wigglesworth & Storch, 2012). A closer examination of our pair talk data, using case studies (Storch & Wigglesworth, 2010b), revealed the importance of affective factors in explaining uptake and retention of the feedback received. These affective factors include the learners' goals, their attitudes towards the form of feedback, and beliefs about certain language rules shaped by previous instruction. These affective factors influenced not only whether the learners' heeded the feedback, but the strategies they adopted to deal with the feedback received (e.g., memorization) and whether ultimately they retained the feedback information.

In a 2010 paper which reviewed the body of extant research on corrective feedback, I called for research on feedback that is more ecologically valid in terms of research design and which takes students' perspectives into consideration when interpreting the results. A number of my current PhD students have now embarked on this kind of research into feedback on L2 writing.

My research on collaborative writing, and subsequently on feedback on writing has been informed by sociocultural theory. I believe that this theoretical perspective can deepen our understanding of the impact of feedback on L2

---

1 The research project was supported by an Australian Research Council Grant, DP0450422.

writing because it considers learners, and particularly adult L2 learners, as agents who are actively involved in language learning, who can decide whether to heed the feedback they receive or reject it, and the strategies to help them retain the feedback information. It is only via studies which attempt to access how students process the feedback they receive that we can gain these valuable insights.

Getting learners to compose and process feedback in pairs has also been an invaluable research tool. Pair talk provides researchers with a window into the important cognitive processes involved in composing texts, in deliberating about language choice, in determining whether to accept or reject feedback received. With L2 learners it seems a more suitable research tool than think aloud protocols and provides perhaps a more accurate representation of these processes than retrospective interviews.

Conclusion

The aim of this paper was to review and showcase research on L2 writing conducted in Australia, by established and novice researchers. The review attempted to explain the directions this research has followed by reference to Australia's linguistically diverse society and government policy initiatives. I hope that the review has shown that despite the relatively small size of the Australian population and by extension the relatively small number of L2 writing scholars, we are making a significant contribution to L2 writing scholarship. To use an apt sporting metaphor, given Australians' love of sport, I believe that we are punching well above our weight.

The future of L2 writing research in Australia looks promising. For example, the number of students enrolling in the L2 writing course I offer at the University of Melbourne in our Masters of Applied Linguistics program has grown exponentially. There is also a growing interest from prospective PhD applicants in conducting research on topics related to L2 writing, particularly writing development and feedback on writing.

References

About Australia. (2013). Australia facts. www.about-australia.com/facts. Accessed 5 October, 2013.

Australian Education International. (2012). Statistics on international students. Available at http://aei.des.gov.au/AEI/MIP/Statistics/StudentEnrolment AndVisaStatistcs/Recent.htm. Accessed 5 October, 2013.

Benevento, C. & Storch, N. (2011). Investigating writing development in secondary school learners of French. *Assessing Writing, 16*(2): 97-110.

Brindley, G. (2000).Task difficulty and task generalisability in competency-based writing assessment. In G. Brindley (ed.), *Studies in immigrant English language assessment.* Vol. 1 (pp. 125-157). Sydney: NCELTR.

Cadman, K. (1997). Thesis writing for international students: A question of identity? *English for Specific Purposes, 16,* 3-14.

Cadman, K. (2002). English for academic possibilities: The research proposal as a contested site in postgraduate genre pedagogy. *Journal of English for Academic Purposes, 1,* 85-104.

Cadman, K. (2005). Towards a "pedagogy of connection" in critical research education: a real story. *Journal of English for Academic Purposes, 4,* 353-367.

Cargill, M. & O'Connor, P. (2006). Developing Chinese scientists' skills for publishing in English: Evaluating collaborating-colleague workshops based on genre analysis. *Journal of English for Academic Purposes, 5,* 207-221.

Chandrasoma, R., Thompson, C. & Pennycook, A. (2004). Beyond plagiarism: transgressive and non-transgressive intertextuality. *Journal of Language, Identity, and Education, 3,* 171-193.

Clyne, M., Fernandez, S., Chen, I. & Summo-O'Connell, R. (1997). *Background Speakers: Diversity and Its Management in LOTE Programs.* Belconnen, ACT: The National Languages and Literacy Institute of Australia.

Cumming, A., Kantor, R., Baba, K., Erdosy, U., Eouanzoui, K. & James, M. (2005). Differences in written discourse in independent and integrated prototype tasks for next generation TOEFL. *Assessing Writing, 10,* 1-75.

Department of Immigration and Citizenship—Australian government. (nd). Everyone belongs. www.harmony.gov.au/schools/students/aussie -fact.htm. Accessed 5 October, 2013.

Dovey, T. (2010). Facilitating writing from sources: A focus on both process and product. *Journal of English for Academic Purposes, 9,* 45-60.

Dunworth, K. (2010). Clothing the emperor: Addressing the issue of English language proficiency in Australian universities. *Australian Universities' Review, 52,* 5-10.

Elder, C. (1996). The effect of language background on "foreign" language test performance: The case of Chinese, Italian and Modern Greek. *Language Learning, 46,* 233-282.

Elder, C., Kim, H. & Knoch, U. (2012). Documenting the diversity of learner achievements in Asian languages using common measures. *Australian Review of Applied Linguistics, 35,* 251-170.

Elder, C. & O' Loughlin, K. (2003). Investigating the relationship between intensive EAP training and band score gains on IELTS. *IELTS* research reports, *4,* 207-254.

Ha, P. L. (2009). Strategic, passionate but academic: Am I allowed in my writing? *Journal of English for Academic Purposes, 8,* 134-146.

Ha, P. L. (2011). The writing and culture nexus: Writers' comparisons of Vietnamese and English academic writing. In P. L. Ha & B. Baurain (eds.), *Voices, Identities, Negotiations, and Conflicts: Writing Academic English Across Cultures* (pp. 23-40). Bingley, UK: Emerald.

Halliday, M. A. K. (1978). *Language as Social Semiotic: The Social Interpretation of Language and Meaning.* London: Edward Arnold.

Hood, S. (2006). The persuasive power of prosodies: Radiating values in academic writing. *Journal of English for Academic Purposes, 5,* 37-49.

Hyland, K. (2005). Stance and engagement: A model of interaction in academic discourse. *Discourse Studies, 7,* 172-192.

Ivaniç, R. (1998). *Writing and Identity: The Discoursal Construction of Identity in Academic Writing.* Amsterdam: John Benjamins.

Iwashita, N. (2012). Cross-linguistic influences as a factor in the written and oral production of school-age learners. *Australian Review of Applied Linguistics, 35,* 290-311.

Iwashita, N. & Sekiguchi, S. (2008). Effects of learner background on the development of Japanese writing skills. *Australian Review of Applied Linguistics, 32,* 1-20.

Jones, A. (2009). Business discourse as a site of inherent struggle. In A. Mahboob & C. Lipovsky (eds.), *Studies in Applied Linguistics and Language Learning* (pp. 85-106). Newcastle, Australia: Cambridge Scholars.

Kim, S. H. O. (2012). Learner background and the acquisition of discourse features of Korean in the Australian secondary school system. *Australian Review of Applied Linguistics, 35*(3), 339-358.

Knoch, U., Macqueen, S. & O'Hagan, S. (forthcoming). An investigation of the effect of task type on the discourse produced by students at various score levels in the TOEFL iBT writing test. TOEFL report.

Knoch, U., Rouhshad, A. & Storch, N. (2014). Does the writing of undergraduate ESL students develop after one year of study in an English medium university? *Assessing Writing, 21,* 1-17.

Knoch, U., Rouhshad, A., On, S. P. & Storch, N. (2015). What happens to ESL students' writing after three years of study at an English medium university? *Journal of Second Language Writing, 28,* 39-52.

Kramsch, C. (2001). Language, culture, and voice in the teaching of English as a foreign language. *Novelty: A Journal of English Language Teaching and Cultural Studies in Hungary, 8,* 4-21.

Lo Bianco, J. (2009). Return of the good times? Japanese teaching today. *Japanese Studies, 29,* 331-336.

Lo Bianco, J. (2012). Afterword: Tempted by targets, tempered by results. *Australian Review of Applied Linguistics, 35,* 359-361.

Lo Bianco, J. & Slaughter, Y. (2009). *Second Languages and Australian Schooling: Review and Proposals.* Australian Education Review (white paper no. 54), Camberwell, Vic: Australian Council of Education Research.

Macqueen, S. (2012). *The Emergence of Patterns in Second Language Writing: A Sociocognitive Exploration of Lexical Trails*. Berlin: Peter Lang.

Martin, J. (2000). Design and practice: Enacting functional linguistics. *Annual Review of Applied Linguistics, 20*, 116-126.

McNamara, T. F. (2001). The roots of applied linguistics in Australia. *Australian Review of Applied Linguistics, 24*, 13-29.

Moore, S. H. (2007). Researching appropriate assessment for low/pre-literacy adult ESL learners: Results, issues and challenges. *Prospect: An Australian Journal of TESOL, 22*, 25-38.

Moore, S. H. & Hargreaves, M. (2009). A case study of an assessment task bank. *Prospect: An Australian Journal of TESOL, 24,* 3-16.

Moore, T. & Morton, J. (2005). Dimensions of difference: a comparison of university writing and IELTS writing. *Journal of English for Academic Purposes, 4*, 43-66.

O'Loughlin, K. & Arkoudis, S. (2009). Investigating IELTS exit score gains in higher education. *IELTS Research Reports, 10*, 95-180.

Orton, J. (2008). *The Current State of Chinese Language Education in Australian Schools*. Melbourne: Education Services Australia

Paltridge, B. (2002). Thesis and dissertation writing: An examination of published advice and actual practice. *English for Specific Purposes, 21*, 125-143.

Paltridge, B. (2004). The exegesis as a genre: an ethnographic examination. In L. Ravelli & R. Ellis (eds.), *Analyzing Academic Writing: Contextualised Frameworks* (pp. 84-103). London: Continuum.

Paltridge, B. (2007). Beyond the text: A textography of Chinese College English writing. *University of Sydney Papers in TESOL, 2*, 149-166.

Paltridge, B. (2008). Textographies and the researching and teaching of writing. *Iberica, 15*, 9-24.

Paltridge, B. (2013a). Narrative inquiry and the researching of academic and professional genres. In M. Gotti and C. S. Guinda (eds.), *Narratives in Academic and Professional Genres* (pp. 497-501). Bern: Peter Lang.

Paltridge, B. (2013b). Genre and English for specific purposes. In B. Paltridge and S. Starfield (eds.), *Handbook of English for Specific Purposes* (pp. 347-366). Boston: Wiley-Blackwell.

Paltridge, B. & Woodrow, L. (2012). Thesis and dissertation writing: Moving beyond the text. In R. Tang (ed.), *Academic Writing in a Second or Foreign Language: Issues and Challenges Facing ESL/EFL Academic Writers in Higher Education Contexts.* (pp. 88-104), London: Continuum.

Pennycook, A. (1996). Borrowing others' words: Text, ownership, memory and plagiarism. *TESOL Quarterly, 30*, 201-230.

Pennycook, A. (1997). Vulgar pragmatism, critical pragmatism, and EAP. *English for Specific Purposes, 16*(4), 253-269.

Roushad, A. & Storch, N. (forthcoming). A focus on mode: Patterns of interaction in face-to-face and computer-mediated modes. In S. Ballinger & M. Sato (eds). *Peer Interaction and L2 Learning.* John Benjamins.

Scarino, A. (2012). A rationale for acknowledging the diversity of learner achievements in learning particular languages in school education in Australia. *Australian Review of Applied Linguistics, 35*(3), 231-150.

Scarino, A., Elder, C., Iwashita, N., Kim, S. H. O., Kohler, M. & Scrimgeour, A. (2011). Student achievement in Asian languages education. Part 1: Project Report. Report prepared for the Department of Education, Employment & Workplace Relations (DEEWR). Available from www.saale.unisa.edu.au.

Scrimgeour, A. (2012). Understanding the nature of performance: the influence of learner background on school-age learner achievement in Chinese. *Australian Review of Applied Linguistics, 35*, 312-228.

Sheldon, E. (2009). From one I to another: Discursive construction of self-representation in English and Castilian Spanish research articles. *English for Specific Purposes, 28*, 251-265.

Starfield, S. & Ravelli, L. (2006). "The writing of this thesis was a success that I could not explore with the positivistic detachment of the classical sociologist": Self and structure in New Humanities research theses. *Journal of English for Academic Purposes, 5*, 222-243.

Storch, N. (1997). The editing talk of adult learners. *Language Awareness, 6,* 221-232.

Storch, N. (1998a). Comparing second language learners' attention to form across tasks. *Language Awareness, 7,* 176-191.

Storch, N. (1998b). A classroom-based study: Insights from a collaborative, text reconstruction task. *ELT Journal, 52,* 291-300.

Storch, N. (1999). Are two heads better than one? Pair work and grammatical accuracy. *System, 27,* 363-374.

Storch, N. (2001a) Comparing ESL learners' attention to grammar on three different collaborative tasks, *RELC Journal, 32,* 104-124.

Storch, N. (2001b) How collaborative is pair work? ESL tertiary students composing in pairs, *Language Teaching Research, 5,* 29-53.

Storch, N. (2002). Patterns of interaction in ESL pair work. *Language Learning, 52,* 119-158.

Storch, N. (2003a). Tasks for focus on form in classroom-based research. *Ilha Do Desterro, 41,* 121-154.

Storch, N. (2003b). Relationships formed in dyadic interaction and opportunity for learning. *International Journal of Educational Research. 37,* 305-322.

Storch, N. (2004). Using activity theory to explain differences in patterns of dyadic interactions in an ESL class. *The Canadian Modern Language Review, 60,* 457-480.

Storch, N. (2005). Collaborative writing: Product, process, and students' reflections. *Journal of Second Language Writing, 14,* 153-173.

Storch, N. (2007a). Development in L2 writing after a semester of study in an Australian university. *Indonesian Journal of English Language Teaching, 3, 173-189.*

Storch, N. (2007b). Investigating the merits of pair work on a text editing task in ESL classes. *Language Teaching Research, 11,* 143-161.

Storch, N. (2008). Metatalk in pair work activity: Level of engagement and implications for language development. *Language Awareness, 17,* 95-114.

Storch, N. (2009). The impact of studying in a second language (L2) medium university on the development of L2 writing. *Journal of Second Language Writing, 18,* 103-118.

Storch, N. (2010). Critical feedback on written corrective feedback. *International Journal of English Studies, 10,* 29-46.

Storch, N. (2013). *Collaborative Writing in L2 Classrooms.* Bristol, UK: Multilingual Matters.

Storch, N. & Aldosari, A. (2010). Learners' use of first language (Arabic) in pair work in an EFL class. *Language Teaching Research, 14,* 355-375.

Storch, N. & Aldosari, A. (2013). Pairing learners in pair-work activity. *Language Teaching Research, 17,* 31-48.

Storch, N. & Hill, K. (2008). What happens to international students' English after one semester at university? *Australian Review of Applied Linguistics, 31,* 1-17.

Storch, N. & Tapper, J. (2009). The impact of an EAP course on postgraduate writing. *Journal of English for Academic Purposes, 8,* 207-223.

Storch, N. & Wigglesworth, G. (2007). Writing tasks and the effects of collaboration. In M. Pillar (ed). *Investigating Tasks in Formal Language Settings* (pp. 157-177). Multilingual Matters.

Storch, N. & Wigglesworth, G. (2010a). Students' engagement with feedback on writing: the role of learner agency/beliefs. In Batstone R (ed.), *Sociocognitive Perspectives on Language Use and Language Learning* (pp. 166-185). Oxford, United Kingdom: Oxford University Press.

Storch, N. & Wigglesworth, G. (2010b). Learners' processing, uptake, and retention of corrective feedback on writing. Case studies. *Studies in Second Language Acquisition, 32,* 303-334.

Swales, J. (1990). *Genre Analysis. English in Academic and Research Settings.* Cambridge: Cambridge University Press.

Swales, J. (2004). *Research Genres: Explorations and Applications.* Cambridge: Cambridge University Press.

Tan, L., Wigglesworth G. & Storch N. (2010). Pair interactions and mode of communication: Comparing face-to-face and computer mediated communication. *Australian Review of Applied Linguistics, 33,* 1-24.

Thompson, C. (2011). Plagiarism, intertextuality and the politics of knowledge, identity and textual ownership in undergraduate ESL/EFL students' academic writing. In Ha, P. L. & Baurain, B. (eds.), *Voices, Identities, Negotiations, and Conflicts: Writing Academic English Across Cultures* (pp. 157-177). Bingley, UK: Emerald.

Thompson, C., Morton, J. & Storch, N. (2013). Where from, who, why and how? A study of the use of sources by first year L2 university students. *Journal of English for Academic Purposes, 12*, 99-109.

Tovey, J. (2013). Students stop taking Asian languages in senior years. *The Age*, 8 October.

Viete, R. & Ha P. L. (2007). The growth of voice: expanding possibilities for representing self in research writing. *English Teaching: Practice and Critique*, 6, 39-57.

Walsh, M. & C. Yallop, C. (2005). *Languages and Culture in Aboriginal Australia*. Canberra: Aboriginal Studies Press.

Wigglesworth, G. & Storch, N. (2009). Pairs versus individual writing: Effects on fluency, complexity and accuracy. *Language Testing, 26*, 445-466.

Wigglesworth, G. & Storch, N. (2012). Feedback and writing development through collaboration: A socio-cultural approach. In R. Manchon (ed.), *L2 Writing Development: Multiple Perspectives* (pp. 69-100). Boston: de Gruyter.

Chapter 2

Studies of Second-Language Writing in Canada: Three Generations

Alister Cumming

Ontario Institute for Studies in Education, University of Toronto and Beijing Foreign Studies University

Introduction

Canada's social and educational policies have always involved immigrant settlement and English-French bilingualism. Research on writing in second languages emerged in the 1980s from graduate programs of education and applied linguistics at major universities in Toronto, Montreal, Ottawa, and Vancouver, particularly done by scholars investigating cognitive and learning processes and rhetorical characteristics of writing in English as a mother tongue. In the 1990s several Canadian scholars established systematic programs of research focused on L2 composing processes, writing for academic purposes, assessment, and innovative educational programs—spawning, in turn, in the 2000s a third generation of L2 writing researchers who have now established themselves across Canada and around the world.

Canadians often joke with Americans that most of the best and funniest comedians in movies and television in the USA are really Canadians. Examples include actors such as Martin Short, Andrea Martin, John Candy, Catherine

O'Hara, and Eugene Levy, who all started their careers in Canada in the 1970s on a comedy program called *Second City Television*. In China, too, there is the famous comedian, Dashan, who similarly grew up and resides in Ontario as Mark Rowswell. Admittedly, researchers of second-language (L2) writing in Canada do not tend to be particularly funny, but like their comedian counterparts, they have been exceptionally well represented, illustrious, and influential internationally. The reputations of the few hundred or so people who have researched L2 writing in Canada certainly exceed expectations proportional to the size of Canada's population (currently just over 35 million people). Whereas some articles in the present volume address situations in countries where studies of L2 writing have been underrepresented, the situation in Canada seems almost the contrary: Research on L2 writing seems almost disproportionally overrepresented. Why might this be so?

Education in Canada has always involved immigrant settlement, policies of English/French bilingualism, and cities with cultural and linguistic diversity (Burnaby, 1997; Cumming, 1997). These three issues have been prominent in the earliest (e.g., Anderson, 1918) to the most recent (e.g., Vaillancourt, Coche, Cadieux & Ronson, 2012) analyses of educational policies and practices in Canada. Indeed, Canada was formed as a nation in 1867 on the premises of, and its government policies continue to emphasize, two official languages (English and French, with equal status federally since 1969 but varying status in each of 10 provinces and three territories) and continuing immigration, initially from Europe mostly but in recent decades increasingly from Asia and diverse other parts of the world. Census data indicate that English or French are the mother tongues of, respectively, 57% or 21% of the Canadian population, and the six and a half-million people with mother tongues other than English or French (who are not indigenous peoples) have settled in or around just a few of the largest cities: Montreal, Toronto, Ottawa, Calgary, Edmonton, and Vancouver (Statistics Canada, 2013).

Given these societal, policy, and historical factors, analyses of language education, learning, and policies have long featured in Canadian scholarship, research, and curricula in schools as well as in higher and non-formal education. This focus has been most evident in research and graduate programs at the larger universities in the major Canadian cities where most recent immigrants have settled and been educated. A focus specifically on writing in second languages, however, developed only over the past few decades. The remainder of this article describes this development, observing foundations established by scholars of educational psychology, rhetoric, and applied linguistics in the 1980s, the emergence of a second generation of researchers in the 1980s and 1990s focused specifically on L2 writing, and then the establishment of a third generation of L2 writing researchers in the 2000s at universities across Canada and around the world. The article closes by describing six trends and concepts prominent in studies of L2 writing in Canada in recent years.

Foundations in the 1980s

Research on writing emerged and flourished across all English-dominant countries in the 1980s as cognitive psychologists put forward new models to explain the processes of composing and its development (e.g., Flower & Hayes, 1984), educators articulated inspiring principles for teaching composition (e.g., Graves, 1983), and scholars surveyed educational practices internationally (e.g., Gorman, Purves & Degenhart, 1988) and synthesized the available research (e.g., Hillocks, 1986). Numerous researchers at universities across Canada participated actively in the movement to analyze, explain, and improve the learning and teaching of writing. Their studies of, ideas about, and graduate level courses on writing in English as a first language (L1) established the intellectual foundations and research orientations for a subsequent generation of scholars to focus later on parallel studies of L2 writing.

A vibrant strand of research about English L1 writing in Canada emerged from the field of applied cognitive science in the 1980s. Theories and the extensive program of research by Carl Bereiter and Marlene Scardamalia at the

Ontario Institute for Studies in Education (OISE), University of Toronto are still commonly cited as models of inquiry and explanations of the psychological dimensions of writing processes and development (Bereiter & Scardamalia, 1987). Other researchers active in cognitive science and studies of English L1 literacy at OISE included David Olson (e.g., 1994), Suzanne Hidi, and Val Anderson (e.g., Hidi & Anderson,1986). Related programs of research based on cognitive science, but focused on a comprehensive scheme for discourse analysis, were developed in the 1980s at McGill University in Montreal by Carl Frederisken and Janet Donin (e.g., Frederiksen, Donin, Décary, Émond & Hoover, 1992) as well as Robert Bracewell (e.g., Bracewell & Witte, 2003). The ideas and approaches to research instantiated by these scholars and their counterparts in the U.S. and Europe are well represented in the journal *Cognition and Instruction*, now in its 31st year of publication.

Inquiry about English L1 writing from scholars of rhetoric and applied linguistics emerged around the same time at McGill University and at Carleton University in nearby Ottawa. Aviva Freedman and Ian Pringle conducted linguistic analyses of students' compositions to study their writing development (c.g., Freedman & Pringle, 1980b) and edited several influential collections of articles from conferences (e.g., Freedman & Pringle, 1980a). Freedman later analyzed writing development through genre and activity theories, working in parallel to studies of workplace writing in English by Patrick Dias and Anthony Paré at McGill University (e.g., Dias, Freedman, Medway & Paré, 1999). Their and others' research in the 1980s was promoted through the Canadian Council of Teachers of English (which later added the term, Language Arts, to its name), particularly by its journal, *English Quarterly*, which produced its 42nd volume in 2011 (though it remains to be seen if new volumes may still appear after that date).

In Vancouver, Bernie Mohan promoted Halliday's theories of systemic-functional linguistics as a basis for analyzing students' writing development and organizing teachers' curricula for language programs (e.g., Mohan, 1986). Other applied linguists who studied English L1 writing at the University of British

Columbia included Marion Crowhurst (e.g., 1983) and Joe Belanger (e.g., Yau & Belanger, 1984). Gordon Wells, at OISE in Toronto from the early 1980s, also adopted theories of systemic-functional linguistics (e.g., Wells, 1980) but reoriented his subsequent research toward elaborating Vygotskian socio-cultural theories to explain and foster English L1 writing development (e.g., Wells, 1999).

Studies of L2 Writing in the 1980s and 1990s

These English L1 writing researchers soon spawned, through their teaching as university professors and thesis supervisions, a subsequent generation of students and colleagues who applied their foundational theoretical orientations and research methods to illuminate the multiple complexities and processes of L2 writing development. That so many of these English L1 writing researchers worked and published in pairs (e.g., Bereiter and Scardamalia, Frederiksen and Donin, Freedman and Pringle, Mohan and Early) makes me think of them fondly as "grandparents" for the next generation of L2 writing researchers. The intellectual foundations for studies of L2 writing were also created in Canada by the many scholars whose research focused on second language acquisition and bilingualism in the 1980s. Notably, Jim Cummins' (1984) interdependence hypothesis provided a principled basis for investigating how complex cognitive abilities and orientations associated with literacy transfer across first and second languages. Numerous large-scale projects, following from educational reforms to promote the learning and teaching of both official languages (e.g., Lambert & Tucker, 1972), were examining the development of bilingual proficiency from comprehensive perspectives while elaborating theories of communicative competence to include both spoken and written language abilities (e.g., Canale & Swain, 1980; Harley, Allen, Cummins & Swain, 1990). Several journals provided national forums for such research while also attracting international attention, including the *Canadian Modern Language Review*, established almost 70 years ago, the *Canadian Journal of*

Applied Linguistics, established in 1998 (but preceded by the *Bulletin of the CAAL* from 1978 to 1991 and then appearing as the *Journal of the CAAL* from 1992 to 1997), and the newer *TESL Canada Journal*, established in 1984.

This confluence of factors prompted Canadians to produce some of the first systematic studies of L2 writing. Certain researchers applied methods, established by Bereiter and Scardamalia (1987), of process-tracing through think-aloud protocols or video recordings of text inscription to document and analyze unique characteristics of L2 composing processes (e.g., Cumming, 1989; Jones & Tetroe, 1987). Others employed text analyses and interviews to reveal educational and developmental factors that challenged the then dominant premises of contrastive rhetoric (e.g., Mohan & Lo, 1985; Yau & Belanger, 1984). An initial focus on psychological issues and task analyses in the 1980s shifted to socio-cognitive perspectives during the 1990s, involving naturalistic, multi-method, longitudinal studies of L2 writing in real educational or workplace settings rather than in experimental or laboratory conditions. Notable in this regard, among the publications about L2 writing that proliferated in the 1990s, were analyses illuminating factors in the development of L2 writing abilities in schools (Early, 1992), pre-university ESL programs (Cumming, 1992), or settlement programs (Cumming & Gill, 1991) in Vancouver; universities in Ottawa (Currie, 1993) or Toronto (Riazi, 1997; Shi, 1998), and workplaces in Montreal (Parks & Maguire, 1999). A focus of inquiry that seems almost uniquely (but not exclusively) Canadian has been analyses of bilingual's switching strategically between their two languages to make decisions, particularly to select words or phrases, while they compose. Interest in this phenomenon may be related to the relatively large populations in Canada of either English-French bilinguals (e.g., Cumming, 1990, 2013) or English-Chinese bilinguals (e.g., Qi, 1998; Wang, 2003). Whereas the publications cited above, and much of the research on L2 writing familiar to readers of English, have focused on the learning and teaching of English, a continuing, parallel body of inquiry in Canada has focused on the writing of French as a second language in schools and higher education. Much of this inquiry has focused on analyses of students' development of language features in their written texts (e.g., Bournot-Trites, 2007; Le Bouthillier & Dicks, 2013; Lapkin & Swain, 2000) along with studies of writing processes (Hall, 1993) and of innovative computer software for writing development (Hamel, 2005).

A Third Generation of L2 Writing Researchers in the 2000s

In the 2000s, students of the initial generation of Canadian L2 writing researchers established themselves in positions at universities, each developing unique programs of inquiry into L2 writing as well as distinguished international reputations for their research and teaching. Most have been immigrants to Canada themselves, and so capitalized on their multi-lingual, multicultural abilities and perspectives. Most studied in the large PhD programs at the University of Toronto, McGill University, or University of British Columbia. At the University of British Columbia, Ling Shi, originally from China, has conducted a programmatic series of studies into textual borrowing in L2 writing (Shi, 2004, 2010). Ryoko Kubota recently joined Ling Shi as a colleague in Vancouver after many years in the U.S. following from her PhD in Toronto in the 1990s, from which she developed ideas about a critical contrastive rhetoric (Kubota, 1997; Kubota & Lehner, 2004). At Carleton University, Guilliame Gentil, originally from France, is notable for his research into individuals' development of biliteracy and their relations to larger issues of language and educational policies (Gentil, 2005, 2011). At the University of Ottawa, Jérémie Séror has researched the socially constructed nature of academic literacy and multiliteracies education (Séror, 2009, 2011). At York University, Khaled Barkaoui, originally from Tunisia, has established a specialized expertise in the assessment of L2 writing (Barkaoui, 2010a, 2010b). His colleague at York University, Brian Morgan, focuses his research on critical community-based ESL writing, following a path of combining the teaching and studying of L2 writing with other interests in language learning and teaching established by numerous predecessors in a previous generation at York University such as Nick Elson, Neil Naiman, and David Mendelsohn. At Concordia University in Montreal, Heiki Neumann is establishing a program of research on teachers' attention to grammatical issues in L2 writing (Neumann, 2014).

Numerous others have, after completing doctoral studies in Canada, gone on to establish programs of research on L2 writing in other parts of the world. Notable among these scholars are Kyoko Baba at Kinjo College in Nagoya, Japan (Baba, 2009); Mari Haneda, now at Pennsylvania State University after several years at Florida State University and Ohio State University in the USA (Haneda, 2004); Mark James at Arizona State University (James, 2009); Mehdi Riazi, now at Macquarie University in Australia after many years at Shiraz University in Iran (Riazi, 1997); Manami Suzuki at Dokkyo University, Japan (M. Suzuki, 2008); Jennifer Shade Wilson at Rice University (Wilson, 2013); Luxin Yang at Beijing Foreign Studies University, China (Yang, 2010); and Ally Zhou at Oklahoma City University (Zhou, Busch & Cumming, 2014). Various other educators have resided and taught in Canada for a time before establishing careers focused on L2 writing elsewhere, such as Icy Lee, now at the Chinese University of Hong Kong (e.g., Lee, 1998).

Trends in L2 Writing Research in Canada in the 2010s

Research on L2 writing is firmly established and now even thriving in Canada. Several trends currently prominent are certain to propel this inquiry well into the 2010s and beyond. Merrill Swain has articulated theories of "languaging" from her initial formulations about "comprehensible output" (e.g., Swain, 2010), and many of her students are applying these concepts in innovative ways to studies of L2 writing (e.g., Suzuki, 2012). Other researchers have likewise adopted Vygotskian socio-cultural theories of learning to investigate adolescent students' and teachers' development of zones of proximal development focused on writing abilities over a full year of schooling

(Cumming, 2012; Parks, Huot, Hamers & Lemonnier, 2005). Addressing young students with multilingual literacies, Jim Cummins, Margaret Early, and many collaborating teachers have developed the practice of students writing and reading about "identity texts" as a means to assert, share, and discuss their unique biliterate abilities and cultural heritages in culturally diverse schools in Toronto and Vancouver (Cummins & Early, 2011) as well as Calgary (Naqvi, Thorne, Pfitscher, Nordstokke & McKeough, 2013).

Systematic syntheses of prior research on specific aspects of L2 writing are another current trend among Canadian scholars, for example, evaluating and providing new insights into longstanding as well as innovative educational practices such as literacy tutoring (Jun, Ramirez & Cumming, 2010) and concordancing tools for L2 writing (Yoon, 2011) (and, I suppose, including the review of issues in the present article, too). Also notable are recent examples of design-based research, which try out and refine, through iterative cycles and formative evaluations with real students and teachers, such pedagogical innovations as individual diagnostic profiles of language abilities (Jang, Dunlop, Park & van der Boom, 2015) and personalized approaches to computer referencing tools (Yoon, 2013). Equally promising for the improvement of pedagogical practices have been the organization and analyses of learning communities among groups of teachers focused on writing among, for example, teachers of French as a Second Language (Kristmanson, Dicks & Bouthillier, 2009) and of multiliteracies in English in culturally diverse schools (Simon, 2013).

References

Anderson, J. (1918). *The Education of the New-Canadian: A Treatise on Canada's Greatest Educational Problem*. Toronto: J. M. Dent & Sons.

Baba, K. (2009). Aspects of lexical proficiency in writing summaries in a foreign language. *Journal of Second Language Writing, 18*, 191-208.

Barkaoui, K. (2010a). Variability in ESL essay rating processes: The role of rating scale and rater experience. *Language Assessment Quarterly, 7*, 54-74.

Barkaoui, K. (2010b). Explaining ESL essay holistic scores: A multilevel modeling approach. *Language Testing, 27,* 515-535.

Bereiter, C. & Scardamalia, M. (1987). *The Psychology of Written Composition.* Mahwah, NJ: Erlbaum.

Bournot-Trites, M. (2007). Qualité de l'écrit au niveau intermédiaire en immersion française: Effet d'un programme intensif et hypothèse d'un effet de plateau. [Writing proficiency at the intermediate level in French Immersion: Effects of an intensive program and the hypothesis of a plateau effect.] *Canadian Journal of Applied Linguistics, 10,* 7-23.

Bracewell, R. J. & Witte, S. P. (2003). Tasks, ensembles, and activity: Linkages between text production and situation of use in the workplace. *Written Communication,* 20, 511-559.

Burnaby, B. (1997). Language policy and education in Canada. In R. Wodak & D. Corson (Eds.) *Encyclopedia of Language and Education*, Vol. 1, Language policy and political issues in education (pp. 149-158). Dordrecht, Netherlands: Springer.

Canale, M. & Swain, M. (1980). Theoretical bases of communicative approaches to language teaching and testing. *Applied Linguistics, 1,* 1-47.

Crowhurst, M. (1983). Syntactic complexity and writing quality: A review. *Canadian Journal of Education, 8,* 1-16.

Cumming, A. (1989). Writing expertise and second language proficiency. *Language Learning, 39,* 81-141.

Cumming, A. (1990). Metalinguistic and ideational thinking in second language composing. *Written Communication, 39,* 482-511.

Cumming, A. & Gill, J. (1991). Learning ESL literacy among Indo-Canadian women. *Language, Culture and Curriculum, 4,* 181-200.

Cumming, A. (1992). Instructional routines in ESL composition teaching. *Journal of Second Language Writing, 1,* 17-35.

Cumming, A. (1997). English language-in-education policies in Canada. In W. Eggington & H. Wren (Eds.) *Language Policy: Dominant English, Pluralist Challenges* (pp. 91-105). Amsterdam: John Benjamins.

Cumming, A. (Ed.) (2012). *Adolescent Literacies in a Multicultural Context.*
New York: Routledge.

Cumming, A. (2013). Multiple dimensions of academic language and literacy
development. In L. Ortega, A. Cumming & N. Ellis (Eds.) *Agendas for
Language Learning Research.* Supplement 1 to *Language Learning, 63,*
130-152.

Cummins, J. (1984). *Bilingualism and Special Education: Issues in Assessment
and Pedagogy.* Clevedon, UK: Multilingual Matters.

Cummins, J. & Early, M. (Eds.). (2011). *Identity Texts: The Collaborative
Creation of Power in Multilingual Schools.* London, UK: Trentham Books.

Currie, P. (1993). Entering a disciplinary community: Conceptual activities
required to write for one introductory university course. *Journal of Second
Language Writing, 2,* 101-117.

Dias, P., Freedman, A., Medway, P. & Paré, A. (Eds.) (1999).*Worlds Apart: Acting
and Writing in Academic and Workplace Genres.* Mawah, NJ: Lawrence Erlbaum.

Early, M. (1992). Aspects of becoming an academically successful ESL student.
In B. Burnaby & A. Cumming (Eds.), *Sociopolitical Aspects of ESL Education
in Canada* (pp. 265-275). Toronto: OISE Press.

Flower, L. & Hayes, J. R. (1984). Images, plans, and prose: The representation of
meaning in writing. *Written Communication, 1,* 120-160.

Frederiksen, C. H., Donin, J., Décary, M., Émond, B. & Hoover, M. L. (1992).
Semantic discourse processing and tutorial systems for second-language
learning. In M. L. Swartz & M. Yazdani (Eds.), *The Bridge to International
Communication: Intelligent Tutoring Systems for Foreign Language Learning.*
Amsterdam: Springer.

Freedman, A. & Pringle, I. (Eds.) (1980a). *Reinventing the Rhetorical Tradition.*
Ottawa: Canadian Council of Teachers of English.

Freedman, A. & Pringle, I. (1980b). Writing at the college level: Some indices of
growth. *College Composition and Communication, 31,* 311-324.

Gentil, G. (2005). Commitments to academic biliteracy: Case studies of
francophone university writers. *Written Communication, 22,* 421-471.

Gentil, G. (2011). A biliteracy agenda for genre research. *Journal of Second Language Writing, 20,* 6-23.

Gorman, T., Purves, A. & Degenhart, R. (Eds.) (1988). *The International Writing Tasks and Scoring Scales: The International Study of Achievement in Writing.* Oxford, UK: Pergamon.

Graves, D. (1983). *Writing: Teachers and Children at Work.* Exeter, NH: Heinemann.

Hall, K. (1993). Process writing in French Immersion. *Canadian Modern Language Review, 49,* 255-274.

Hamel, M. J. (2005). Grammaire de texte en contexte d'ALAO: une année avec le didacticiel FreeText. [Text grammar in the context of computer-assisted language teaching: A year with the computer courseware Free Text.]. *The Canadian Modern Language Review, 62,* 221-233.

Haneda, M. (2004). The joint construction of meaning in writing conferences. *Applied Linguistics, 25,* 178-219.

Harley, B., Allen, J. P. B., Cummins, J. & Swain, M. (Eds.) (1990). *The Development of Second Language Proficiency.* New York: Cambridge University Press.

Hidi, S. & Anderson, V. (1986). Producing written summaries: Task demands, cognitive operations, and implications for instruction. *Review of Educational Research, 56,* 473-493.

Hillocks, G. (1986). *Research on Written Composition: New Dimensions for Teaching.* Urbana, IL: National Conference on Research in English/ERIC Clearinghouse.

James, M. (2009). "Far" transfer of learning outcomes from an ESL writing course: Can the gap be bridged? *Journal of Second Language Writing, 18,* 69-84.

Jang, E., Dunlop, M., Park, G. & van der Boom, E. (2015). How do young students with different profiles of reading skill mastery, perceived ability, and goal orientation respond to holistic diagnostic feedback? *Language Testing, 32,* 359-383.

Jones, S. & Tetroe, J. (1987). Composing in a second language. In A. Matsuhashi (Ed.), *Writing in Real Time: Modeling the Production Processes* (pp. 34-57). Norwood, NJ: Ablex.

Jun, S. W., Ramirez, G. & Cumming, A. (2010). Tutoring adolescents in literacy: A meta-analysis. *McGill Journal of Education, 45,* 219-238.

Kristmanson, P., Dicks, J. & Bouthillier, J. (2009). Pedagogical applications of a second language writing model at elementary and middle school levels. *Writing & Pedagogy, 1,* 37-62.

Kubota, R. (1997). Reevaluation of the uniqueness of Japanese written discourse: Implications for contrastive rhetoric. *Written Communication, 14,* 460-480.

Kubota, R. & Lehner, A. (2004). Toward critical contrastive rhetoric. *Journal of Second Language Writing, 13,* 7-27.

Lambert, W. E. & Tucker, G. R. (1972). *Bilingual Education of Children: The St. Lambert Experiment.* Rowley, MA: Newbury House.

Lapkin, S. & Swain, M. (2000). Task outcomes: A focus on Immersion students' use of pronominal verbs in their writing. *Canadian Journal of Applied Linguistics, 3,* 7-19.

Le Bouthillier, J. & Dicks, J. (2013). L'emploi d'un modèle d'enseignement systématique d'écriture: Une étude de cas en 7e anneé de l'immersion précoce. [Using a systematic model for teaching writing: A case study in 7th grade early immersion]. *Canadian Modern Language Review, 69,* 298-323.

Lee, I. (1998). Enhancing ESL students' awareness of coherence-creating mechanisms in writing. *TESL Canada Journal, 15,* 36-49.

Mohan, B. (1986). *Language and Content.* Reading, MA: Addison-Wesley.

Mohan, B. & Lo, W. (1985). Academic writing and Chinese students: Transfer and developmental factors. *TESOL Quarterly, 19,* 515-534.

Morgan, B. (1998). *The ESL Classroom: Teaching, Critical Practice, and Community Development.* Toronto, ON: University of Toronto Press.

Morgan, B. (2002). Critical practice in community-based ESL programs: A Canadian perspective. *Journal of Language, Identity, and Education, 1,* 141-162.

Naqvi, R., Thorne, K., Pfitscher, C., Nordstokke, D. & McKeough, A. (2013). Reading dual language books: Improving early literacy skills in linguistically diverse classrooms. *Journal of Early Childhood Research, 11*, 3-15.

Neumann, H. (2014). Teacher assessment of grammatical ability in second language academic writing: A case study. *Journal of Second Language Writing, 24*, 83-107.

Olson, D. R. (1994). *The World on Paper: The Conceptual and Cognitive Implications of Writing and Reading.* Cambridge, UK: Cambridge University Press.

Parks, S. & Maguire, M. (1999). Coping with on-the-job writing in ESL: A constructivist-semiotic perspective. *Language Learning, 49*, 143-175.

Parks, S. Huot, D., Hamers, J. & Lemonnier, F. (2005). "History of theatre" websites: A brief history of the writing process in a high school ESL language arts class. *Journal of Second Language Writing, 14*, 233-258.

Qi, D. (1998). An inquiry into language-switching in second language composing processes. *Canadian Modern Language Review, 54*, 413-435.

Riazi, M. (1997). Acquiring disciplinary literacy: A social-cognitive analysis of text production and learning among Iranian graduate students of education. *Journal of Second Language Writing, 6*, 105-137.

Séror, J. (2009). Institutional forces and L2 writing feedback in higher education. *The Canadian Modern Language Review/la Revue canadienne des langues vivantes, 66*, 203-232.

Séror, J. (2011). Alternative sources of feedback and second language writing development in university content courses. *Canadian Journal of Applied Linguistics (CJAL)/Revue canadienne de linguistique appliquée (RCLA), 14*, 118-143.

Shi, L. (1998). Effects of prewriting discussions on adult ESL students' compositions. *Journal of Second Language Writing, 7*, 319-345.

Shi, L. (2004). Textual borrowing in second-language writing. *Written Communication, 21*, 171-200.

Shi, L. (2010). Textual appropriation and citing behaviors of university undergraduates. *Applied Linguistics, 31*, 1-24.

Simon, R. (2013). "Starting with what is": Exploring response and responsibility to student writing through collaborative inquiry. *English Education, 45,* 115-146.

Statistics Canada. (2013). Language highlight tables, 2011 Census. Ottawa: Statistics Canada. Retrieved October 4, 2013 from http://www12.statcan. gc.ca/census-recensement/2011/dp-pd/hlt-fst/lang/index-eng.cfm? Lang=E

Swain, M. (2010). Talking it through: Languaging as a source of learning. In R. Batstone (Ed.), *Sociocognitive Perspectives on Second Language Learning and Use* (pp. 112-130). Oxford, UK: Oxford University Press.

Suzuki, M. (2008). Japanese learners' self revisions and peer revisions of their written compositions in English. *TESOL Quarterly, 42,* 209-233.

Suzuki, W. (2012). Written languaging, direct correction, and second language writing revision. *Language Learning, 62,* 1110-1133.

Vaillancourt, F., Coche, O., Cadieux, M. & Ronson, J. (2012). *Official Language Policies of the Canadian Provinces: Costs and Benefits in 2006.* Calgary, AB: Fraser Institute.

Wang, L. (2003). Switching to first language among writers with differing second language proficiency. *Journal of Second Language Writing, 12,* 347-375.

Wells, G. (1980). *Learning Through Interaction.* Cambridge, UK: Cambridge University Press.

Wells, G. (1999). *Dialogic Interaction: Towards a Sociocultural Practice and Theory of Education.* Cambridge, UK: Cambridge University Press.

Wilson, J. S. (2013). The role of social relationships in the writing of multilingual adolescents. In L. de Oliveira & T. Silva (Eds.), L2 *Writing in Secondary Classrooms: Student Experiences, Academic Issues, and Teacher Education* (pp. 87-103). New York: Routledge.

Yang, L. (2010). Doing a group presentation: Negotiations and challenges experienced by five Chinese ESL students of Commerce at a Canadian university. *Language Teaching Research, 14,* 141-160.

Yau, M. & Belanger, J. (1984). The influence of mode on the syntactic complexity of EFL students at three grade levels. *TESL Canada Journal, 2,* 65-76.

Yoon, C. (2011). Concordancing in L2 writing class. *English for Academic Purposes, 10,* 130-139.

Yoon, C. (2013). Web-based concordancing and other reference resources as a problem solving tool for L2 writers. Unpublished PhD thesis, University of Toronto.

Zhou, A., Busch, M. & Cumming, A. (2014). Do adult ESL learners' and their teachers' goals for improving grammar in writing correspond? *Language Awareness, 23*(3), 234-254.

Chapter 3

An Ecology of Studies on EFL Writing in the Chinese Context

Junju Wang

Shandong University

Introduction

The last few decades have seen L2 writing become an explosively growing field. With many venues devoted exclusively to L2 writing research, such as the *Journal of Second Language Writing* and the Symposium on Second Language Writing, L2 writing has evolved into an important academic field with a range of subfields, theories of its own, and cross-disciplinary interfaces (Kroll, 2003; Silva & Matsuda, 2001, 2010; Zhan, 2007). Over last half century, L2 writing has become an interdisciplinary field drawing primarily on work in second language studies and applied linguistics.

Such rapid development has made it difficult even for specialists to have a complete, state-of-the-art picture of this field. As a result, the need to review and synthesize research findings in its sub-areas has become ever stronger, not only for reflection on the past but also for a look into the future. Early in the 1990s, Silva (1993) made one of the first attempts, examining 72 reports of empirical research for the distinctive features of L2 writing by comparing studies on L1 and L2 writing available at the time. Similar studies include Silva,

Brice, and Reichelt (1999) and Matsuda, Canagarajah, Harklau, Hyland, and Warshauer (2003). More importantly, Leki, Cumming and Silva (2008) synthesized twenty-five years of the most significant and influential findings of published research on second language writing in English and provided access to research developments in the field.

Similarly, Chinese scholars have made efforts to review and synthesize research on L2 writing. As of December 2014, over 100 review articles were published in Chinese journals, and their focal areas range from L2 writing processes (e.g., He, 2007; Wang, 2007) to L2 writing instruction (Jiang, 2007; Ren, 2008), to L2 writing assessment (Xiu, 2002). Among these review articles, over 20 have examined the status quo of L2 writing studies in the Chinese context. Table 1 presents a selection of these studies. Li and Li (2003), for example, found a steady increase in the number of papers published in eight linguistics journals with a wide range of topics and a small percentage of empirical studies. Further analysis revealed certain problems, such as repetitious research on some topics, disproportionate use of empirical research methods, inadequate attention paid to the learner, and a lack of scientific and objective means of evaluation and testing. Wang and Wang (2004) found that empirical studies of L2 writing in the Chinese context had investigated various aspects pertaining to L2 writing, but little attention had been paid to L2 writing theory or writing pedagogy.

In addition, Qin (2009) provided an overview of studies on college English writing in China. The results showed that although research on L2 writing was generally on the rise with increasingly diversified topics, most work was done in the areas of teaching L2 writing, students' finished products, and writing contexts. So, problems existed, such as repetition of similar research and a lack of empirically oriented research on the teaching of L2 writing. To find out if the trend for the most recent five-year period was consistent with the general tendency of L2 writing studies, Huang and Yu (2009) selected and compared two sets of data, one being a collection of 229 papers published in 17 journals in foreign language studies from 2003 to 2007, and the other a collection of 251 papers from 9 key journals in foreign language studies from 1993 to 2007. Results show a tremendous increase in the number of EFL writing studies since 1993 and an obvious change in what topics these studies covered. They suggested that more attention be paid to empirical studies, writing textbooks, and learners other than college students. Guo (2009) found that the domestic research on L2 writing presented characteristics of scientific, multi-faceted, and rational development. It was proposed that future studies on L2 writing focus more on the use of multimedia and on the influence of the learning environment on learners. According to Meng, Li and Dou (2010), despite the fact that the gap between non-empirical and empirical studies was narrowing, empirical studies still made up a small percentage of all studies. Additionally, studies on L2 writing in China were found not to be evenly distributed with regard to subject matter and focal area.

Table 1   Major Meta-Studies on L2 Writing in China

Study	Time range	Source journals	Focus
Li & Li (2003)	1993-2002	8 key FL journals	Studies on L2 writing
Wang &Wang (2004)	1993-2003	Not specified	Empirical studies on L2 writing
Yao & Cheng (2005)	1980-2003	7 key FL journals	Studies on L2 writing
Tang & Yao (2008)	2003-2007	9 key FL journals	Studies on L2 writing
Qin (2009)	2000-2007	8 key FL journals	Studies on L2 writing at tertiary level
Huang & Yu (2009)	1993-2007 2003-2007	9 key FL journals 17 other FL journals	Studies on L2 writing
Guo (2009)	1991-2008	8 key FL journals	Studies on L2 writing
Meng, et al (2010)	1989-2008	10 key FL journals	Studies on teaching EFL writing

It has to be noted that the above review articles mostly involve publications retrieved from key journals in FL studies, particularly those appearing earlier than the 1990s. Using a similar framework for data analysis, they tried to capture the big picture but were largely partial and duplicative, thus failing to represent the multiple facets of the L2 writing research in the Chinese context.

To develop a state-of-the-art understanding of the L2 writing field in China, this study will take a meta-disciplinary approach to examine in depth the actual progression of the history of this specialized field (Matsuda, et al., 2003). This study is aimed at providing a historical and multi-faceted overview of L2 writing research in China by focusing on the general developmental pattern, level of scholarship, subject matter, and focal areas of relevant previous studies. It is hoped that the results of the study can help professionals gain a meaningful and insightful knowledge of L2 writing research in China in order to develop novel scholarship in the future.

Methodology

The data for the study were collected from the three largest Chinese periodical databases: the China Academic Journals Database (CAJ), the China Online Journal Database (COJ), and the Chinese Technology Periodical Database (CTP). As of April, 2015, CAJ had a pool of 35.2 million articles from more than 7,500 journals, starting from 1915; COJ contained 15.9 million records from over 6,400 periodicals from 1986 onward; and CTP had over 20 million articles in over 8,000 periodicals from 1989 onward.

The data collection and validation were done in three steps. First, the researcher did a "basic search" in all the journals with over 19 key words, trying to exhaust the possibilities. The key words included "English writing", "L2 writing", "foreign language writing", "second language writing, "L2 composition", etc. A total of 9,542 articles were retrieved. Then, the researcher did a "standard search" with 10 more generic key words in the 42 identified journals on foreign language studies and foreign language education. The key words included "writing", "composition", "essay", "narrative", etc. Altogether, 2,716 articles were obtained. The retrieval was done on April 12, 2015 and updated on May 20, 2015. After that, the researcher combined the two groups of data and deleted the identical articles, articles on writing other than English writing, and irrelevant records like calls-for-papers for conferences. A total of 11,889 articles were finally found valid. These articles were published in 1,417 journals, between 1962 and 2015.

When analyzing the data, the researcher did a pilot study on 500 articles by using the categorical classification in Leki, Cumming and Silva (2008), Huang and Yu (2009), and Meng, et al (2010). Four major themes were first identified, including developmental pattern, level of scholarship, subject matter, and focal area. After several revisions of categories and the application of the resulting classification system to another 500 articles, a coding scheme for data analysis was finally worked out for the needs of this particular study.

When the category of an article was not readily determinable, the full text of this particular article was referred to for a more sound judgment. Totals and percentages were counted up for patterns, features, and tendencies. Details of categorization and criteria for classification are described together with results in the next section.

Results and Discussion

The following section presents the findings of the survey of literature and a discussion of the development and current state of L2 writing research in the Chinese context.

Developmental Tendency

A chronological analysis of the data shows that studies on L2 writing in the Chinese context started in the 1960s, about three decades earlier than what was previously noted (e.g., Li & Li, 2004), In general, such studies have been done over five decades and indicate an accelerating developmental pattern. Ever since the 1990s, there has been a steady rise in the number of studies published in various journals.

As Table 2 shows, among the 11,889 articles published before May 2015, two were published in the 1960s, two in the 1970s, 68 in the 1980s, and 799 in the 1990s. There was a sharp increase of 6,272 publications between 2001 and 2010 and a steady rise of 4,746 publications in the last five years. This shows that studies on L2 writing in China in the 21st century have flourished, the number of which makes up 92.67% of all studies, over 12.65 times larger than the total of the studies from the 1960s to the 1990s. In this sense, the history of L2 writing studies in China could be divided into three phrases of development, namely, the "early period" (1961-1980), the "developmental period" (1981-2000), and the "flourishing period" (2001-2015).

Table 2   The Chronology of the Publications on L2 Writing in China

Year	1961	1962	1963	1964	1965	1966	1967	1968	1969	1970	Subtotal
Size	0	1	0	0	0	1	0	0	0	0	2

Year	1971	1972	1973	1974	1975	1976	1977	1978	1979	1980	Subtotal
Size	0	0	0	0	0	0	0	0	1	1	2

Year	1981	1982	1983	1984	1985	1986	1987	1988	1989	1990	Subtotal
Size	1	3	2	10	7	12	5	8	13	7	68

Year	1991	1992	1993	1994	1995	1996	1997	1998	1999	2000	Subtotal
Size	10	30	32	50	62	84	87	116	161	167	799

Year	2001	2002	2003	2004	2005	2006	2007	2008	2009	2010	Subtotal
Size	204	273	355	376	464	590	887	986	1,073	1,064	6,272

Year	2011	2012	2013	2014	2015*						Subtotal
Size	1,191	1,123	1,093	1,027	312						4,746
Total	11,889										

* The number only reflects publications for the first quarter of the year.

Understandably, the 1960s and the 1970s saw a tiny number of sporadic studies on L2 writing, since the "Cultural Revolution" (1966-1976) turned many fields of study into deserts. The 1980s saw slow but real growth, with one to thirteen studies published in each year of this period. Despite the small number of studies, growth was continuous, if not systematic. In the 1990s, the development of Chinese studies on L2 writing became steady and took on an accelerating tendency. In this decade, the number of published articles increased from 10 papers in 1991 to 167 papers in 2000. After 2001, the number of publications grew exponentially. The number of published articles sharply increased from 204 in 2001 to 1,064 in 2010. The last five years have seen continued growth in L2 writing studies with large numbers of articles, ranging from 1,027 to 1,191, published each year in various periodicals.

Level of Scholarship

In this study, the level of scholarship is determined mainly by discipline relevance and periodical type. In terms of relevance to L2 writing studies, disciplines were classified into foreign language studies and education (FL); arts, humanities and social sciences (ART); common areas (COM); and science and technology (ST). "Common areas" in this list refers to those papers that are focused on people's daily life or popular topics. Papers of this kind are usually non-academic or non-empirical.

With regard to level of authority, periodicals were classified as authoritative journals (AUT), key journals (KEY), ordinary journals (ORD) and marginal journals (MAR). In China, the top indexes for evaluation are the CSSCI[1] developed by Nanjing University and the PKU top journal list established by Peking University. In this study, authoritative journals refer to those listed in both of the two top indexes; key journals are those listed in one of the two top indexes; ordinary journals are those not listed in either of the two indexes; and

---

1 The Chinese Social Sciences Citation Index (CSSCI) is an interdisciplinary citation index program developed by Nanjing University since 1997 and established in 2000. This citation database covers more than 2,700 Chinese academic journals of humanities and social sciences. Now many leading Chinese universities and institutes use CSSCI as a basis for the evaluation of academic achievements and promotion.

marginal journals are those not particularly suited for academic affairs.

With regard to periodical type, this study found that among all the source journals for L2 writing studies, 63 were authoritative journals; 104 were key journals; 1,059 were ordinary journals; and 190 were marginal journals. As indicated in Table 3, authoritative journals had a relatively small number of publications (578) on L2 writing studies but had a relatively high publication rate (9.17) whereas ordinary journals had the largest number of publications (6,088) but had a relatively small publication rate (5.75). Interestingly, marginal journals outperformed authoritative journals and key journals in number of publications and publication rate. This suggests that authoritative and key journals had become important sources for advanced studies on L2 writing whereas ordinary journals were the main sources for publication due to the large numbers of periodical types and number of publications. Also, marginal journals, though primarily not academically-oriented, make up quite a large proportion of publications on L2 writing studies in the Chinese context.

Table 3   Levels of Scholarship and Distributions of Publications

	By Periodical Type				By Discipline Relevance			
	AUT	KEY	ORD	MAR	FL	ART	COM	ST
No. of periodicals	63	104	1059	190	42	1176	91	101
No. of articles	578	105	6088	4177	1192	6308	3662	727
Percentage (%)	5.71	8.02	51.21	35.13	10.03	53.06	30.80	6.11
Publication rate (a/p)	9.17	1.01	5.75	21.89	28.38	5.36	40.24	7.19

*Publication rate refers to the average number of papers published by each journal.

In terms of discipline relevance, it was found that the 42 journals in foreign language studies and pedagogy (FL) have published 1,192 articles, making up 10.03% of all publications; journals in arts, humanities, and social sciences (ART) have published 6,308 papers (53.06%); journals for common studies (COM) have published 3,662 articles (30.80%); and the journals in the area of science and technology (ST) 727 articles (6.11%). On average, each FL journal has published 28.38 papers, with ART journals averaging 5.36; COM

Journals 40.24; and ST journals 7.19. These numbers suggest that journals in arts, humanities, and social sciences, as well as ordinary journals are where most studies on L2 writing are published. Consequently, the published papers have a relatively low level of scholarship and are comparatively less influential in academia. To make necessary changes, there is a need to promote the competitiveness of studies on L2 writing for key and authoritative journals.

Focus of Study

Based on studies like Wang (2013), this study has identified 10 kinds of study focuses in previous studies on EFL writing in the Chinese context. These focuses of study include writing process, written texts, writing ability, writing assessment, teaching of writing, influential factors on writing, approaches to writing, textbooks on writing, studies on writing, and others.

Table 4　**Focal Areas and Distribution of Publications**

Focus of Study	Topic Range	Subtotal	%
Teaching of writing	Classroom teaching, teacher feedback, peer feedback, process approach, genre approach	5595	47.06
Written text	Error analysis, textual structure, linguistic features	2068	17.40
Approaches to writing	Writing skills, writing techniques, rhetorical devices	1257	10.58
Writing ability	Writing competence, writing proficiency	1215	10.11
Influential factors	Negative transfer, thinking modes, cultural differences	938	7.89
Writing process	Subprocesses, strategy use, anxiety in writing	332	2.80
Writing assessment	Writing tests, formative assessment	296	2.49
Textbooks on writing	Textbooks, exercise books	451	0.38
Meta-studies on writing	Reviews of previous studies	110	0.09
Others	Other focus than the abovementioned	78	0.06

Table 4 shows that the teaching of EFL writing is the best investigated area since 47.06% of the previous studies were focused on classroom instruction, teacher/peer feedback, and teaching with process and genre approaches. Different from Huang and Yu (2009), this study found that nearly 17.40% of all the studies were focused on students' written products in English, with analysis of mistakes and errors, textual structure, and linguistic features as the most popular topics explored. In addition, a large number of studies were on how to develop writing abilities (10.11%), approaches to writing (10.58%), and the influential factors (7.89%) on both writing processes and written products. By contrast, studies on EFL writing processes, writing assessment, and writing textbooks were relatively small in number, with 2.80% of them investigating the subprocesses of writing, 2.49% on writing tests and the formative approach to assessing writing, and 0.38% of them on reviews of textbooks available to Chinese EFL students at all levels.

A closer examination of the studies indicates that most studies on the teaching of writing were actually summaries of teaching experiences, and those on writing approaches and writing abilities were exclusively suggestions for developing more effective writing methods and better writing abilities. Also, many studies on written texts presented lists of errors and mistakes made by students, together with examples to illustrate such mistakes and errors. Empirical studies make up only a small portion of all the studies, with most of them being on writing processes and writing assessment.

Subject Matter

Based on the context and the object of study, subject matter was classified into ten categories, namely L2 writing of primary students, L2 writing of secondary students, L2 writing of vocational students, L2 writing of undergraduate students, L2 writing of postgraduate students, L2 writing of students in continuing education, L2 writing of students in general, L2 writing for specific and academic purposes, L2 writing in general, and others. Sample titles of each type of articles are illustrated in Table 5.

Table 5   Subject Matter and Distribution of Publications

Subject Matter	Example	Subtotal	%
Undergraduate L2 writing	Attributions of errors in English writing by college students	3863	32.49
L2 writing of unspecified students	Coherence in students' English writing: a perspective of discourse analysis	2564	21.57
L2 writing in general sense	Psycholinguistics and English writing	1920	16.15
Approaches to writing	Writing skills, writing techniques, rhetorical devices	1257	10.58
Professional L2 writing	The writing of English articles on medical research	1166	9.81
Secondary L2 writing	The cultivation of English writing ability of junior secondary students	971	8.16
Vocational L2 writing	The application of error analysis in the teaching of English writing for vocational students	512	4.31
Primary L2 Writing	Effective practice of the teaching of English writing at primary level	473	3.97
Postgraduate L2 writing	On the teaching strategies of English writing for non-English major master's students	154	1.30
L2 writing of adult part-time students	The process approach in the teaching of English writing for adult students	146	1.23
Others (e.g., minority students)	Error analysis of English writings by Tibetan minority students	120	1.1

Table 5 shows that with regard to L2 writing by students of different kinds, a large portion of studies (32.49%) were on EFL writing by undergraduate students at tertiary level, followed by studies on writings by unspecified students (21.57%) and EFL writing in general sense (16.19%). The least investigated subject matter areas include L2 writing at primary and secondary levels (3.97% and 8.16% respectively), followed by vocational students (4.31%), postgraduate students (1.30%), and part-time adult students (1.23%).

It can be suggested that studies on L2 writing in China address a complete range of subject matter in terms of object of investigation. In addition to professional writing and writing in a general sense, L2 writing at different educational levels and in educational modes has been covered. However, a lack of balance was found among the studies of different categories: the largest number of studies were focused on English writing at college and university level while studies on other students received much less attention.

Discussion

An historical review of the studies on EFL writing in China shows that relevant studies started in the 1960s and have gone through steady development for the past two decades. Focusing on a broad range of areas, these studies are mostly non-empirical investigations and have primarily remained in the domain of writing teaching at the tertiary level. Hence, disproportionateness and off-balance phenomena are evident.

Disproportionateness refers to the sharp contrast between the number of journals specializing in foreign language studies and pedagogy and those in arts and humanities, the contrast between the number of source journals for publication and the population of English teachers, and the contrast between the number of studies on primary and secondary students and those on tertiary students. Statistics show that, in China, there are over a million of English teachers teaching 180,000,000 students in primary and secondary schools and around 120,000 English teachers teaching 20,000,000 students at tertiary level. It is also the case that relatively few published papers on L2 writing show up in journals of foreign language studies and that relatively few studies have been done on EFL writing at the primary and secondary levels. It is a sad fact that the smallest portion of studies (3.97%) were on the largest group of students and that the largest group of teachers (English teachers, as opposed to teachers of other subjects) had the smallest number of journals available for publication on L2 writing.

Off-balance phenomena, refers to the large body of publications on the teaching of EFL writing and the fact that most of them were non-empirical studies. This indicates that pedagogical issues have become a very important part of the studies on EFL writing in the Chinese context (Huang & Yu, 2009; Wang, 2013). While these pedagogical studies are helpful for perceptual and methodological upgrades and for a better understanding of Chinese studies on EFL writing, it should be noted that studies of this kind are mostly limited to summaries of what the authors have experienced in their actual classroom teaching. Without sufficient support from theories and empirical data, the viewpoints conveyed are not very convincing, and the conclusions of the studies are, more often than not, shaky (Fan & Zhu, 2004).

Theoretically oriented studies have tried to approach relevant topics from the perspectives of justification and construction. Although they are not systematic to a large extent, they help to confirm the idea that "no single theory or pedagogical approach by any means applies to and validates L2 writing scholarship" (Fujieda, 2006, p. 66).

Empirical studies mostly address writing processes and strategy use. They have confirmed the transferability of L1 writing strategies, the proficiency threshold for thinking in English, and the socially and contextually bound nature of work on sub-processes and strategy use (Wang, 2013). In addition, they have indicated that L2 writing processes are naturally bilingual and that various factors can have an effect on the progression of writing behaviors. Although limited in number, these empirical studies have justified the important role of L1 in L2 writing processes and the positive transfer of L1 writing competence for the improvement of the quality of English writing.

Despite the huge number of studies on EFL writing in the Chinese context produced over a half century, it has to be admitted that important and significant studies are not strong in terms of methodology, originality and theoretical localization. In those insufficiently investigated areas (Wang, 2013), more studies can be conducted with diversified methodologies and sufficient theoretical backup (Sun, 2013). What is also needed is the localization of the theories introduced from the West to tailor models to the characteristics of Chinese EFL learners.

It can be argued that studies in the Chinese context have to pay due attention to both pedagogical and professional issues. To balance the focal areas and promote the quality of relevant studies, interdisciplinary research should be encouraged for a more comprehensive understanding of EFL writing processes. It is clear that interface studies will be promising for future research.

Conclusion

This study has synthesized the studies of EFL writings in the Chinese context. By analyzing the features of relevant studies in terms of developmental tendency, level of scholarship, subject matter, and focal area, it has been found that enormous efforts have been made in developing theories and practice in the area of L2 writing. Despite inadequacies in several aspects, relevant studies have made great contributions to both academic research and practical teaching. This study concludes that L2 writing in China is a young, active, and promising area of studies. To improve the ecology of studies in this area, Chinese researchers need to develop their own theories, diversify their methodology, balance the focal areas, and promote quality in studies. The need of interface and interdisciplinary studies calls for more synergistic investigations.

It has to be pointed out that this study only looks at advanced studies on EFL writing in the Chinese context. The publications selected for analysis are all articles from Chinese journals. Future studies could take a comprehensive look at research in the area by including studies in the forms of monographs, dissertations, edited books, and conference proceedings. Comparative work could also be done with studies in other contexts in the future to develop a better picture of EFL writing in general.

Acknowledgements

This study is supported by The Program of National Social Science Foundation of China [10BYY026].

References

Fan, L. & Zhu, L. (2004). A synthesis of the psychological process of writing planning in the West. *Foreign Language Education, 25*(4), 65-70.

Fujieda, Y. (2006). A brief historical sketch of second language writing studies: A retrospective. [Online] Available:www.kyoai.ac.jp/college/ronshuu/no-06/fujieda.pdf

Guo, S. (2009). A review of China's second language writing research in the past 18 years (1991-2008). *Shandong Foreign Language Teaching Journal, 30*(5), 38-41.

Huang, J. & Yu, S. (2009). Reflections on EFL writing researches in China. *Foreign Languages in China, 6*(4), 60-65.

Kroll, B. (2003). *Exploring the Dynamics of Second Language Writing.* Cambridge: Cambridge University Press.

Leki, I., Cumming, A. & Silva, T. (2008). *A Synthesis of Research on Second Language Writing in English: 1985-2005.* New York: Routledge.

Li, Z. & Li, S. (2003). Reflections on contemporary research on EFL writing in China: A survey of articles published in eight of the major linguistic journals in China in the past decade. *Foreign Language World, 24* (6), 55-60+78.

Matsuda, P. K., Canagarajah, A. S., Harklau, L., Hyland, K. & Warshauer, M. (2003) Changing currents in second language writing research: A colloquium. *Journal of Second Language Writing, 12*(2), 151-179.

Matsuda, P. K & Silva, T. (2005) (Eds). *Second Language Writing Research: Perspectives on the Process of Knowledge Construction.* Mahwah, New Jersey: Lawrence Erlbaum.

Meng, X., Li L. & Dou, Q. (2010). A review of domestic [research?] on English writing for the past 20 years. *Neijiang Science and Technology, 21*(3), 31-32.

Qin, Z. (2009). An overview of college English writing studies in China between 2000 and 2007. *Modern Foreign Languages, 32*(2), 195-204+220.

Silva, T. (1993). Toward an understanding of the distinct nature of L2 writing: The ESL research and its implications. *TESOL Quarterly, 27*(4), 657-677.

Silva, T. & Matsuda, P. K. (Eds.) (2001). *On Second Language Writing.* Mahwah, NJ: Lawrence Erlbaum Associates.

Silva, T. & Matsuda, P. K. (Eds.). (2010). *Practicing Theory in Second Language Writing.* West Lafayette, IN: Parlor Press.

Silva, T., Brice, C. & Reichelt, M. (Eds.) (1999). *Annotated Bibliography of Second Language Writing: 1993-1997.* Stamford: Ablex.

Sun, Y. (2013). Sociocultural perspectives and second language writing research. Paper presented at the 2013 ELT Conference in China, Wuhan.

Wang, W. & Wang, L. (2004). L2 writing research in China: An overview. *Foreign Language World, 25*(3), 51-58.

Wang, L. (2005). Empirical studies on L2 writing in China: A review. *Foreign Languages in China, 2*(1), 40-46.

Wang, J. (2006). A study of strategy use in L2 writing processes. *Journal of Shandong University, 56*(6), 61-66.

Wang, J. (2013). A synthesis of the studies on L2 writing in the Chinese Context. *Journal of EFL Writing Teaching and Research, 1*(1), 11-24.

Wen, Q. (2001). *Applied Linguistics: Research Methods and Thesis Writing.* Beijing: Foreign Language Teaching and Research Press.

Zhan, J. (2007). ESL writing in the U.S.: From pedagogical practice to theoretical research. *Foreign Languages in China, 4*(2), 42-47.

Chapter 4

Teaching, Learning and Assessment of Writing in Schools of Hong Kong, China: Bridging the Idealism-Realism Gap

Icy Lee

The Chinese University of Hong Kong

Introduction

With increasing emphasis on EFL writing programs and earlier starting ages for EFL education (Reichelt, 2009) in different parts of the world, writing in English as a foreign language has been receiving more and more attention. While research on EFL writing has been mushrooming since the turn of the century, there is an under-representation of work conducted in the school context (Ortega, 2009). As a result, we have scant knowledge about the theory, research and pedagogy of EFL writing that affect younger students learning to write in school contexts. This paper sets out to examine the teaching, learning and assessment of EFL writing in Hong Kong schools, with a specific focus on the "best practices" advice that has informed the writing curriculum vis-à-vis teachers' actual practices in local classrooms. The review uncovers a number of areas in which teachers' practices are at odds with the "best practices" recommendations. The paper discusses such disjunctures and concludes with recommendations to bridge the idealism-realism gap.

EFL Writing in Hong Kong Schools

In Hong Kong, although English is one of the two official languages (Chinese is the other official language) and often referred to as a second language (whereas Japanese, French, Spanish etc. are referred to as foreign languages), the diminishing role of English in society has become a fact of life since 1997. While English writing is introduced early in the primary school curriculum, students in Hong Kong rarely write in English outside the classroom. In writing, therefore, English mainly plays the role of a foreign language (Lee, 2011).

In Hong Kong schools, English is one of the most important subjects for both primary and secondary students, who usually have an English lesson almost every day of the week. They learn writing throughout the twelve years of schooling, six years primary and six years secondary. The skills students are expected to learn range from "the basic conventions of written English" (Curriculum Development Council, 2004, p. 57) at lower primary to "a broad range of text types, so as to deepen their understanding of the use of different methods of organization in different types of discourse" (Curriculum Development Council & Hong Kong Examinations and Assessment Authority, 2007, p. 85) at senior secondary.

Although the teaching of integrated language skills (instead of their compartmentalization) is advocated (Curriculum Development Council, 1999), schools in Hong Kong have designated writing lessons starting in upper primary, during which in-class writing is conducted. Grades 3, 6 and 9 students take part in territory-wide assessments that require them to write 30, 80, and 150 words, respectively, based on a picture or mind-map prompt, while Grade 12 students sit for a high-stakes university-entrance examination that requires them to write two essays of 200 words and 400 words, respectively. To prepare for public examinations, teachers usually require students to write a composition every two to three weeks in the school year. Writing topics are often taken from English textbooks, which the majority of teachers use to guide their classroom teaching.

The teaching syllabuses in schools are informed by local curriculum documents, which are developed by the Curriculum Development Council, an advisory body set up to give advice to the Education Bureau regarding matters relating to curriculum development in local schools. Although it is not mandatory for teachers to base their teaching on the curriculum guides, these documents are considered to be blueprints for teaching and learning in schools. The next section will examine the major recommendations for the teaching of writing provided by local curriculum documents, which constitute the "best practices" advice for teachers of English in Hong Kong.

"Best Practices" Recommendations From Hong Kong Curriculum Documents

A review of several major curriculum documents that guide the teaching of writing in Hong Kong schools reveals a number of salient principles, which are by and large supported by major findings in the L2 writing literature.

Multifarious Functions of Writing

To start with, the teaching of writing is grounded in a perspective that views writing as a multi-faceted concept. In the Hong Kong context, writing is seen to perform multifarious functions (Grabe & Kaplan, 1996). First, it is used to communicate ideas and present information for different purposes and audiences:

> In real life, people often communicate with each other in writing, whether through paper-and-pen or electronic means. Through writing, people can communicate at a distance with each other. They can also record information which will last over time, and present

information, ideas and feelings for a variety of purposes and audiences. (Curriculum Development Council, 2004, p. 152)

Second, the use of writing as a vehicle for language reinforcement is emphasized, as writing "enhances oral development and reinforces the language structures and vocabulary that learners acquire" (Curriculum Development Council, 2004, p. 152).

Also, writing serves an important cognitive function. As students engage in the writing process, they generate and explore ideas, compose, organize, re-organize ideas, and engage in knowledge transformation (Bereiter & Scardamalia, 1987; Hayes & Flower, 1980):

In the process of writing, learners activate their knowledge, take in information, generate ideas, organize and recognize ideas, and sometimes recreate meanings. (Curriculum Development Council, 2004, p. 152)

Finally, apart from being a tool that serves a variety of social purposes ranging from informing and entertaining (Sperling, 1996; Weigle, 2002), writing can enable students to develop their creativity and critical thinking:

Writing provides learners with the opportunity to develop their communication skills to inform, influence and entertain others as well as to demonstrate their creativity and critical thinking. (Curriculum Development Council, 2004, p. 152)

Teaching Methodologies and Expected Learning Outcomes

Given the multi-facetedness of writing, methodologies in the writing classroom should be geared towards helping students develop a range of writing skills. These skills, which are expressed as the expected learning outcomes for students, include the following at senior secondary level (grades 10-12):

- Write texts for different contexts, audiences, and purposes with relevant content and adequate supporting detail;
- Convey meaning using a range of vocabulary, linguistic devices and language patterns appropriately and accurately;
- Plan and produce coherent and structured texts with ideas effectively presented and developed; and
- Write texts using appropriate tone, style and register and the salient features of different genres (Curriculum Development Council & Hong Kong Examination and Assessment Authority, 2007, p. 48).

It is noteworthy that "methodologies entirely focusing on language errors are hardly adequate in improving learners' abilities" (Curriculum Development Council, 1999, p. 95). Thus, teachers are advised against adopting conventional approaches that focus primarily on language form. Instead, it is suggested that strategies and activities for developing students' writing skills should include pre-writing, drafting, revising and editing (Curriculum Development Council, 1999). Therefore, "a process approach to writing is recommended" (Curriculum Development Council & Hong Kong Examination and Assessment Authority, 2007, p. 83).

Process and Text-based Approaches

Although it is suggested that teachers develop students' writing skills at different stages of the writing process, it is recognized that "there should be an emphasis on the process of writing as well as the product" (Curriculum Development Council, 2004, p. 152). Hence, process pedagogy can be adopted alongside a text-based or genre-based approach that focuses on helping students develop texts that are coherent and appropriate for the target genre (Badger & White, 2000). For instance, at the pre-writing stage, it is suggested that students be helped with idea generation through a range of activities (e.g. brainstorming, free writing, reading or listening to texts on the topic), as well as with planning of ideas by taking into account the purpose, audience and structure of the target genre through text-based activities (e.g. reading and analyzing sample texts) (Curriculum Development Council & Hong Kong Examination and Assessment Authority, 2007).

Peer/Self-Evaluation as an Integral Part of Process Pedagogy

In the writing classroom, aside from the teacher, students themselves are considered an important resource for providing support to their peers during the writing process (Yang, Badger & Yu, 2006; Zhao, 2010). It is suggested that students "work interactively in pairs or small groups to review each other's draft through questions, suggestions or comments" (Curriculum Development Council & Hong Kong Examinations and Assessment Authority, 2007, p. 85-86). Also, students can be "encouraged to respond critically to their own work by practicing self-feedback" (Curriculum Development Council & Hong Kong Examinations and Assessment Authority, 2007, p. 85-86).

Teacher-Student Conferences

In addition to peer/self-evaluation, it is suggested that students participate actively in teacher-student conferences:

> The teacher conducts a conference with learners individually or in small groups to discuss their drafts. Learners can participate actively in negotiating and clarifying meaning before proceeding to revise their work. (Curriculum Development Council & Hong Kong Examination and Assessment Authority, 2007, p. 86)

Conferencing is seen as an important pedagogical procedure that can help students improve their revisions through engaging in a dialogue with the teacher (Hyland & Hyland, 2006).

Teacher Feedback

Teacher feedback plays a pivotal role in the writing classroom. A few pieces of advice are provided in the local curriculum documents:

- Teachers "must avoid providing detailed editing comments on the surface form without paying attention to organizational and content issues" (Curriculum Development Council, 1999, p. 94).

- "Teachers need not correct all the mistakes in learners' work. Total correction is time-consuming for the teacher and discouraging for the learners, particularly when the latter see their papers full of red ink" (Curriculum Development Council, 1999, p. 95).

- "When marking compositions, it is advisable to provide learners with comprehensive feedback on content, accuracy, appropriateness, presentation and organization" (Curriculum Development Council & Hong Kong Examination and Assessment Authority, 2007, p. 106).

- "Teachers should give comments on the drafts they have collected from learners … They should make suggestions which will enable learners to carry out revisions in the areas of organization, grammar and mechanics" (Curriculum Development Council & Hong Kong Examination and Assessment Authority, 2007, p. 83).

The above quotes show that it is important that teachers deliver feedback to intermediate drafts, rather than single drafts, and that feedback should have balanced coverage on all important aspects of writing. An error-focused approach is not recommended. Instead, it is suggested that teachers should respond to errors selectively in order not to discourage students (Ferris, 2002, 2003).

Assessment for Learning

Teacher feedback to intermediate drafts of student writing is intended to help students improve their writing. Such feedback is formative and serves the purpose of assessment for learning (Black, Harrison, Lee, Marshall & Wiliam, 2004; Black & Wiliam, 1998), which is another recommended principle for the local writing curriculum (also for the English language curriculum in general). In the writing classroom, assessment for learning strategies such as the use of continuous, qualitative feedback through portfolios, student involvement in assessment through self-/peer assessment, and conferencing are advocated (Curriculum Development Council, 2007). Assessment for learning is ongoing, i.e., it occurs during the process of writing. Additionally, the teacher "needs to observe learners' behavior and skills, assess progress, and give feedback and suggestions on drafting and revising" (Curriculum Development Council, 2004, p. 157).

Teachers' Actual Practices in the Writing Classroom

As the above section has shown, in Hong Kong there is no shortage of advice about how best to teach writing. The recommendations are all in line with the "expert" advice given in the L2 writing literature. In reality, to what extent do teachers follow the advice and put the recommendations into practice? This section attempts to answer this question by drawing upon recent local research.

Writing for Language Reinforcement

Although Hong Kong teachers are advised against paying too much attention to accuracy in writing, their classroom and feedback practices appear to be primarily language-focused. Teachers' pre-writing input, which is limited, is dominated by a focus on grammar and vocabulary (Lo & Hyland, 2007). When giving feedback, teachers pay most attention to language form (Lee, 2008), and the bulk of their time is spent on responding to written errors. In a real sense, they play the role of composition slaves (Hairston, 1986).

Product-Oriented Writing

As in other EFL contexts, the large majority of Hong Kong teachers adopt a product-oriented approach in the writing classroom, where single drafts are collected (Furneaux, Paran & Fairfax, 2007; Lee, 2004, 2008). In fact, since process writing was first introduced in Hong Kong in the 1990's, significant research efforts have focused on the implementation of process writing in Hong Kong classrooms (Brock, 1995; Curtis, 2001; Curtis & Heron, 1998; Hamp-Lyons, 2006; Hamp-Lyons, Chen & Mok, 2001; Pennington, Brock & Yue, 1996). Results of the studies reveal the difficulties involved in implementing process writing in local classrooms. Obstacles include the heavy examination culture and lack of support from school leaders (Hamp-Lyons, Chen & Mok, 2001). In a recent school-based writing curriculum reform project in a primary school in Hong Kong (Lee & Wong, under review), which tells of a success story, the teachers started process writing in 2006, sustained their efforts, and witnessed very positive change in teaching and learning. The process writing teaching team also won the 2010 Chief Executive's Award for Teaching Excellence in Hong Kong. The teachers' innovation was recognized locally and reported in a Radio Hong Kong Television program broadcast in early September 2013, where process writing was referred to as a new approach to teaching writing. Although the benefits of process writing have been promulgated in local curriculum documents since the 1990's, it has remained unpopular with Hong Kong teachers.

Under-Development of Creativity and Critical Thinking

Creativity is expressed in not only "what a student's writing is saying", but also "how it is saying it" (Choi, 2009, p. 281). In Hong Kong writing classrooms, however, due to a heavy focus on written accuracy, students feel discouraged from experimenting with new language to express creative ideas, for fear that they will make more mistakes in writing. An error-focused approach in local writing classrooms, therefore, is a major impediment to the development of creativity. In Lee's (2012) recent study about genre-based teaching and assessment, even though students find the genre-based explicit instruction useful, some feel that they have to follow the "template" provided by the teacher in order to meet teachers' expectations of good writing (Lee, 2012), and as a result, creativity in writing is stifled.

Developing critical thinking through writing is, similarly, much easier said than done. In a recent study conducted by Mok (2009), the classroom observation data reveal that critical thinking is lacking in the writing classroom due to ineffective questioning techniques (that focus mainly on lower-order questions), lack of attention to the writing process, as well as a teacher-dominated, product-centered, and quantity-driven approach that encourages a surface approach to learning. The teachers in the study failed to create the space for learning to facilitate students' critical thinking development. Given the primacy of written accuracy in local classrooms and the fact that many students are still struggling with linguistic expression in their writing, developing critical thinking through writing is a goal that seems difficult to achieve.

Passive Student Involvement

A consequence of a teacher-dominated, product-centered, and error-focused approach in local writing classrooms is that students are reduced to passive recipients in the learning-to-write process. This reality stands in stark contrast to the recommendation that students should be actively involved through engaging in peer/self-evaluating and conferencing. The problem of single drafting is that students need not act upon teacher feedback to revise their drafts and can remain passive throughout. An error-focused approach, on the other hand, sees teachers working very hard to provide detailed error feedback, and oftentimes such error feedback is direct—i.e., correct answers are given to students (Lee, 2004, 2008). Hence, there is little opportunity for students to engage in self-editing and to develop editing skills.

Students' passive role in the writing classroom can also be ascribed to their own entrenched beliefs about teacher and student roles in the writing classroom, as revealed in previous local research on peer evaluation (Sengupta, 1998). Students tend to value teacher feedback more than peer feedback since they believe in the important role the teacher plays as reader and evaluator of student writing (Sengupta, 1998; Tsui & Ng, 2000).

Writing as an Assessment Rather than Learning Tool

With the preponderance of a product-oriented approach, writing in Hong Kong classrooms serves primarily as an assessment tool (Lee & Coniam, 2013), where writing is treated as a test rather than an opportunity for learning. Teacher instructional support and scaffolding are limited, especially during the writing process (Lo & Hyland, 2007). Classroom writing assessment serves the purpose of assessment of learning rather than assessment for learning. Lee's (2007) analysis of the feedback delivered to 174 student texts by 26 secondary teachers indicates that teacher feedback serves mainly summative purposes—as it is retrospective in nature and focuses largely on scores/grades, conveying teachers' judgment of student performance rather than being used for diagnostic purposes to help students improve their writing. Although teachers are advised to implement assessment for learning, assessment of learning dominates in the writing classroom. There is a lack of alignment between assessment and instruction, where writing is assessed according to broad criteria like content, language and organization, and feedback communicated mainly through scores and detailed error feedback that does not require much student engagement.

Bridging the Idealism-Realism Gap

The preceding section has uncovered a clear disjuncture between the "best practices" recommendations provided in local curriculum documents and the reality of teaching as illustrated in local research. Such a chasm can be best summarized by re-visiting an important piece of advice offered as early as 1999, which remains unheeded:

> Teachers should, therefore, avoid adopting solely traditional product-based approaches to writing which are mainly preoccupied with the teaching of form and usage, with the finished product seen as a display of learners' ability in accurately manipulating grammar, vocabulary and mechanics (such as spelling, punctuation and handwriting). (Curriculum Development Council, 1999, p. 95)

Indeed, there is a tremendous gap between idealism and realism. How can the gap be bridged? This section attempts to provide some answers to this conundrum.

Broaden Teachers' Conceptualization of Writing Ability

In view of Hong Kong teachers' heavy language focus in the writing classroom, it is imperative to broaden their perspectives on writing, helping them reflect on fundamental questions about what writing is and how the notion of "writing ability" should be defined. Teachers need to acquire a broader view of writing that entails multiple types of knowledge, in addition to knowledge of the language system—e.g., knowledge of content, process/composing, genre, and context. Without broadening teachers' conceptualization of the notion of writing ability, it is hard to expect a change in their instructional and assessment focus.

Implement a Focused Approach to Error Feedback

One striking characteristic of Hong Kong English teachers' job is that they spend a massive amount of time marking student writing, mainly responding to errors. This aspect of their work has not only eaten into their time but also demotivated them and diminished their interest in teaching writing. Therefore, it is urgently necessary to help teachers appreciate the advice provided in curriculum documents regarding the need to respond to errors selectively. Once this is achieved, teachers will have more time to respond to other areas of student writing. Teachers can also be freed up to engage in other meaningful aspects of their work, such as providing instructional scaffolding and peer review training for students.

Interweave Assessment with Instruction

Teachers' current practice in the writing classroom reveals a lack of connection between assessment and instruction, where assessment entails primarily summative functions expressed in terms of detailed error feedback and scores/grades. To better align assessment with instruction so that assessment is used to improve student learning, teachers should strengthen pre-writing instruction by sharing learning goals with students and establishing criteria of good writing. Apart from teaching what they are going to assess, they should assess what they teach—e.g. using rubric-based assessment. Through interweaving assessment with instruction, teachers can facilitate the delivery of formative, diagnostic feedback to help students understand their strengths and weaknesses in writing.

Implement a Context Approach to Change

As teachers consider the "best practices" advice in the curriculum documents and the wider research literature, and how best to bridge the idealism-realism gap, it is important for them to first critically examine the feasibility of recommended pedagogies (which are imported from the West) and assess the contextual factors in their own classroom and institutional context. In some classrooms, for instance, a combination of process and product approaches may be necessary, where two or three essays are subjected to single drafting in a timed impromptu format (so as to give students examination practice)—e.g. at the beginning and the end of the academic year. For selective error feedback, some teachers may feel uncomfortable about not telling students all the errors they make in their writing. Instead of giving selective error feedback to all essays, viable options include selective error feedback to all full-length essays but comprehensive error feedback to paragraph-level writing, or selective error feedback to most essays but comprehensive error feedback to two or three essays done at the beginning and end of the academic year. These examples show that bridging the idealism-realism gap does not mean that teachers should embrace the "best practices" advice uncritically, without any consideration for their own teaching context.

Take Account of Sociocultural Forces

In addressing the idealism-realism gap, it is equally important to take account of the sociocultural forces that influence the teaching and learning of writing. Tsui and Ng (2010) suggest that teachers "construct local understanding of their work embedded in the local cultural traditions and to explore possibilities for student learning in the context of constraints" (Tsui & Ng, 2010, p. 364). In peer review, for instance, typical constraints in the local Hong Kong Chinese context include issues relating to face and group harmony, which may stop students from offering critical comments. The study by Tsui and Ng (2010), however, shows that students can be helped to benefit from peer review through teachers' sensitive exploitation of possibilities of learning rooted in cultural Chinese traditions—e.g., taking advantage of notions like collective responsibility and public praise to help students engage with peer review. To give another example, some teachers in Hong Kong find it hard to conduct peer review in English, particularly for students of lower language proficiency. Given this, and given the importance of sensitive exploitation of sociocultural factors, teachers may consider allowing the use of L1 when students conduct peer review, since the Ll is "an essential tool for making meaning of text, retrieving language from memory, exploring and expanding content, guiding their action through the task, and maintaining dialogue" (Villamil & de Guerrero, 1996, p. 60).

Strengthen Teacher Training

In order to realize the above suggestions, teacher training has to be significantly strengthened. In many parts of the world, language teachers are under-prepared to teach writing (Johns, 2009). This is also true in Hong Kong, where teachers feel that they lack knowledge and skills to teach and assess writing. Recent studies by Lee (2010, 2013a) have demonstrated that teacher education can help enhance teachers' preparedness to teach writing—e.g., helping them think outside the box and challenge their pre-existing assumptions about writing and how writing should be taught and assessed. In order that teachers' practices in the writing classroom can be brought more in line with the recommended principles, writing teacher education definitely merits more attention.

Encourage School-Based Professional Learning and Classroom-Based Research

Lastly, to bridge the idealism-realism gap it is crucial that school-based professional learning be encouraged, where teachers get together to examine the contextual factors that influence teaching and learning in their own situation, share concerns, work out solutions to their own problems, and develop a common vision to guide their practice. Additionally, there is a need to produce local knowledge about the teaching and learning of writing through ethnographic, longitudinal classroom/school-based research, as such knowledge can be used to further inform practice (Lee, 2013b). While university researchers can continue to investigate thorny issues concerning the idealism-realism gap, teachers themselves should be encouraged to take an active part in classroom-based research, playing the role of teacher-researchers or co-researchers in collaboration with university researchers. To advance our knowledge about how best the idealism-realism gap can be bridged, teacher perspectives and voices need to be heard (see Min, 2013).

Conclusion

This paper has shown that Hong Kong teachers' practices in the writing classroom deviate hugely from "expert" recommendations as suggested in official curriculum documents and scholarly research. Such "best practices" advice has remained unheeded and failed to get through to classroom teaching. The paper has provided a number of suggestions to bridge the idealism-realism gap, including the importance of consideration for the contextual and sociocultural factors that influence teachers' work. To find answers to this important yet taxing question about the idealism-realism gap, teachers have to be involved in school-based professional learning and encouraged to take part in classroom-based research. There is also a need to broaden our understanding of research and seek alternative research methodologies to include non-replicable research, ecological studies, and longitudinal qualitative research. Through these endeavors, we will be able to shed light on what *could* be achieved in our quest for best practice, rather than what *should* be implemented in local writing classrooms.

References

Badger R. & White G. (2000). A process genre approach to the teaching writing. *ELT Journal 54*, 153-160.

Bax, S. (2003). The end of CLT: A context approach to language teaching. *ELT Journal, 57*(3), 278-287.

Bereiter, C. & Scardamalia, M. (1987). *The Psychology of Written Composition.* Hillsdale, NJ: Lawrence Erlbaum Associates.

Black, P., Harrison, C., Lee, C., Marshall, B. & Wiliam, D. (2004). The nature and value of formative assessment for learning. Unpublished manuscript, Educational Testing Service. Princeton, NJ. Retrieved from http://www.kcl. ac.uk/content/1/c4/73/57/formative.pdf

Black, P. & Wiliam. D. (1998). Assessment and classroom learning. *Assessment in Education, 5*(1), 7-74.

Brock, M. N. (1995). Resistance and change: Hong Kong students and the process approach. *Perspectives, 7*(2), X-69. Hong Kong: City University of Hong Kong, Working Papers of the Department of English. Paper also presented at the Annual TESOL Conference (1995, March), Long Beach, CA.

Choi, T. H. (2009). Power and the subversion of stories. *Power and Education, 1*(3), 282-294.

Curriculum Development Council. (1999). *Syllabuses for Secondary Schools: English Language Secondary 1-5.* Hong Kong: Hong Kong Government Printer.

Curriculum Development Council. (2004). *English Language Education: Key Learning Area Curriculum Guide (Primary 1-6).* Hong Kong: Hong Kong Government Printer.

Curriculum Development Council. (2007). *English Language Curriculum and Assessment Guide (Secondary 4-6).* Hong Kong: Hong Kong Government Printer.

Curriculum Development Council & Hong Kong Examinations and Assessment Authority. (2007). *English Language Curriculum and Assessment Guide (Secondary 4-6).* Hong Kong: Hong Kong Government Printer.

Curtis, A. (2001). Hong Kong student teachers' responses to peer group process writing. *Asian Journal of English Language Teaching, 11,* 129-143.

Curtis, A. & Heron, A. (1998). On being less innovative: Peer groups and process writing in Hong Kong. *Asia Pacific Journal of Language in Education, 8,* 99-117.

Ferris, D. R. (2002). *Treatment of Error in Second Language Student Writing.* Ann Arbor: University of Michigan Press.

Ferris, D. R. (2003). *Response to Student Writing: Implications for Second Language Students.* Mahwah, NJ: Lawrence Erlbaum.

Furneaux, C., Paran, A. & Fairfax, B. (2007). Teacher stance as reflected in feedback on student writing: An empirical study of secondary school teachers in five countries. *International Review of Applied Linguistics in Language Teaching, 45*(1), 69-94.

Grabe, W. & Kaplan, R. B. (1996). *Theory and Practice of Writing.* London: Longman.

Hairston, M. (1986). On not being a composition slave. In C. W. Bridges (Ed.), *Training the New Teacher of College Composition* (pp. 117-124). Urbana, IL: NCTE.

Hamp-Lyons, L. (2006). The impact of testing practices on teaching: Ideologies and alternatives. In J. Cummins & C. Davison (Eds.), *International Handbook of English Language Teaching* (Vol. 1) (pp. 487-504). Norwell, MA: Springer.

Hamp-Lyons, L., Chen, J. & Mok, J. (2001). Introducing innovation incrementally: Teacher feedback on student writing. Thai TESOL Bulletin: Selected papers from the 21st Annual Thai TESOL International Conference, *14*(2), 59-66.

Hayes, J. R. & Flower, L. S. (1980). The dynamics of composing: Making plans and juggling constraints. In L. W. Gregg & E. R. Steinberg (Eds.), *Cognitive Processes in Writing* (pp. 31-50). Hillsdale, NJ: Lawrence Erlbaum Associates.

Hyland, K. & Hyland, F. (2006). *Feedback in Second Language Writing: Contexts and Issues.* Cambridge: Cambridge University Press.

Johns, A. (2009, November). The future of second language writing instruction. Paper presented at the Symposium on Second Language Writing, Tempe, AZ.

Lee, I. (2004). Error correction in L2 secondary writing classrooms: The case of Hong Kong. *Journal of Second Language Writing, 13*(4), 285-312.

Lee, I. (2007). Feedback in Hong Kong secondary writing classrooms: Assessment for learning or assessment of learning? *Assessing Writing, 12* (3), 180-198.

Lee, I. (2008). Understanding teachers' written feedback practices in Hong Kong secondary classrooms. *Journal of Second Language Writing, 17,* 69-85.

Lee, I. (2010). Writing teacher education and teacher learning: Testimonies of four EFL teachers. *Journal of Second Language Writing, 19*(3), 143-157.

Lee, I. (2011). Issues and challenges in teaching and learning EFL writing: The case of Hong Kong. In T. Cimasko & M. Reichelt (Eds.), *Foreign Language Writing Instruction: Principles and Practices* (pp. 118-137). West Lafayette, IN: Parlor Press.

Lee, I. (2012), Genre-based teaching and assessment in secondary English classrooms. *English Teaching: Practice and Critique, 11*(4), 120-136.

Lee, I. (2013a). Becoming a writing teacher: Using "identity" as an analytic lens to understand EFL writing teachers' development. *Journal of Second Language Writing, 22*(3), 330-345.

Lee. I. (2013b). Second language writing: Perspectives of a teacher educator-researcher. *Journal of Second Language Writing, 22*(4), 435-437.

Lee, I. & Coniam, D. (2013). Introducing assessment for learning for EFL writing in an assessment of learning examination-driven system in Hong Kong. *Journal of Second Language Writing, 22*(1), 34-50.

Lee, I. & Wong, K. (under review). Bringing innovation to the EFL writing classroom: The case of a Hong Kong primary school. *The Asia-Pacific Education Researcher.*

Lo, J. & Hyland, F. (2007). Enhancing students' engagement and motivation in writing: The case of primary students in Hong Kong. *Journal of Second Language Writing, 16,* 219-237.

Min, H. T. (2013). A case study of an EFL teacher's belief and practice about written feedback. *System, 41,* 625-638.

Mok, J. (2009). From policies to realities: Developing students' critical thinking in Hong Kong secondary school English writing classes. *RELC Journal, 40*(3), 262-279.

Ortega, L. (2009). Studying writing across EFL contexts: Looking back and moving forward. In R. M. Manchón (Ed.), *Writing in Foreign Language Contexts: Learning, Teaching, and Research* (pp. 232-255). Clevedon: Multilingual Matters.

Pennington, M., Brock, M. C. & Yue, F. (1996). Implementing process writing in Hong Kong secondary schools: What the students' responses tell us. *Perspectives, 8*(1), 150-217.

Reichelt, M. (2009). A critical evaluation of writing teaching programmes in different foreign language settings. In R. Manchón (Ed.), *Writing in Foreign Language Contexts: Learning, Teaching, and Researching* (pp. 183-206). Clevedon, UK: Multilingual Matters.

Sengupta, S. (1998). Peer evaluation: "I am not the teacher". *ELT Journal, 52,* 19-28.

Sperling, M. (1996). Revisiting the writing-speaking connection: Challenges for research on writing and writing instruction. *Review of Educational Research,* 66, 53-86.

Tsui, A. B. M. & Ng, M. M. Y. (2000). Do secondary L2 writers benefit from peer comments? *Journal of Second Language Writing,* 9, 147-170.

Tsui, A. B. M. & Ng. M. M. Y. (2010). Cultural contexts and situated possibilities in the teaching of second language writing. *Journal of Teacher Education, 61*(4), 364-375.

Villamil, O. & de Guerrero, M. (1996). Peer revision in the L2 classroom: Social-cognitive activities, mediating strategies, and aspects of social behavior. *Journal of Second Language Writing,* 5, 51-75.

Weigle, S. C. (2002). *Assessing Writing.* Cambridge: Cambridge University Press.

Yang, M., Badger, R. & Yu, Z. (2006). A comparative study of peer and teacher feedback in a Chinese EFL writing class. *Journal of Second Language Writing, 15* (3), 179-200.

Zhao, H. (2010). Investigating learners' use and understanding of peer and teacher feedback on writing: A comparative study in a Chinese English writing classroom. *Assessing Writing, 15,* 3-17.

Chapter 5

English Writing Instruction in Senior High Schools in Japan: A Historical Ecological Approach

Miyuki Sasaki

Nagoya City University

Introduction

This study was motivated by the results of a series of studies (e.g., Sasaki, 2004, 2007, 2011) that investigated the development of English writing ability in Japanese university students. In these studies, most participants reported that they had not learned how to write a coherent paragraph-long text[1] in their high school English classes. For example, in Sasaki (2013), which followed the development of 22 Japanese students' views about writing in both Japanese and English, all the respondents said that they had not learned how to organize a coherent paragraph in English in high school and that during their high school days, they believed that writing in English meant "filling in blanks with appropriate words or phrases" or "translating one to two Japanese sentences into English," especially in test situations. Similarly, Rinnert and Kobayashi

---

1 In this chapter, I define the word "coherent" as "sequentially logical" (adapted from Ferris & Hedgcock, 2014, p. 166).

(2009) reported that a substantial number of Japanese university students did not receive sufficient training in how to write a coherent text in English when they entered university. Because studying English has been virtually compulsory in both junior and senior high schools in Japan since 1962 (Sasaki, 2008), this suggests that many graduating high school students with at least six years of English education[1] may not be able to write a coherent paragraph, to say nothing of a longer text. Moreover, now that over 95% of Japanese junior high school graduates proceed to senior high school (e.g., 98.4% in 2014; Ministry of Education, Science, Sports, and Culture, Japan, 2014, henceforth, MEXT),[2] this is probably a fair representation of the overall English writing ability of 18-year-old Japanese students. With the increased importance of English as a means of communication in this rapidly globalizing world, this (if true) is not desirable. However, these results may be confined to the participants in my own studies as well as in Rinnert and Kobayashi's because our numbers were small and our participants were not randomly selected from the wider population of Japanese senior high school graduates.

The present study thus examines the goals of English writing instruction in Japanese senior high school, paying special attention to the goal of teaching how to write coherent texts as well as to the English writing ability of graduating senior high school students as the ultimate product of such instruction. Of course, examining the true state of English education even at a particular grade level in one country is a formidable task (cf., Wall, 1996), and space is limited. However, since no study (to my knowledge) has ever addressed this question, this study should be a useful first step. Furthermore, this hope may be aided by the fact that Japanese education is centrally controlled by the government through legally-binding curriculum guidelines known as the "Course of Study"

---

1 Until 2011, English education in Japanese public schools started in the first year of junior high school (at the age of 12). Since April 2012, it now starts in the fifth grade (at the age of 11) as part of a new subject termed "Foreign Language Activities," which was put into effect by the 2012 Course of Study.

2 On January 6, 2001, Japan's Ministry of Education, Science, Sports, and Culture changed its name to Ministry of Education, Culture, Sports, Science, and Technology, with MEXT as its official abbreviation.

(see below). Examining the objectives of these guidelines should therefore explain a great deal about the current situation nationwide. That is, if we examine the results of a nationwide survey of English writing abilities and the goals set by the curriculum guidelines, we may be able to have at least a general idea of the current state of English writing instruction as implemented in the country. Although the findings of this study are bound to be provisional, the selected methodology and materials (see the Method section) are designed and selected with such a first step in mind.

In the study, I thus ask the following two questions:

(1) What skills and knowledge are expected to be achieved by the third (final) year of senior high school English classes by the current Course of Study, that is, the legally-binding curriculum guidelines promulgated by the government?

(2) To what extent do the ability and skills of Japanese senior high school students reflect the goals set by the Course of Study? If there is a discrepancy, what might be possible reasons for it?

I hope that answering these questions will provide practical hints on how to improve the current state of English writing instruction in Japan, which is the ultimate purpose of this study.

Method

In the following section, I outline the methods used in carrying out this review of the ecological setting in which English writing instruction is often carried out in Japanese schools. The following will outline the chosen theoretical lens, the historical ecological approach, as well the use of retrocasting to analyze materials in order to better understand the social setting of L2 writing instruction in Japan.

Gaddis' (2002) Historical Ecological Approach

I chose an ecological perspective as the theoretical framework for the present study because I have learned that educational practices can be affected by multiple and unexpected factors such as "socio-political, economic, academic, and historical/cultural factors in different periods" (Sasaki, 2008, p. 64). Such a belief concurs with the basic principles of many ecological perspectives (e.g., van Lier, 2004). Among various types of ecological approaches, I selected Gaddis' (2002) historical-ecological method because it is unique in its claim that a study should be designed to serve the researcher's intended purpose, which best fits the fact that I do have a specific purpose for conducting the study. To explain how one can design a study according to one's purpose, Gaddis uses a map-making metaphor, whereby a study should focus on a particular set of variables necessary to explain a given phenomenon so that the results will most effectively serve the given purpose, just as a "highway map will exaggerate certain features of the landscape and neglect others" (p. 33). However, the resulting map and the representation of "reality" it constructs must of course be a valid one, supported by evidence convincing enough for the reader to feel that the results are usable. Lastly, Gaddis claims that this act of "reality" representation should be revised through constant verification in light of changes brought about by the study itself, an approach that is highly suitable for the present study as a first and provisional step. Lastly, Gaddis' approach was helpful when I analyzed the data because, unlike some ecological approaches, he illustrates how his theory can be put into practice through a method he calls "retrocasting" (p. 65), accompanied by several practically usable techniques (see below).

Retrocasting Techniques Used in the Study

Retrocasting, which has been used mainly in historical studies, means tracing the history of the targeted phenomenon through our "imagination with logic" (Gaddis, 2002, pp. 40-41). A researcher uses "surviving structures" that remain in the present to infer how they reached their current state. Because multiple and unexpected factors may have influenced the end-product (i.e., the current structure), researchers can include *ex post facto* as many variables as they like if they seem relevant. The inference does not have to be correct (if anything can ever be called "correct"). However, as mentioned above, the results of the restoration should be in the form that can best serve the intended purpose of the study.

To summarize, researchers start with existing evidence (the current structure) and infer how it came about (the processes). While imagining these processes, researchers can include as many potential explanatory variables or factors as they like. However, the choice should be based on how useful the end-product of the analysis is. To decide which variables should be focused upon, Gaddis suggests following two rules, adapting the strategies used by historian Clayton Roberts (cited on pp. 98-99 in Gaddis, 2002):

1) Assign greater importance to immediate rather than distant causes; and

2) Find a "point of no return" at which the target phenomenon became the present state as a result of changing from a stable state to an unstable state (the current state), and find what critically caused the unstable state.

In this study, the remaining structures are the students' English writing ability as compared with the intended goals set by the Course of Study (i.e., the structures' background). If the students' ability turns out to be too far removed from the intended goals (especially in terms of writing coherent texts), I will explore why this happened (the processes) by searching for possible causes among the most immediate ones that may have critically influenced the discrepancy between the instructional goals and the students' ability. To make my analysis convincing, I will use the students' own (emic) accounts in addition to the historical background surrounding the current structure.

Goals Set by the Current Course of Study (2003 to 2012) as the Background

Before describing the state of the English writing ability of Japanese senior high school students (i.e., the remaining structure as the target of this study), I present the goals intended to be met by the Course of Study, the official set of curriculum guidelines, as the sociocultural background to be compared with that ability.

The Course of Study is a set of curriculum guidelines promulgated by Japan's Ministry of Education, Science, Sports, and Culture (MEXT) for primary to secondary education, covering kindergarten to senior high school. The first Course of Study was issued in 1947 for the new school system, starting in April of that year, after Japan was defeated in World War II. At the time, Japan was under the control of the General Headquarters (GHQ) of the Allied Powers, and starting a new school system was one of the democratizing actions conducted under GHQ guidance (see Sasaki, 2008). Modeled on the US school system, Japan's system changed to six single-track years in elementary school, three years each in junior and senior high school, and two or four years in college or university. Since then, the Course of Study has been revised six times at approximately ten-year intervals to accommodate sociocultural change. The Course of Study for senior high schools was promulgated in 1947, 1960, 1970, 1978, 1989, 1999 and 2009, and except for the first one, all were put into effect three to five years later (1963, 1973, 1982, 1994, 2003 and 2013, respectively). Henceforth, to avoid confusion, I will use the years during which each Course of Study was effective instead of its promulgation year. Except for the initial 1947 document, the other six Courses of Study have had legally-binding force, and the curricular content as well as the textbooks used in all primary and secondary schools in Japan were devised according to the Course of Study in force at the time.

The most current Course of Study for senior high schools came into effect in April, 2013. However, since it has not been in place for very long, this is too short a period to gauge its effect, and I therefore target the last Course of Study, which was put into effect in 2003. This Course of Study was promulgated in 1999, a time "characterized by the introduction of the government's new educational policies, followed by public criticism of the results of these policies" (Sasaki, 2008, p. 73). However, while conceding the potential importance of the social background, I focus here on the Course of Study as the most immediate influence.

For this Course of Study, the overall objective for English education for senior high schools, which I translated as no official translation is available, is as follows (Ministry of Education, Science, Sports and Culture, 1999):

To develop students' practical communication abilities such as understanding information, intentions, and ideas, expressing one's own ideas, deepening one's understanding of language and culture, and fostering a positive attitude toward communication through foreign languages.

The term "communication" was used for the first time in the 1994-2002 Course of Study, whereas prior to that, the words "understand" and "express" were used, and it was taken up again in the 2003-2012 version. This was supposed to respond to the societal need for schools to cultivate more practical English skills for a rapidly globalizing society rather than knowledge and appreciation of the language itself (Sasaki, 2008). Another common feature between these versions was the focus on "fostering a positive attitude toward communication through foreign languages," which was also added to the 1994-2002 document for the first time in the history of Courses of Study as a result of a paradigm shift in education from treating academic ability as consisting of knowledge and skills as opposed to having a positive attitude toward a given task (Abiko, 1996). This was in reaction, starting in the 1980s, against the excessive past emphasis on cramming facts in school, especially for university entrance examinations, which was believed to cause various educational problems such as bullying and dropping out (Sasaki, 2008). To reduce such a burden on students, the 2003-2012 Course of Study also cut about 30% of the content of the syllabus across all subjects. Thus, for English, the number of new words to be introduced in senior high school fell from 1,900 to 1,300, and the number of elective subjects was reduced from seven to six (one subject equals about 29 class hours). Finally, in terms of the skills to be taught, the objectives for the 2003-2012 Course of Study promote the four skills of speaking, listening, reading, and writing with equal weight. However, the fact that the two required subjects for graduation among the six English subjects were Oral (but not Written) Communication I and English I (emphasizing all four skills) suggests that written communication was not seen as being as important as oral communication.

Steering our focus toward writing instruction, we can see that the general objective described above only mentions "appropriately conveying information, ideas, etc.," which is quite vague. Furthermore, the description of one of the two required subjects, labeled "English I," only suggests an activity consisting of "writing by sorting out one's own ideas or the information gained through listening and reading in English" and makes no mention of learning how to organize a coherent text specifically. We can thus infer that the minimum English writing ability required by the government for high school graduation is not necessarily related to writing in a manner that is "sequentially logical" (Ferris & Hedgcock, 2014, p. 166), especially as the minimum level for the other three skills seem similarly vague. On the other hand, given that the elective subject of English Writing is taken by most senior high school students unless they are in a vocational school (Yamamoto, 1999), the goal for this subject is probably the highest level Japanese senior high school students are expected to achieve. Let us therefore examine the most relevant part of the description (which I underline below) in the Course of Study for Writing (which I translated as no official translation is available):

A) Objectives:

To further develop students' writing ability to appropriately convey information and ideas according to the given situation and purpose and to foster a positive attitude toward communication through this ability.

B) Content:

1) Language activities:

Conduct the following communication activities by creating actual language use situations in which students can send and receive information and ideas by:

a) Summarizing content heard or read in a manner appropriate to the given situation and purpose;

b) Writing one's own ideas by synthesizing what one hears or reads;

c) Organizing the content one wants to convey and writing in a manner appropriate to the given situation and purpose so that readers can understand it easily.

2) Treatment of language activities:

a) Points to consider in teaching:

To effectively conduct communication activities mentioned in 1) above, teachers should consider the following points, as appropriate:

i) Dictating spoken and written texts;

ii) Using necessary phrases and expressions to convey ideas

and feelings;

   iii) Writing while paying attention to the organization and development of the text.

  b) Language use situations and functions:

Teachers should select and practically combine situations and functions as appropriate to achieving the goals mentioned in A) when conducting the activities mentioned in 1). In such cases, teachers should create opportunities for the students to experience actual communication by selecting language use situations such as letter or email writing.[1]

We can see here that the two underlined sections clearly indicate that the Course of Study expects a majority of senior high school students to have gained the ability to write a coherent text in English by the time they graduate, even though the chosen examples of letter and email writing suggest that these imagined texts may not be academic but practical.

Japanese Senior High School Students' Ability to Write a Coherent Text

As mentioned earlier, all 22 participants in Sasaki (2013) reported that they had never learned how to write a text beyond the paragraph level while in high school. However, it is possible that these participants may in fact be exceptional. Therefore, as a more solid "remaining structure" worth analyzing, I present the results of a nationwide test (henceforth, the "Senior High School Test") conducted by the National Institute for Educational Policy Research (NIEPR) in 2005. In the past, NIEPR conducted two nationwide tests targeting all pubic and private senior high schools in order to check whether the Course

---

1 These two writing modes have now been replaced by "various situations according to the students' needs" in the equivalent subject of "English Expression I" in the 2013 Course of Study.

of Study in force at the time had been properly implemented. The 2005 test applied to the 2003-2012 Course of Study, and the 2002 test covered for the 1994-2002 Course of Study. Because 27.5% of the 2005 items overlapped with those of the 2002 test, we can also compare the changes in these items between the two tests.

For the 2005 test, over 150,000 graduating senior high school students (or 13% of all such full-time students for the given year in Japan) were randomly selected from 2,333 departments in all public and private senior high schools in the country. All the test-takers had studied under the 2003-2012 Course of Study since their first year in senior high school. These students took the test in one of two versions (A or B)[1] in up to three out of 12 subjects (50 minutes per subject), including English, from six fields (e.g., math, science, foreign languages, etc.). Some test items differed in content or specifications according to the versions while others shared the same content or specification across versions. For the English test, the items seemed to differ in content across the two versions (though the content was not revealed) but shared common specifications for all items (see Table 1). A total of 29,880 students took Version A or B of the English test. Both versions consisted of 26 items, with 10 listening items (Items 1 to 10; multiple choice), 9 reading items (Items 11 to 19; multiple choice), and 7 writing items (Items 20 to 26; descriptive). All items were related to the content of English I, one of the two courses required by the 2003-2013 Course of Study for senior high school graduation (recall the previous section). Furthermore, when the test was given, the participating students and their teachers also answered questionnaire items about their motivation to study, their perception and understanding of the given school subjects, and their learning or teaching activities.

Table 1 presents brief specifications, (averaged) percentages of those who answered the item correctly (henceforth, accuracy rates), and expected accuracy rates (the accuracy rates expected if the teacher spends the standard amount of

---

1 NIEPR (2007) does not mention the reason(s) for using two versions.

Table 1 Specifications, Accuracy Rates, and Related Information Regarding the English Items in Versions A and B of the Senior High School Test

Version	Item number	Main skill to be measured	Ability to be tested	Item type	Average % of those who answered the item correctly (accuracy rate)	Expected (average) accuracy rate	% of no answer
A (n=14,915)	1-3	Listening	Ability to respond when spoken to in English	Multiple Choice (MC)	63.0	68.3	Not reported (NR)
	4-6		Ability to comprehend the details of a spoken text	MC	66.0	66.7	NR
	7-10		Ability to comprehend the main point of a spoken text	MC	65.2	60.0	NR
	11-12	Reading	Ability to comprehend the details of a written text	MC	63.6	65	NR
	13-15		Ability to comprehend the main point of a coherent written text	MC	61.1	60	NR
	16-17		Ability to understand the logical development of a written text	MC	61.7	60	NR

(to be continued)

(continued)

Version	Item number	Main skill to be measured	Ability to be tested	Item type	Average % of those who answered the item correctly (accuracy rate)	Expected (average) accuracy rate	% of no answer
A (n=14,915)	18-19		Ability to understand the writer's intention in a written text	MC	59.4	67.5	NR
	20	Writing	Ability to write a coherent text consisting of more than 3 sentences	Descriptive	21.7	45.0	28.5
	21-23		Ability to fill in blanks with an appropriate word or phrase	Descriptive	43.8	58.3	NR
	24-26		Ability to write a sentence using scrambled words	Descriptive	63.2	61.7	NR
B (n=14,965)	1-3	Listening	Ability to respond when spoken to in English	MC	60.8	70	NR
	4-6		Ability to comprehend the details of a spoken text	MC	51.3	63.3	NR
	7-10		Ability to comprehend the main point of a spoken text	MC	64.5	66.3	NR

(to be continued)

(continued)

Version	Item number	Main skill to be measured	Ability to be tested	Item type	Average % of those who answered the item correctly (accuracy rate)	Expected (average) accuracy rate	% of no answer
B (n=14,965)	11-12	Reading	Ability to comprehend the details of a written text	MC	69.3	62.5	NR
	13-15		Ability to comprehend the main point of a coherent written text	MC	72.7	63.3	NR
	16-17		Ability to understand the logical development of a written text	MC	69.3	60	NR
	18-19		Ability to understand the writer's intention in a written text	MC	66.3	62.5	NR
	20	Writing	Ability to write a coherent text consisting of more than 3 sentences	Descriptive	25.0	45	22.8
	21-23		Ability to fill in blanks with an appropriate word or phrase	Descriptive	51.7	53.3	Not reported
	24-26		Ability to write a sentence using scrambled words	Descriptive	48.4	60	Not reported

time covering activities suggested by the Course of Study for the given year for the 26 English items in Versions A and B) (NIEPR, 2007). For the purpose of this study, I present below a more detailed explanation of the seven Writing items (Items 20 to 26) shared by the two versions (NIEPR, 2007).

- Item 20 requires the students to write a coherent text using more than three sentences about a given topic. The opening of the sentence was given. This item is intended to measure the students' ability to write such a coherent, and responses were evaluated in terms of quantity and organization (coherence). The presence of this item in this test implies that students were in fact expected to write a short coherent text even at the required English I level.
- Items 21 to 23 require the students to explain a picture or situation by filling in blanks using appropriate words and phrases.
- Items 24 to 26 require the students to form a sentence from four to six scrambled words occurring in a conversation between two people.

The figures presented in Table 1 suggest that final-year senior high school students were weakest at writing a coherent text consisting of more than three sentences (Item 20). First, the accuracy rates for Item 20 in Versions A and B were the lowest among all the items (21.7% and 25%, respectively). Moreover, they were much lower than the expected accuracy rates. That is, the students failed to achieve the level of ability expected (i.e., writing a short coherent text) if teaching the particular skill successfully met the goals set by the Course Study for English I. Moreover, about one in four students wrote nothing for Item 20. Of course, we have to take into consideration the fact that the participants in this survey included students from various types of high schools, some of which did not require English classes beyond the required English I level. In fact, the survey revealed that 36.6% of these students did not take the Writing class, while 27.9% did not take the Reading class. Yet, Table 1 shows that even a majority (63.3%) of those final-year senior high school students who took the Writing class (which clearly required the ability to write a coherent text, as mentioned above) could not write a text consisting of more than three related sentences.

How did this come about? Recall that the 22 participants in Sasaki (2013) said that their perception of writing during senior high school consisted of filling in blanks with appropriate words or phrases or translating Japanese sentences into English in tests. The averaged accuracy rates for Items 21 to 23 (in both versions of the test), which show the students' ability to fill in blanks, and the accuracy rates for Items 24 to 26 (also in both versions), which show the students' ability to form a correct sentence from scrambled words were both much higher than the accuracy rates for Item 20, which requires them to write a coherent text (again in both versions), thus concurring with these accounts. Furthermore, the teachers' questionnaire ($n = 887$) reveals that only 18.8% ("agree" and "agree to some extent" combined) had conducted the activity consisting of "writing by sorting one's own ideas or the information gained through listening and reading in English," as was suggested by the description of the required English I subject in the 2003-2012 Course of Study. The fact that this figure is lower than those for similar items for listening (38.2%) and reading (66.3%) suggests that high school teachers are not enthusiastic about cultivating the students' ability to write a coherent text compared to their ability to listen or read such a text. (Note, however, that the figure for speaking was only 16.7%.)

These results bring to mind the fact that many participants in my previous studies (e.g., Sasaki 2004, 2011) also reported during interviews that their high school English classes tended to emphasize what was likely to be asked in university entrance exams. In fact, many teachers and researchers report similar views (e.g., Negishi et al., 2010). The teachers' responses to the questionnaire items regarding writing activities administered alongside the 2005 Senior High School Test may be a natural reaction on their part if we consider that about half of these students—for example, 49.3% in 2006 (MEXT, 2006)—proceeded to tertiary education while the 2003-2012 Course of Study was in effect. We can easily imagine that in a meritocratic society such as Japan, effectively preparing students to enter prestigious universities was most appreciated by the students as well as their parents (Kanatani, 2009). If writing and speaking coherently was not measured in the university entrance exams, we cannot blame the teachers for not teaching these skills even if they were required to do so by the Course of Study. With this in mind, we will now check what was tested in the university entrance exams taken by the participants in the 2005 Senior High School Test as a possible "immediate" cause. Because space is limited, I will focus mainly on the 2006 "Center Exam," which many participants in this test must have taken to enter university the following year.

Content of the English Test in the 2006 Center Exam

The Center Exam is given by the National Center for University Entrance Examination (NCUEE) to university applicants in January for the year during which they hope to enter university. The first test, known as the Common Test, was given in 1979 for public universities only. The test was originally created at the government's initiative in response to the public sentiment that the entrance exams asked too many questions that were beyond what the Courses of Study required of senior high school education, which caused excessive competition among university applicants (Sasaki, 2008). The Common Test (and its successors, known as "Center Exams" since 1990) is given once every year, and the NCUEE claims that the test given each year covers only the content suggested by the Course of Study in force at the time (NCUEE, 2015). After the test was renamed "Center Exam" in 1990, more and more private universities started to use it. Today, all public universities and a majority of private universities use this test for admission. For example, in 2013, 573,271 applicants took the test in an average number of 5.69 subjects to apply for places in 163 (or 100%) public and 520 (or 86%) private universities.

All items in the Center Exam are multiple-choice, and a test in one subject lasts from 60 to 80 minutes. All tests are given over two days. After taking the test, the applicants calculate their scores on their own to decide which university to apply to (see Sasaki, 2008 for details of the procedure). While some universities require no further exams, others require yet another test in written or multiple-choice form (usually given in February and March). Based on this, we can safely say that the Center Exam is the most influential university entrance exam in present-day Japan. I would therefore like to examine the 2006 Center Exam as a possible explanatory variable for the writing ability of those who took the 2005 Senior High School Test, which was not only "immediate" but also "convincing" as well as "usable" (in Gaddis' terms) for the purpose of this study.

The 2006 English Center Exam was a special case because for the first time in its 26-year history, it included a listening subtest, which was given as a separate test from the main English test (i.e., some universities did not require scores on both the main English test *and* the listening test for admission, though the number of such universities was small). The main test lasted 80 minutes and consisted of 50 multiple-choice items for a maximum score of 200. The listening test lasted 30 minutes, followed by a 30-minute practice period using earphones, and had 25 multiple-choice items for a maximum score of 50. As claimed in the very name of the test, all 25 listening test items mainly measured the participants' ability to listen to English, although they also required other skills and knowledge (e.g., reading the instructions as well understanding the oral texts). In contrast, what the 50 main items (Items 1-50) measured is not as obvious. I therefore present their content below, with my interpretation of what abilities these items mainly measured in parentheses:

Items 1-2: Find the correct location of the stress in each word (pronunciation, but indirectly through written forms);

Items 3-6: Find the part of words that carries the most stress in given contexts (speaking, but indirectly through written forms);

Items 7-16: Insert the most appropriate word or phrase in the blanks in a sentence (grammatical knowledge);

Items 17-19: Insert the most appropriate sentence in the blanks in a 4-sentence conversation between 2 people (speaking, but indirectly through written forms);

Items 20-25: Sort scrambled words to form a sentence (grammatical knowledge);

Items 26-27: Fill in the two blanks in a 100-word text with appropriate phrases (reading);

Items 28-29: Fill in the blanks in a 50-word text with an appropriate sentence (10 to 20 words long) (reading);

Items 30-32: Fill in the most appropriate three blanks out of six in a 300-word text with an appropriate sentence (10 to 20 words long) each (reading);

Item 33: Find the most appropriate word or phrase to fill in the blank in a sentence related to a given text (measuring the ability to comprehend a text) (reading);

Items 34-37: Find a particular piece of information in a given text (about 400 words) and a related graph (reading);

Items 38-42: Read a 400-word long conversation between two people and answer questions related to its content (reading);

Items 43-50: Read a 700-word long text and answer comprehension questions (by searching for information or inferencing) (reading).

Overall, 18% of the 50 main English test items appear to measure mainly abilities related to speaking (but indirectly through written texts), while 32% measure grammatical knowledge, and the rest (50%) measure abilities related to reading. Meanwhile, no item in the main test appears to measure writing ability, especially in the sense of writing a coherent text. After taking the Center Exam, some students may have taken exams that required descriptive answers for the universities of their choice. However, according to Kanatani (2009), who investigated additional exams given in 2007 (the following year) by 18 major public and private universities, 11 of them (or 61.1%) required translation of Japanese sentences, and only seven (or 38.9%) required applicants to write a coherent text either additionally or exclusively. As Kanatani notes, these are some of the most prestigious universities in Japan out of 756 universities in operation in 2007. Moreover, those universities were exceptional in requiring written answers as the entrance exams of many other universities had been moving in the opposite direction and required no written answers (i.e., consisting entirely of multiple-choice items) in order to decrease the rating burden.

To summarize the above information concerning the Center Exam and the additional entrance exams, most university applicants in 2006, including the participants in the 2005 Senior High School Test, probably did not have to write a coherent text similar to the one tested in the Senior High School Test for their university entrance exams. No wonder that only 18.8% of the 882 teachers who responded to the questionnaire reported having their students write a text "by sorting out one's own ideas or the information gained through listening and reading." This is in sharp contrast with the fact that 66.3% of the same teachers had their students "read to understand the writer's intention and the main point of the given text," or that 38.2% of them had their students "listen to understand the speaker's intention or the main point" (NIEPR, 2007). Given this, I speculate that whether or not a given skill is required in university entrance exams is probably the most immediate "point of no return" that lowers the students' ability to write a coherent text compared to their reading ability (see Table 1). This speculation is further confirmed by the questionnaire results, which shows that as few as 16.7% of the teachers had the students practice speaking coherently because speaking performance is also rarely required in university entrance exams (Kanatani, 2009). Finally, recall that Sasaki's participants' view of writing during their high schools days was filling in blanks or translating Japanese sentences in tests. Given the results presented here, we can infer that such a view was probably formed through repeated classroom activities as their teachers must have known that these activities, but not writing a coherent text, would be tested in the university entrance exams. In fact, many items in the 2006 Center Exam required filling in blanks activities (e.g., Items 26-32), and over half of the 18 prestigious universities investigated by Kanatani (2009) required their applicants to translate Japanese sentences into English in their additional exams following the Center Exam.

Conclusions and Suggestions for the Future

The findings of this study can be summarized as follows:

1) The Course of Study required teachers to teach "appropriately conveying information and ideas" (the overall objective) and how to "write while paying attention to the organization and development of the text" (for the subject of Writing taken by about 65% of all senior high school students);

2) However, only about 25% of test takers could write a coherent text consisting of four or more sentences, while another 25% could write nothing;

3) Only 18.8% of the teachers taught how to write a coherent text;

4) The Center Exam had no section requiring the applicants to write a coherent text, and very few universities required this ability in their additional entrance exams, which is probably one of the main causes for the gap between the goals stated in 1), the students' actual proficiency stated in 2), and the teachers' attitude stated in 3).

Following Gaddis (2002), I started with the government-mandated goals as the background for the structure of the English writing ability of Japanese senior high school students. Noting a gap between these goals and the students' ability, I concluded that the content of the university entrance exams, and especially the nationwide Center Exam, is the most likely cause for this gap. Although I could not identify any other factor that seemed as powerful, the results of this study are subject to further revision (as mentioned earlier), and I expect future studies to uncover other factors as convincing as pressure from the entrance exams (for example, the lack of the kind of training that would enable teachers to teach their students to write coherent texts might be a good candidate; see Oi, 2012). Leaving such further investigation to future studies, I would now like to conclude by pursuing its ultimate purpose, which was to make suggestions on how to improve the current situation. Because the findings of the study summarized above indicate that the current situation may not improve unless educational policies at governmental level change, I suggest a number of measures the government might take to improve the situation, hoping that these will be the most effective and useful.

First, if the Center Exam were to include descriptive items similar to those in the Senior High School Test, the situation might change dramatically. In fact, this is what happened to the high school students' listening ability when they took the 2005 Senior High School Test. In March, 2000, the NCUEE announced the introduction of a listening section in the Center Exam, starting in 2006. Hence, the participants' performance on the 2005 Senior High School Test (described in this study) was especially relevant because many of them must have had extra preparation for this newly-added listening subsection. In fact, the effects of such preparation are apparent when we compare the changes in the scores for overlapping items (see above) between the 2002 and 2005 Senior High School Tests. Of the 52 items on the 2005 test, 21 (7 listening, 8 reading, 6 writing) overlapped with the 2002 items. The results reveal that among these overlapping items, four (57.1%) of the seven listening items were the only items whose scores were significantly higher in 2005 than in 2002 (NIEPR, 2007). That is, the students' listening ability significantly improved between 2002 and 2005, whereas their reading and writing ability did not. We could easily attribute these results to the introduction of the listening section in the Center Exam in 2006, whereas other sociocultural or academically-related events surrounding these students during the years between 2002 and 2005 do not seem as immediate (Sasaki, 2008). For these students, the introduction of a listening section in the Center Exam was clearly a "point of no return" in terms of improving their English listening ability.

My second suggestion also relates to university entrance exams because it seems crucial if teaching practices are to change in Japan. I suggest that the NCUEE use external and well-established commercial measures (e.g., TOEFLiBT, IELTS, TOEIC Speaking/Writing) that require the ability to write a coherent text as additional components of the Center Exam. If submitting a writing score to a university of choice in addition to the overall Center Exam score worked in favor of those who did so (e.g., a maximum of 50 additional points, as in the listening subtest), this would surely provide an incentive for some applicants to practice writing a coherent text. Clearly, we must also consider whether the purpose of each of these tests may match that of the university entrance exams (i.e., to measure how successfully each applicant might function as a university student in a given academic field) in order to avoid an invalid use of the test (Messic, 1988). However, I would still recommend that the NCUEE consider including some kind of a measure of the ability to write coherently even though this would be conducted by an external organization. If such as test measured the students' ability to write based on information gained through other skills (i.e., an integrative type of test), as recommended by the 2003-2012 and the 2013 Courses of Study, it would be even more advantageous (although we would also have to consider the difficulty level of the test). Considering that it took the NCUEE at least five years to introduce the listening subtest, using an external measure as a makeshift response might be better than having no such test because even a makeshift test could create a washback effect similar to that related to the students' listening skills, as we saw above.

Finally, publicizing the importance of writing ability in today's world in an EFL (English as a Foreign Language) country such as Japan may have a beneficial impact. Fortunately, the 2013 Course of Study has begun to emphasize the four skills more equally than did the 2003-2012 Course of Study, which put greater emphasis on oral proficiency. For example, as part of the general objectives, the aim of writing and speaking is now to "convey information and one's ideas appropriately" as opposed to "expressing one's ideas" in the 2003-2012 version. Furthermore, in Communication English I, one of the two required subjects in the 2013 Course of Study, one activity that seems to cultivate students' ability to write coherently, namely "Reading and writing while paying attention to the main point or topic sentence and words and phrases that make the text cohere," has been added. In these descriptions, we can see that even at the minimum required subject level, the 2013 version of

Course of Study values the students' ability to write a coherent text more clearly than did the previous Courses of Studies. This might be a manifestation of the government's awareness of the fact that such skills have become particularly important as a result of developments in IT that are making this shrinking world intensely competitive (e.g., MEXT, 2002, but see also Kubota, 2013). If so, I hope that such awareness at government level will influence English teachers so that a greater number of them will try activities that aim to improve their students' ability to write coherently, as suggested by the 2013 Course of Study, even though such skills may not be tested in university entrance exams in the near future.

Acknowledgements

An earlier version of this paper was presented at the Symposium on Second Language Writing, Shandong University, Jinan, China, on October 18, 2013. I would like to thank Paul Bruthiaux for his valuable comments and suggestions. The preparation of this paper was aided by Research Grant No. 24520666 for the 2013-2015 academic year from the Ministry of Education, Culture, Sports, Science, and Technology of Japan.

References

Abiko, T. (1996). *Shin gakuryokukan to kisogakuryoku: Nani ga towareteiruka* [New perspective on academic ability and basic academic ability: What has been questioned?]. Tokyo: Meijitosho.

Ferris, D. R. & Hedgcock, J. S. (2014). *Teaching L2 Composition: Purpose, Process, and Practice* (3rd ed.). New York: Routledge.

Gaddis, J. (2002). *The Landscape of History: How Historians Map the Past*. Oxford: Oxford University Press.

Kanatani, K. (2009) (Ed.). *Kyokasho dakede daigakunyuushi wa toppa dekiru* [You can pass university entrance exams with English textbooks only]. Tokyo: Taishuukan.

Kubota, R. (2011). Questioning instrumentalism: English, neoliberalism, and language tests in Japan. *Linguistics and Education, 22,* 248-260.

Messic, S. A. (1988). Validity. In R. L. Linn (Ed.), *Educational Measurement* (3rd ed.), (pp. 13-103). New York: American Council on Education.

Ministry of Education, Culture, Science, Sports, and Technology (MEXT). (2002). *Japanese Government Policies in Education, Culture, Sports, Science, and Technology.* Retrieved from: http://www.mext.go.jp/b_menu/hakusho/html/hpac200201

Ministry of Education, Culture, Science, Sports, and Technology (MEXT). (2006). *Heisei 18 nendo gakkoku kihon chosa* [2006 School Basic Survey]. Retrieved from: http://www.mext.go.jp/b_menu/toukei/chousa01/kihon/kekka/k_detail/1279800.htm

Ministry of Education, Culture, Science, Sports, and Technology (MEXT). (2014). *Heisei 26 nendo gakkoku kihon chosa* [2014 School Basic Survey]. Retrieved from: http://www.mext.go.jp/component/b_menu/other/__icsFiles/afieldfile/2014/12/19/1354124_2_1.pdf

Ministry of Education, Sports, Science, and Culture. (1999). *Koutougakkou gakushuushidou youryou dainishou daihassetsu gikokugo* [Chapter 2, Section 8: English for the 2003 Course of Study]. Retrieved from: http://www.mext.go.jp/a_menu/shotou/cs/1320221.htm

National Center for University Entrance Examination (NCUEE). (2015). *Sentaa shiken no yakuwari* [The role of the Center Exam]. Retrieved from: http://www.NCUEE.ac.jp/center/shiken_gaiyou

National Institute for Educational Policy Research (NIEPR). (2007). *Heisei juunananendo koutougakkou kyouiku katei jisshi joukyou chousa* [Results of the 2005 survey of the implementation of the senior high school curriculum]. Retrieved from: http://www.nier.go.jp/kaihatsu/katei_h17_h

Negishi, M., Matsuzawa, S., Sato, R., Toyota, Y. & Nakano, T. (2010). Daigaku nyuushi ga kawareba eigokyouiku mo kawarunoka: Zadankai [Will English instruction in Japan change if university entrance exams change? A discussion]. *The English Teachers' Magazine, August,* 10-19.

Oi, K. (2012). Matomari no aru bunsho o kakaseru shidou [Instructions on making students write a coherent text]. *The English Teachers' Magazine, June,* 17-20.

Rinnert, C. & Kobayashi, H. (2009). Situated writing practices in foreign language settings: The role of previous experience and instruction. In R. M. Manchón (Ed.), *Writing in Foreign Language Contexts: Learning, Teaching, and Researching* (pp. 23-48). Clevedon, England: Multilingual Matters.

Sasaki, M. (2004). A multiple-data analysis of the 3.5-year development of EFL student writers. *Language Learning, 54,* 525-582.

Sasaki, M. (2007). Effects of study-abroad experiences on EFL writers: A multiple-data analysis. *The Modern Language Journal, 91,* 602-620.

Sasaki, M. (2008). The 150-year history of English language assessment in Japanese education. *Language Testing, 25,* 63-83.

Sasaki, M. (2011). Effects of varying lengths of study-abroad experiences on Japanese EFL students' L2 writing ability and motivation: A longitudinal study. *TESOL Quarterly, 45,* 81-105.

van Lier, L. (2004). *The Ecology and Semiotics of Language Learning: A Sociocultural Perspective.* Boston, MA: Kluwer Academic.

Wall, D. (1996). Introducing new tests into traditional systems: Insights from general education and from innovation theory. *Language Testing, 13,* 334-354.

Yamamoto, R. (1999). Gakkokugenba dewa kouyomu: Kitai to fuan [This is how senior high school teachers interpret the new Course of Study: Expectations and worries]. *The English Teachers' Magazine, June,* 20-21.

Chapter 6

The Research Context of L2 Writing in South Korea: Historical Development, Issues, and Future Directions

Yeon Hee Choi

Ewha Womans University

Introduction

L2 writing in South Korea began with the use of Chinese as a written language as early as the beginning of the Three Kingdoms' period in the first Century BC (Lee, 2000) due to the nonexistence of a written language. Since the beginning of the Western style school education in the late 19th century, English has been taught as the major second/foreign language (Choi, 1979; Choi, 2007; Moon, 1976; Pae, 2002), except during the Japanese colonial period, when Japanese filled this role. English writing was first taught by American missionaries and was one of the key subjects in some missionary universities (Choi, 2007). However, the strong impact of the Grammar-Translation Method during the Japanese colonial period (from 1910 to 1945) resulted in the stagnation of English-L2 writing education (Choi, 1979; Choi, 2007), which continues until today. Thus, historically, L2 writing, including English-L2 writing, has not gained much attention in institutional, pedagogical, and research contexts within South Korea. Secondary-level L2 nationwide direct writing tests have not been administered, which has led to the lack of writing instruction, due to an assessment dominant educational culture of South Korea (Kwon, Yoshida, Watanabe, Negishi & Nagamura, 2004; Lee, 2007). The South Korean government has highly controlled and centralized primary and secondary school education, including the national curriculum, which has strongly influenced L2 learning content (Choi, 2007). The government has attempted to include direct sentence- and paragraph-level English writing assessment in the college entrance examination for the past six years (Im et al., 2011; Jin, Shin & Si, 2012; Lee et al., 2011). This promoted high school students' English writing practices, which led to an expectation of fostering English-L2 writing research (Lee et al., 2013). Recently, however, the government has decided not to officially administer such direct writing assessment as part of the college entrance examination due to the expansion of private education for English-L2 writing.

The lack of L2 writing instruction in the secondary school context has affected the number and status of L2 writing studies in South Korea, but the growth of L2 writing research suggests a promising future for its status. Due to the increasing number of English-mediated undergraduate or graduate courses (Choi, 2008), tertiary-level EAP writing courses and clinics have been established since the beginning of the 21st century. This seems to have focused L2 writing studies on academic writing, parallel to the development of international L2 writing instructional practices and research (Matsuda & Silva, 2010).

The research context of L2 writing in South Korea has not been recognized outside of South Korea. Local voices have rarely been presented in the global context. L2 writing in South Korea is mainly writing in English as a foreign language (EFL), as noted in other countries and reflected by the number of articles published in the *Journal of Second Language Writing* (Reichelt, 1999). Nonetheless, research on L2 writing in languages other than English, including Korean, has been emerging in recent years.

This chapter will explore the research context of L2 writing in South Korea, which will be defined as writing in a language other than Korean as the first language. It will provide a historical overview of L2 writing studies and a sketch of their recent development. It will mainly deal with L2 writing research published in South Korea. The chapter will also discuss the interweaving relations of L2 writing studies with L2 writing institutional and pedagogical contexts (including the influence of government policies) and with international L2 writing theories, practices, and research trends. It will present unique features of L2 writing research context and address its issues and challenges in South Korea. Finally, it will end with a discussion on future directions and development of South Korea-based L2 writing studies.

The Research Context of L2 Writing in South Korea

Graduate theses (including master's and doctoral theses) and journal articles on L2 writing in South Korea from 1970 until 2012 were collected to analyze their research topics and target subjects with an ultimate goal of exploring the historical development and current trends and the influence of international L2 writing theories and research. The relevant studies published in South Korea were located through an online government research database (www.riss.kr) using keywords such as *writing, composition, foreign language, second language, text,* and *written text.* The articles analyzed were published in 56 journals, including L2-specific journals. None of them is an L2 writing-specific journal, which implies a lack of L2 writing-specific professional organizations.

The Number of L2 Writing Studies

The number of master's and doctoral theses and journal articles on L2 writing is presented by the target second language in Table 1. Writing in various second languages has been studied over the last few decades. However, English has been the most frequently and actively researched language among them, making up 82.2% of the total number of graduate theses on L2 writing (647 out of 787); approximately 93.7% of research articles on L2 writing issued in major journals in South Korea were written on English-L2 writing (490 out of 523). Recently, Korean-L2 composition has been actively explored and published in master's and doctoral students' theses, and thus, the number of the related theses amounts to 93 studies, which is a significant number, compared to second languages other than English (i.e., 47 theses on second languages other than Korean and English).

Table 1　The Number of Master's and Doctoral Theses and Journal Articles
on L2 Writing

	English	Chinese	Japanese	German	French	Spanish	Russian	Thai	Korean	Total
Master's	606	25	11	2	2	2	2	1	89	740
Doctoral	41	0	0	1	1	0	0	0	4	47
Articles	490	1	9	4	3	2	2	1	11	523
Total	1137	26	20	7	6	4	4	2	104	1310

The first graduate thesis and journal article on L2 writing instruction were issued in 1970 and 1971, respectively; they were literature-based studies dealing with pedagogical ideas or frameworks of English-L2 writing rather than empirical studies. The first doctoral dissertation, on the other hand, was published in 1987, 16 years later; it was an error analysis of English-L2 composition. Generally, the number of studies on L2 writing in the Korean context has steadily increased since 1990, and the number has been soaring since 2000, as illustrated by the number of graduate theses and journal articles

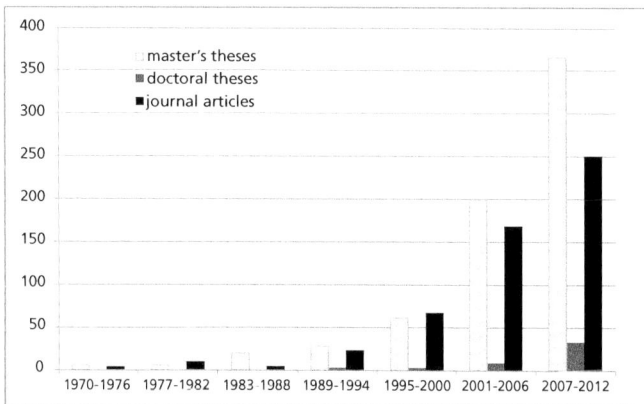

Figure 1. The number of graduate theses and journal articles from 1970 to 2012

every six years from 1970 or 1971 to 2012 in Figure 1. This suggests L2 writing is emerging as a key research area.

The frequency of the articles on L2 writing published in the main English-L2 journal in South Korea, entitled *English Teaching,* also illustrates that more studies on L2 writing have been published in recent years, as shown below.

1975 - 1984: 3 writing studies out of 80 articles (3.8%)

1985 - 1994: 3 writing studies out of 176 articles (1.7%)

1995 - 2004: 25 writing studies out of 509 articles (4.9%)

2005 - 2012: 44 writing studies out of 417 articles (10.6%)

Approximately 10 percent of the articles are writing studies in 2012, though only two to five percent of the articles used to be on writing research. The nearly doubled ratio of the writing studies (4.9% in 1995 to 2004 and 10.6% in 2005 to 2012) suggests that L2 writing has gained attention from Korean English-L2 researchers.

The increasing number of graduate theses and journal articles seems related to the institutional context of L2 writing; that is, the growing number of English-L2 writing specialists with doctoral degrees as university academics and undergraduate or postgraduate courses on L2 writing. Since 1995, English-L2 writing specialists with doctoral degrees from the inner circle of English have been increasing; for example, three specialists were recognized in 2010 and 2011, respectively, whereas one specialist was noted in 1988 and 1989, respectively. Moreover, the Ministry of Education put a focus on teaching skills as a key qualification of school teachers in the mid-1990s. This led to the inclusion of L2 skills education (e.g., teaching reading or writing) in pre- and in-service L2 teacher education in 1994 and 1998, respectively. MA and doctoral courses have also been offered since 2001 and 2003, respectively, which illustrates that teaching L2 writing is recognized as an independent academic area that needs to be explored in graduate studies as well as in teacher education. This might have led to fostering graduate theses and journal articles on L2 writing.

The Target Subject Groups of L2 Writing Studies

When graduate theses and journal articles are analyzed by target subject groups with school levels, they can be categorized into three distinct groups: children (including primary students), secondary students, and adults (including undergraduates and postgraduates). The studies that did not specify the target subject groups were excluded from the review. The number of graduate theses and journal articles per target subject group was counted from 1970 to 2012 and then counted also by six-year periods except for the period from 1970 to 1976, as shown in Figure 2. The first master's thesis, published in 1971, studied secondary English-L2 students. The frequency analysis of graduate theses per year illustrates that approximately 48.3% of the total number of graduate theses (288 of 596 theses) have targeted secondary students, while 36.2% have dealt with adult learners (216 of 596 theses). This can be attributed to the authors of the theses. The majority of master's theses have been written by secondary English-L2 teachers attending graduate schools of education who researched their secondary school students. This seems ironic since writing has rarely been the main learning or testing content of English-L2 education. Secondary English-L2 teachers might research their writing activities or analyze their students' writing for a research purpose rather than a pedagogical purpose. This suggests a dissimilarity between English-L2 writing research foci and institutional or pedagogical L2 writing contexts (see Figures 3 and 4). Figures 3 and 4 are a historical sketch of institutional or pedagogical context of English-L2 writing in South Korea for the past 60 years, respectively, after the first national curriculum of English in 1946 or independence from Japan in 1945. Figure 3 specifically provides chronological information on significant government policies or reforms implemented for English-L2 education in South Korea. Figure 4 illustrates the beginning and ending year of the implementation of an English-L2 pedagogical focus or approach in South Korea in the primary or secondary school context or the university context.

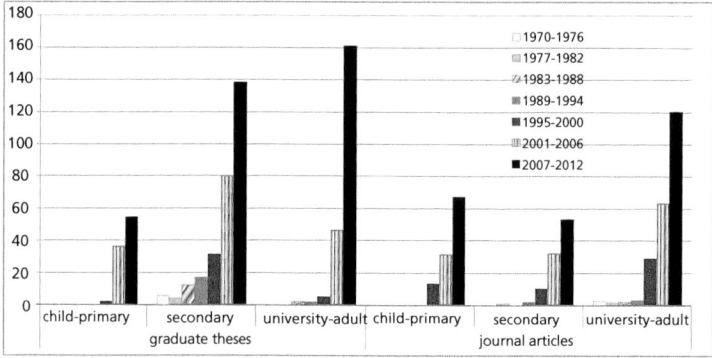

Figure 2. The number of graduate theses and journal articles from 1970 to 2012 per target subject groups

1945	University English composition courses in English-related majors
1994 College Scholastic Aptitude Test (CSAT)	Indirect English writing MCQs in CSAT Pre-service teacher education courses on teaching English writing
1997 The 7th national curriculum	High school English writing classes (elective)
1998	In-service teacher education courses on teaching English writing
1999	English writing-related master programs (text linguistics or ESP writing)
2000	University academic English writing courses and English writing clinics
2007 Revised curriculum	
2009-2013 National English Ability Test (NEAT)	Direct English writing assessment

Figure 3. Historical sketch of the institutional context of English-L2 writing in South Korea

L2 writing context in South Korea	1946	1955	1963	1973	1981	1987	1992	1997	2000	2007	2009	2014
Controlled-to-free writing												
Paragraph Pattern Approach												
Process writing												
Academic writing												
Communicative Approach												
Sentence-level writing												
Paragraph-level writing												
Accuracy												
Fluency												
Dictation												
Error correction												
Translation from L1 to L2												
Letter and journal writing												
Summary writing (reading-writing)												
CALL/MALL												

Figure 4. Historical sketch of pedagogical foci of English-L2 writing in South Korea. Solid lines refer to primary and secondary school context; Broken lines, to university context.

The government has issued national curricula for primary and secondary subjects including second/foreign languages since independence from Japan (e.g., MOE, 1986, 1997; MOE & HRD, 2000, 2006, 2007; MEST, 2009, 2011). As shown in Figure 3, it was with the 7th national curriculum issued in 1997 that English-L2 composition was first offered as a high school elective class (MOE, 1997). Nonetheless, it was chosen by very few regular high schools. The national curriculum issued in 2009 also included two high school elective integrated reading and writing classes entitled *Practical English Reading and Writing and Advanced English Reading and Writing* (MEST, 2009, 2011). However, few high schools have selected these classes. This illustrates a gap between the national curriculum and school practices, as noted in Pae (1999, 2000), Kwon (2003), and Lee (2007). Choi (2007) states "Curriculum reforms are not fundamentally based on the results of the application of the current curriculum" nor on classroom-based research which explores "major problems or limitations of current curricula and solutions for them" (p. 61). Furthermore, secondary students in South Korea have few chances to express their ideas in English-L2 writing. This may have led to the lower writing scores of Korean students compared with those of Japanese and Chinese counterparts which were reported in Kwon, Yoshida, Watanabe, Negishi and Nagamura (2004). Kwon et al. (2004) state that such lower scores may result from the college entrance exam (CSAT), which mainly consists of reading and listening comprehension multiple-choice questions. English writing scores of Korean 11th graders were lower than those of 10th graders due to the lack of English-L2 writing practice in high school and the teachers' and students' neglect of writing education. High school English-L2 teachers' evaluation of Korean students' writing ability reported in Lee (2007) also illustrates the lack of Korean students' writing competence, even in sentence-level grammar and vocabulary use as well as paragraph development. The neglect of L2 classroom writing practices reflects the influence of assessment-dominant school education in South Korea, in which no official school-based or nationwide L2 direct writing assessment is administered. As discussed before, nonetheless, there were a large number of graduate theses written by L2 teachers, which suggests classroom-based L2 writing research may not be a reflection of institutional or pedagogical L2 writing contexts.

Graduate theses on L2 writing have expanded target subject groups, as such expansion was noted in terms of "age groups" in the ESL context (Matsuda & Silva, 2010, p. 238). The first master's thesis on the university context or adults (an error analysis of English-L2 composition) was published in 1988, and the number of theses on this target subject group has been growing since 2003, as academic writing for postgraduates and researchers became the major research focus in the ESL context in the 21st century (Matsuda & Silva, 2010). The growing number of theses on adult learners is strongly related to the undergraduate or postgraduate institutional context. Due to the expansion of English-mediated major or elective courses, academic writing courses have been offered since 2000 (see Figure 3), with the increasing number of EAP courses. English-L2 writing clinics have also been established in 27 out of 204 universities since 2000. The increase of L2 writing studies targeting university students or adults has also been triggered by the expansion of Korean-L2 graduate programs, in which postgraduate students write their MA or doctoral theses targeting under- or post-graduates or adults. The number of graduate theses on university-level L2 writing outnumbered those on the secondary school context in 2009, and this trend has continued since then (see Figure 2).

Graduate theses on L2 writing of children or primary school learners emerged in 1995, when primary English-L2 education officially started. This can be accounted for by the beginning of master's programs for primary English-L2 education at the university of education (an institution for pre- and in-service primary teacher education). It was in the early 2000s when the constant growth of this target subject group was detected (see Figure 2). Nonetheless, the expansion of graduate theses on primary English-L2 writing is ironic since primary English-L2 education puts a focus on oral language education (Choi, 2007; Pae, 2002), and primary English-L2 writing education merely covers learning the English alphabet and writing words or simple sentences learned orally. This suggests discrepancies between the research context and primary classroom practices, as noted between the research foci and secondary L2 writing education.

As for journal articles, more research on university-level writing (51.5% of the total articles on L2 writing) was found than on other target subject groups. This trend is also reported by Kang (2006), Park (2008), and Song and Im (2010), as noted in the articles and dissertations published in the U.S. (Reichelt, 1999) and in Hong Kong, China (Lee, 2011). This may be due to the fact that a significant number of the authors are university academics, as noted in Park (2008). As mentioned before, university-level L2 writing practices have been more prevalent than those in the secondary school context because of the lack of government control on the learning contents, types of teachers (native speakers), including their L2 proficiency and writing competence, and administration of direct writing assessment (see Figure 4). L2 writing research in the tertiary-level context illustrates developments parallel to ESL writing contexts. The majority of journal articles on L2 writing in other languages than English targets university-level learners or adults. Such target subject groups have been studied in approximately 70.2% of the studies on Korean-L2 writing. The dominance of journal articles on the university context is still pronounced in recent years (in 2012, 31 out of 55 articles or 56.4%).

A review of various L2 writing-related journal research articles also reveals that studies on children's or primary-level writing have been salient since 2003 (see Figure 2) though the first article on primary English-L2 writing was published in 1998 (a study on the importance of writing instruction in primary English-L2 education), and English-L2 writing was not the main focus for this target level. As reported in Park (2008), more research articles on primary English-L2 writing were published than those on secondary-level writing in eight major journals on language education in South Korea for the past ten years. This may be accounted for by a particular journal, that is, *Journal of Primary English Education,* which is specifically devoted to articles on primary English-L2 education.

The Topic Areas of L2 Writing Studies

L2 writing studies were also reviewed in terms of their research topics, which were classified into seven categories: error analysis, text analysis (including contrastive rhetoric and cohesion), writing process (focus on the writer), genre (including academic writing)/corpus (focus on the reader), writing instruction (including textbook analysis and curriculum), assessment, and computer assisted language learning (CALL). These categories were selected since some of them, such as error analysis and instruction, are dominant topics addressed in journal articles and graduate theses. Moreover, the frequency of studies on the first four categories can illustrate a research pattern of the Korean L2 writing context, compared with the development of L2 writing theories and research in the ESL writing context, such as focus on text, the writer, and the reader (Hyland, 2002; Raimes, 1991). Some of the studies were coded into more than one topic area. For example, if a study dealt with the effect of pre-writing tasks, it was coded as a study on writing instruction and on writing process.

Frequency of L2 writing studies on the main research topics. Of the seven topic areas, writing instruction has been the most dominant topic explored by L2 writing researchers since 1970 (see Tables 2 and 3). Graduate theses and journal articles on this topic have provided suggestions for pedagogical interventions or the results from the analysis of the effects of such interventions on L2 writing development. In the beginning of L2 writing research, a theoretical overview of L2 writing instruction or review of current instructional situations were dominant in graduate theses and journal articles. The analysis of graduate theses reveals that writing instruction and error analysis were the most popular topics in the early development of L2 writing research until the late 1990s. Although the number of the theses on writing instruction has been constantly increasing, the proportion of such theses is declining due to the emergence of other topics such as writing process and genre. The percentage of teaching instruction has dropped from 100% in 1971, to 40.1% in 1997, to 29.2% in 2012.

Table 2   The Number of Graduate Theses from 1970 to 2012 per Research Topics

	Error analysis	Text analysis	Process	Genre-Corpus	Instruction	Assessment	CALL
1970-1976	1				4		
1977-1982	3				3		
1983-1988	16				4		
1989-1994	18	2			9		
1995-2000	26	3	6		27	2	1
2001-2006	46	15	38	7	83	5	6
2007-2012	50	41	100	44	137	21	12

Table 3   The Number of Journal Articles from 1970 to 2012 per Research Topics

	Error analysis	Text analysis	Process	Genre-Corpus	Instruction	Assessment	CALL
1970-1976					3		
1977-1982	1	1	1		7		
1983-1988	1	1			2		
1989-1994	2	2			6		2
1995-2000	4	8	9	1	27	7	8
2001-2006	12	7	16	13	57	16	24
2007-2012	9	16	33	33	73	17	20

Error analysis is another popular topic studied in graduate theses in early L2 writing research. It was the most dominant topic until the late 1990s. Such popularity appears to have been triggered by the product-oriented instructional approach with a focus on accuracy and sentence-level writing. For example, error correction was specified as a key skill to learn in the national English-L2 curriculum until 2006, as shown in Figure 4. In L2 classroom practices, the time for writing instruction was seldom specifically allotted; even in classes intended for reading and writing, writing in English-L2 is seldom practiced. If it is taught, it is practiced in controlled or guided writing, such as writing sentences including certain grammatical forms or sentence structures (see Figure 4). A survey of secondary English-L2 teachers shows that writing is focused on grammar to practice writing a sentence in order to learn grammatical structures (Kim, 2013). Such a pedagogical orientation has prioritized accuracy and mechanics, as it was noted as a major focus even in the ESL context in 2004 (Silva & Leki, 2004).

Although the proportion of research on error analysis in English-L2 writing has declined, the growing number of the studies on this topic has been recently noted in writing studies in other L2 languages, such as Korean and Chinese. This indicates different development of L2 writing research across second languages in South Korea; research on English-L2 writing is more common than writing studies in other languages. Graduate theses and journal research articles also show different trends on this topic. More specifically, unlike graduate theses, not many journal articles on error analysis have been published since an article on error analysis was first issued in 1979 in *English Teaching* (a study on characteristics of errors in Korean students' composition in English-L2).

Text analysis, including contrastive rhetoric and cohesion, is another research area explored at the early stage of L2 writing research in South Korea. Analyses of discourse and grammar in written texts were put into this category. The first journal article on text analysis was published in 1980 in *English Teaching* (a contrastive analysis of rhetoric and style in English-L2 composition). It was about ten years before the first MA thesis on cohesion was published in South Korea (a study on cohesion and coherence problems in Korean students' writings in English-L2). Text analysis of two different languages (L1 and L2) is often conducted. Such analyses are also steadily growing. Approximately 10 articles on text analysis have been published per year since 2010, which seems triggered by the emergence of genre-based studies (e.g., analysis of organizational patterns of Korean English speakers' request emails).

The writing process is another important and distinct area of L2 writing research in South Korea. This topic includes process-oriented writing instruction. L2 writing researchers have noted that there is a substantial number of studies focusing on L2 writers' composing processes (Matsuda & Silva, 2010). The notion of writing as process was introduced to L2 studies by Vivian Zamel (1976), who argued that advanced L2 writers are similar to L1 writers and can benefit from instruction emphasizing the process of writing (Matsuda, 2003). Such a notion of writing as process was also introduced to the L2 writing academic community in South Korea; as a result, graduate theses on the writing process first came out in 1997 and their number has gradually increased. Since 2007, they outnumbered the theses on error analysis (exceeded error analysis by 2.4% in 2007 and 6.2% in 2012). The popularity of process-oriented studies is also related to changes in the instructional approach, as process writing was first mentioned in the national secondary English-L2 curriculum in 2007 (see Figure 4). The majority of the studies on the process of writing have examined feedback or revision (approximately 62% all graduate theses on writing process), as such studies are prevalent and have dealt with diverse issues such as peer feedback and conferences in the ESL context (Hyland & Hyland, 2006). The writing process was explored in research articles much earlier in graduate theses; the first journal article on this topic was issued in 1980. Interestingly, no journal articles on writing process were present for nearly 5 years until 1995.

A significant portion of graduate theses and journal articles on the writing process has covered the topic of feedback; however, the majority of them have limited their topics to the feedback type and its effects on the development of students' L2 writing ability. While L2 writing research on feedback in the ESL context has pointed out that there should be various feedback modes available for students, such as writing conferences, studies on writing conferences in the Korean context are scarce. The effect of writing conferences in the Korean EFL context was first researched in a doctoral dissertation issued in 2009.

In addition to the three major topics discussed earlier, other topics, such as assessment, CALL and academic writing, have been dealt with in both graduate theses and journal articles. The first articles on CALL and assessment were published in 1989 and 1996, respectively. Although the number of studies on assessment and CALL has been steadily growing since 2000, their number remains smaller than those of studies on the writing process or instruction. This might be accounted for by the secondary L2 writing pedagogical context. With the advent and utilization of technology in the L2 learning environment, Web-based writing has emerged in school contexts since the late 1990s (see Figure 4), including online feedback on L2 writing and online chatting. However, the findings from such research do not seem to be applied to the L2 writing classroom environment due to key obstacles such as a large class size and teachers' inability to teach writing using various computer-based programs.

As for L2 writing research on assessment, positive future development of English-L2 writing research cannot be easily predicted due to the removal of the government policy for nationwide English-L2 writing assessment (NEAT) (see Figure 3). As discussed before, Education in South Korea is strongly influenced by assessment, especially college entrance examinations. The lack of direct writing assessment from the beginning of English-L2 education led to the neglect of L2 writing education. The development of a national English ability test (NEAT), including direct writing assessment, in 2007 fostered high school English-L2 writing education. KICE ([South] Korea Institute of Curriculum & Evaluation) (2013) reported that more middle and high schools administer essay writing tests (about 15.9% in 2012 and 24.3% in 2013) and sentence or paragraph-level writing tests (about 55.3% in 2012 and 55.4% in 2013). Unfortunately, the government has decided not to administer the assessment as part of the college entrance examination from 2014.

In the ESL context, genre studies in L2 writing are growing, and particular genres have been extensively examined (Matsuda & Silva, 2010). For example, the academic writing of graduate students and researchers has become a major topic in L2 writing research (Casanave & Vandrick, 2003; Lillis & Curry, 2006; Matsuda & Silva, 2010; Swales, 2004). Academic writing and genre studies have been growing areas of L2 writing in L2 writing research in South Korea with the expansion of academic English-L2 writing education since 2000. The first journal article on this topic in the Korean context was published in 1999 in *Journal of Applied Linguistics* (a study on the genre analysis approach to teaching composition in English-L2 for academic purposes). These topics appeared relatively late in 2004 in graduate theses (a study on the use of information from source texts in Korean graduate students' English-L2 academic writing), but they have shown a gradual development during the past few years. This implies that researchers in South Korea are increasingly interested in genre-relevant topics, including EAP and genre-based writing instruction. A number of graduate theses and journal articles published in South Korea have addressed genre-based academic writing. Those studies have analyzed academic discourse genres and examined the effect of teaching genre on students' production of texts.

The growing number of graduate theses on the writing process, academic writing or genre and the declining number on error analysis demonstrate the influence of L2 writing theories or research in the inner circle of English on those in the Korean context despite the delayed introduction of updated theories or research topics. However, the fact that the studies on error analysis and text analysis were still found in 2012 implies that written products are still frequently analyzed. Interestingly, the publication year of the first journal article on each research area is five to 10 years earlier than that of the first thesis on them. This may be a result of differences in their major author groups and the larger number of the master's theses than the doctoral dissertations. The journal articles cover newly emerging topics and seem influenced by international L2 writing theories or research because the authors, university academics, need to play a role as an introducer of new or updated international theories or research.

Historical development of L2 writing studies on instruction. As mentioned before, writing instruction has been the dominant topic of L2 writing research. Studies on this topic can be classified into three foci, following L2 writing and writing instruction theory in Raimes (1991) and Hyland (2002): focus on text (written product), the writer (writing process) and the reader (genre) (see

Figures 5 and 6). A master's thesis on product-oriented instruction was first published in 1973, and the first journal article on the same focus came out in 1976. Since then, research on product-oriented pedagogy has been extensively conducted. Writing seen as a product focuses on language structures and writers' grammatical/lexical knowledge. Such aspects of learners' written texts in instruction were analyzed in a large number of graduate theses and journal articles. Writing instruction using a variety of materials, modes, or specific types of writing has been explored in graduate theses as well as journal articles. Such materials or modes include literature, pictures, dialogue journals and the Internet. The majority of such theses and articles are product-oriented. Interestingly, a large number of graduate theses have been written on letter or journal writing in the secondary school context, which seems to result from the fact that such writing has been viewed as a useful writing activity from the beginning of English-L2 writing education in South Korea, as specified in the national curriculum.

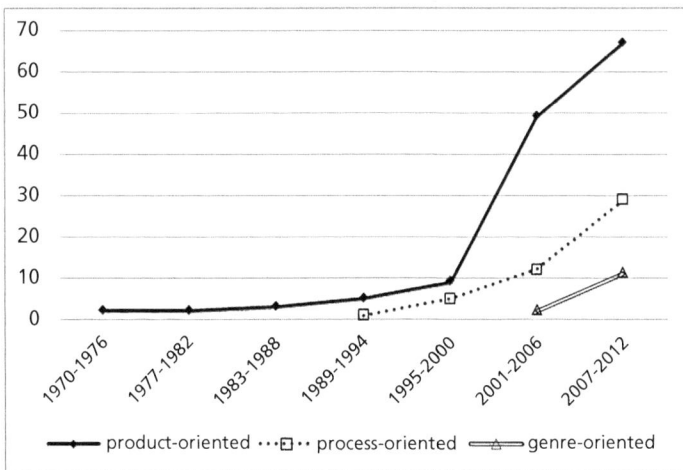

Figure 5. The number of graduate theses on writing instruction from 1970 to 2012 per pedagogical focus

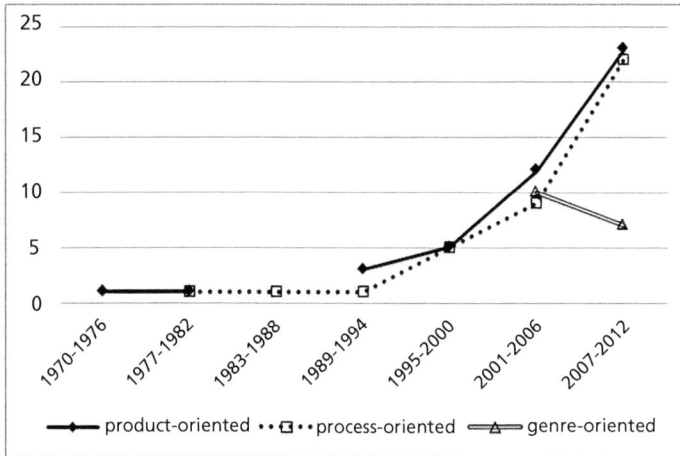

Figure 6. The number of journal articles on writing instruction from 1970 to 2012 per pedagogical focus

Compared to the changes in research and pedagogical foci in the ESL context, certain orientations never fade away in South Korea, as controlled writing is a key classroom or textbook writing activity (see Figure 4). Written texts are still viewed as autonomous objects (Hyland, 2002) without consideration of the relational aspects of writing, such as the relationship between the reader and the writer (Matsuda & Silva, 2010; Silva, 1990). From the beginning of school education, L2 writing was defined as the production of graphic symbols, and it was subordinate to learning language elements such as grammar, vocabulary, and mechanics. Since grammar-centered learning was dominant, writing was viewed as grammar manipulation (Hyland, 2002), and the view of writing as composition was often neglected in classroom-based writing practices, which mainly aimed at decontextualized word- or sentence-level writing. Such an orientation is still noticeable in primary and secondary school contexts. Error correction and translation from Korean to English used to be stated as the learning content in the national primary and secondary school English curriculum in 1996 and 2006, respectively (MOE, 1997; MEST, 2009). This may have resulted from the focus on accuracy. This trend is thus illustrated by the fact that error analysis has been one of the dominant research topics in South Korea.

In South Korea, process-focused theses and journal articles appeared approximately ten years after the first product-focused instruction study (see Figures 5 and 6). The process approach received attention from researchers in the field of L2 writing who were dissatisfied with controlled and paragraph-pattern composition, as noted in North America (Matsuda & Silva, 2010). A substantial body of research in South Korea was devoted to prewriting while a large amount of post writing process research has dealt with feedback, which is either teacher or peer feedback in L2 writing. Process-oriented writing instruction with a particular focus on revision, collaborative writing, and dialogue journal writing is mainly explored in graduate theses and journal articles. The most updated curriculum, which was issued in 2009, also illustrates the influence of L2 writing theories, research, and practices in the inner circle of English: it includes process-oriented activities. Nonetheless, this does not imply that L2 writing practices in South Korea have reflected parallel development to ESL writing practices. There has always been a gap between theory and reality in L2 education, including writing, as discussed in Kwon (2003) and Choi (2007).

Over the last 10 years, research on genre-based L2 writing instruction in the Korean context has developed along with studies on academic writing and EAP. In addition, the studies of genre-based writing instruction published in South Korea have expanded the target subject groups to secondary and even primary students from mainly undergraduate or postgraduate students. Nonetheless, product-based writing instruction still has a place in L2 writing research.

Emergence of new research topics in L2 writing studies. Besides the seven main research areas of L2 writing, five specific topics are recognized as recently developed research areas of L2 writing in South Korea: learners, instructors, academic writing, corpus work, and reading-writing integration. They emerged after 2002 and are growing research areas in L2 writing, which is indicated by the number of graduate theses and journal articles on these topics.

Learner-related journal articles and graduate theses have been gradually increasing in South Korea since 2005, while fewer studies on writing instructors have been conducted during the same period. Learner-related studies have explored student writers' motivation, strategies, and perception about specific instructional techniques or activities. Though journal articles on writing instructors were not found as frequently as those on learner variables, some articles addressed the role of native and non-native teachers in L2 writing classrooms. Research on academic writing has shown a similar developmental pattern with that of genre in terms of the starting point and the number of journal articles and graduate theses. Few graduate theses have been written on corpus work. Moreover, the first thesis on this research area appeared in 2008. On the other hand, journal articles first featured a corpus-based study in 2002 (a corpus-based study on the uses of *make* in Korean EFL learner writing). Lastly, reading-writing integration is another recently growing topic in L2 writing. In spite of its earlier emergence than the other recent topics, it had not been explored until the early 2000s.

Issues and Challenges in L2 Writing in South Korea

The issues and challenges noted from the review of the L2 writing research context in South Korea are interwoven with its institutional and pedagogical context. Lack of L2 writing research needs and practicality is a key issue in the L2 writing research context of South Korea. L2 writing instruction in South Korea is a comparatively young area of instruction in the school context. A gap between the national curriculum and school practices in L2 writing is noticeable, as mentioned before. As illustrated in Figure 7, L2 writing research in South Korea is strongly influenced by the government policy, including assessment and curriculum, more than the theoretical and research context of L2 writing in the inner circle of English. Lack of high-stakes L2 writing tests has led to no need of L2 writing instruction (Lee, 2007). The minor role of L2 writing has resulted in L2 learners' lack of motivation for developing L2 writing

competence and negative attitude toward learning L2 writing; L2 teachers'
professional development as writing teachers; and a lack of resources for
research. Lee's (2007) survey of English-L2 teachers illustrates L2 teachers' lack
of competence for teaching or assessing writing and insufficient time for
teaching writing and providing feedback, mainly due to the large size of classes.
These problems are also noted in other second/foreign language contexts,
including Hong Kong, China (Lee, 2011).

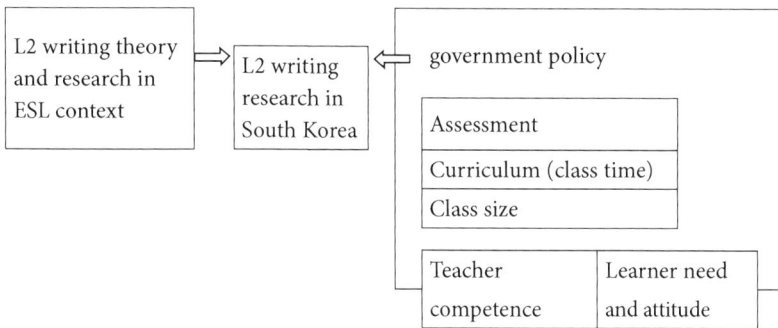

Figure 7. Influential factors of L2 writing research in South Korea

Problems with research practicality are also a demotivating factor for L2
writing research. Since writing is not taught or practiced in L2 classrooms
except for tertiary L2 writing education, it is a challenge to recruit the ideal
target subject group for a study or to conduct a study for investigating a new
teaching technique in real classrooms, especially longitudinally. The institutional,
pedagogical and research context of L2 writing thus creates a vicious cycle.

The pedagogical orientation to L2 writing also causes an imbalance
between pedagogical and research contexts; between secondary school and
university contexts (Sohn, Kim, & Choi, 2006); among different L2 languages;
and among target research subject groups and topics. The pedagogical context
has not yet kept up with the recent changes or developments found in the
research context, especially in the secondary school context. A number of L2
writing studies have investigated various topics in L2 writing, such as error

analysis, text analysis, process writing, genre- or corpus-based writing, writing instruction, writing assessment, and Web or computer-based writing. However, in secondary L2 classrooms, writing activities mainly consist of sentence-level writing focusing on accuracy since writing is still viewed as language manipulation. L2 teachers focus on "teaching about writing" rather than "teaching writing" (Matsuda & Silva, 2010), which leads to Korean L2 learners' misconception of writing as subordinate to other skills and language elements such as grammar and to the dominance of controlled writing activities. Genre- or corpus-based writing has seldom been observed in the secondary classroom context. Nor has Web-based writing been practiced in secondary L2 classrooms. In the university context, to some extent, L2 writing courses adopt some recent developments in research. Their curriculum includes most of the writing activities or approaches prevalent in the ESL context. Nonetheless, writing instruction has not demonstrated parallel development with L2 writing research.

Another issue is concerned with the fact that certain research areas such as reader awareness or conferencing are seldom explored in L2 writing research in South Korea. The process of writing is "a complex web of relationships among the elements of writing, including the writer, the reader, and the text and reality" (Matsuda & Silva, 2010, p. 232). It involves the three aspects of writing: the relational aspect (e.g., consideration of the relationship between the writer and the reader); the strategic aspect (e.g., use of writing strategies such as planning and revising); and the textual aspect (e.g., use of cohesive devices). L2 writing process studies in South Korea do not illustrate balanced exploration among such aspects. The relational aspect has seldom been researched, though genre-based studies have been emerging. This may be accounted for by Hinds' (1987) classification of Korean as a "writer-responsible" language. The reader factor does not seem to be viewed as a key aspect of writing in South Korea, as Choi's (2006) study of Korean university students shows no clear impact of reader awareness on their L2 writing.

The final issue is a lack of research infrastructure including professional organizations and graduate programs. As a discipline, L2 writing is still in an early stage of development and has not been established as an independent academic discipline. Professional organizations have not been established for L2 writing. There are no L2 writing-specific associations, SIGs (Special Interest Groups), conferences, nor journals. This implies that L2 writing including English-L2 writing has not been recognized as an independent academic field in South Korea, unlike L1 and L2 writing in North America (Silva & Leki, 2004). There are also no L2 writing-specific postgraduate programs; rather, L2 writing courses are provided in L2 majors including English education, English culture and communication, and English, French, or Chinese language and literature. There are two specialized master's programs related to English-L2 writing: a professional ESP writing master's program established in 1999 and a master's program on rhetoric including genres, discourse analysis, text linguistics, and corpus linguistics. However, they cannot be classified as L2 writing-specific programs since one of them aims at educating ESP writers, and the other is mainly concerned with rhetoric and text linguistics rather English-L2 writing as an academic discipline.

Few L2 writing-specific professional organizations, journals or postgraduate programs are identified, which may lead to delaying professional development of L2 writing research. Such a delay could result from a lack of constant L2 writing research by university academics after their doctoral studies and of collaborative research with L2 writing scholars. The majority of L2 writing scholars identified by their doctoral dissertations are mainly university academics who specialize in English-L2 writing and are housed in English-related departments, especially English education (28 out of 53). Thirty-nine English-L2 writing scholars did their doctoral studies in the inner circle of English. Less than 50% of the journal articles published by the English-L2 writing scholars have explored L2 writing-specific topics, though they tend to supervise MA and doctoral students who study L2 writing. For example, an English-L2 writing scholar with a doctoral degree from an American university has published 23 articles on English-L2 writing out of 56 articles since 1988 (41.1%), but none of them is a collaborative research with other English-L2 writing scholars. She has supervised 22 of 51 MA theses and seven of eight doctoral theses on English-L2 writing (49.2%). Another scholar has published one article on English-L2 writing out of nine articles since 1995 (11.1%) with no collaborative research with other English-L2 writing scholars. He has supervised 15 MA theses on English-L2 writing of 43 MA and 4 doctoral theses (31.9%). The discontinuity of L2 writing research among L2 writing scholars can be accounted for by their work load (e.g., school textbook construction, government projects, including the development of the national curriculum and nationwide examinations) and also by their research focus shift to L2 educational policies or current educational issues since such research is often funded by the government. Moreover, L2 writing scholars seem to neglect the establishment of a research network among them; thus, little collaborative research is noted among them.

Future Directions of L2 Writing in South Korea

The review of the historical and contemporary research contexts of L2 writing in South Korea has illustrated an interweaving relationship with its institutional and pedagogical context. Though L2 writing is a young area of study and practice in South Korea, it is an emerging academic discipline, as indicated by the growing amount and the topic diversification of L2 writing research. The research context evidences a resemblance to L2 writing research in the ESL context and an influence of the development of L2 writing theory and research rather than L2 writing instruction theories or practices. Nonetheless, this should not be interpreted as a complete lack of L2 writing scholarship in South Korea. Unique features of the Korean context, including pedagogical needs, might foster certain pedagogical approaches or research such as product-oriented instruction and error analysis. By hearing local voices on L2 writing from South Korea, L2 writing specialists in the ESL context can expand their understanding of the second language writing context, as Reichelt (1999) states "FL and ESL writing specialists can learn from each other"

(p. 195). At the same time, Korean L2 writing researchers can gain some insights from the L2 writing theories, practices, and research in other countries including North America, as suggested in Lee (2011). L2 writing theories, practices, and research in the ESL context should not be accepted and implemented in the L2 writing context of South Korea as authoritative answers to issues, as cautioned by Silva and Leki (2004) on the role of parent disciplines (rhetoric, linguistics, composition studies, and applied linguistics) in L2 writing in the ESL context. Korean L2 writing researchers need to develop South Korea-based L2 writing research frameworks which meet local needs, while sharing benefits from L2 writing theories, practices, and research in the ESL context. For example, the Korean L2 writing pedagogical context does not provide a research setting for a longitudinal study or a study exploring implicit instruction or diverse written genres. L2 writing research should reflect such local context and pedagogical needs. At the same time, it should further develop the study of underexplored aspects of writing or pedagogical needs to take a step forward in L2 writing pedagogy as well as L2 writing research.

Future development of L2 writing research cannot be optimistically predicted due to a lack of L2 writing research infrastructure, including professional organizations. Different research patterns in graduate theses and journal articles also appear to indicate a lack of research networks. This seems to reflect their distinctive author groups (postgraduates and university academics) and their pedagogical and institutional context, which influence their target subject groups and topics. The pedagogical and institutional context of L2 writing should be reformed to have a parallel development of the research context and establish research infrastructure; otherwise, there would be limited development of L2 writing as an academic discipline as well as L2 writing research. L2 writing scholars should contribute to the reform of the pedagogical and institutional context; more specifically, they should try to play a leading role as government policymakers in a society where top-down approaches are dominant or education is centrally controlled by the government. Furthermore, they need to establish a research network and professional organizations such as special interest groups (SIGs). Though the number of L2 writing doctoral theses and scholars is growing, no L2 writing scholars have attempted to establish such a research network or organization. They should create a synergistic effect by setting up such a network or organization not only for the benefit of the L2 writing academic community but also for their own research development.

Conclusion

L2 writing in South Korea has not been established as an independent academic discipline, unlike the disciplinary status of L2 writing in North America. The assessment-dominant educational culture in South Korea has been the main cause for negligence of L2 writing instruction in primary and secondary school context. Furthermore, the minimal role of L2 writing leads to a lack of attention pedagogical needs and student motivation and of research needs. The research, institutional, and pedagogical context have created a vicious cycle, which leads to a lack of research infrastructure. However, the growing number of L2 writing studies including graduate theses and journal articles suggests the emergence of the field, which should lead to the future development of L2 writing research infrastructure. The Korean L2 writing research context shares some features with the ESL context, but it also has its own distinctive features due to the institutional and pedagogical context. This implies Korean L2 writing scholars should be devoted to the development of the South Korea-based L2 writing research context by adopting and being adept in L2 writing theories and research in the inner circle of English.

References

Casanave, C. P. (2004). *Controversies in Second Language Writing: Dilemmas and Decisions in Research and Instruction*. Ann Arbor, MI: The University of Michigan Press.

Casanave, C. P. & Vandrick, S. (Eds.) (2003). *Writing for Scholarly Publication: Behind the Scenes in Language Education.* Mahwah, NJ: Lawrence Erlbaum.

Choi, E. K. (1979). Yeongjakmun-gyosubeop: Geuy eojey-wa oneuyl (English writing instruction: The past and the present). *English Teaching,* 18, 1-27.

Choi, Y. H. (2006). Effects of L2 writing proficiency and reader awareness on EFL students' writing product and process on-line: Computer-based observation. *The Journal of Asia TEFL,* 3(2), 37-78.

Choi, Y. H. (2007). The history of and the policy of the English language education in [South] Korea. In Y. H. Choi & B. Spolsky (Eds.), *English Education in Asia: History and Policies* (pp. 33-66). Seoul: Asia TEFL.

Choi, Y. H. (2008). Proficiency-differentiated and discipline-specific student needs for English-medium content-based courses. *English Language & Literature,* 54(6), 953-985.

Hinds, J. (1987). Reader versus writer responsibility: A new typology. In U. Connor & R. B. Kaplan (Eds.), *Writing Across Languages: Analysis of L2 Text* (pp. 141-152). Reading, MA: Addison-Wesley.

Hyland, K. (2002). *Teaching and Researching Writing.* Harlow, UK: Longman.

Hyland, K. (2003). *Second Language Writing.* Cambridge: Cambridge University Press.

Hyland, K. & Hyland, F. (2006). Feedback on second language students' writing. *Language Teaching,* 39, 83-101.

Grabe, W. & Kaplan, R. B. (1996). *Theory and Practice of Writing.* New York: Longman.

Im, C., Jin, K., Lee, M., Chang, K., Kim, M., Lee, B., … Paek, I. (2011). Yeongeo-gwa gyoyuk-gwajeong-gwa gukga-yeongeo-neungryeok-phyeoga-shiheom yeongyey bangan yeongu (Connecting the English national curriculum and the national English ability test) (Report CRE 2011-4). Seoul: KICE.

Jin, K., Shin, D. & Si, G. (2012). Gukga-yeongeo-neungryeok-phyeoga-shiheom-euy chujin-hweonhwang-gwa baljeon-banghyang (A study on the current status and future directions of the national English ability test) (Report ORI 2012-02-07). Seoul: KICE.

Kang, D. (2006). Yeongeo gyoyuk haksulji 40-nyeon yeongjak-yeongu hoego-wa jeonmang (Synthesis of 40 years' writing studies in the journal of English Teaching). *English Teaching,* 61(Special issue), 97-114.

Kim, H. S. (2013). Jungdeung-yeongeo-gyosa-deul-euy sseuy-gi gyosu-ey daehan inshik mit thaedo-ey gwanhan yeongu (Secondary school English teachers' perspectives on and attitudes towards teaching writing). Unpublished master's thesis. Korea University, Seoul, South Korea.

Kwon, O. (2003). (2003, November). Narrowing the gaps between ideals and realities in TEFL. Plenary speech presented at the First Asia TEFL International Conference, Busan, South Korea.

Kwon, O., Yoshida, K., Watanabe, Y., Negishi, M. & Nagamura, N. (2004). A comparison of English proficiency of Korean, Japanese, and Chinese high school students. *English Teaching,* 59(4), 3-21.

Lee, D. (2007). Secondary school teachers' practices, perceptions and problems regarding English writing instruction. *Foreign Languages Education,* 14(2), 37-64.

Lee, I. (2011). Issues and challenges in teaching and learning EFL writing: The case of Hong Kong. In T. Cimasko & M. Reichelt (Eds.), *Foreign Language Writing Instruction: Principles and Practices* (pp. 118-137). West Lafayette, IN: Parlor Press.

Lee, K. S. (2000). Hanguk-eyseo woygukeo gyoyuk-euy yeoksa (The history of foreign language education in [South] Korea). *Journal of German Education,* 21, 53-88.

Lee, M., Shin, D., Cho, B., Park, T., Lee, D., Song, M. Y., ... Kim, S. J. (2011). Mal-ha-gi sseuy-gi phyeongga doip-ey ttareun yeonggeo-gyosu-hakseup-bangbeop gaeseon bangan yeongu (A study on the reform of English instruction for the implementation of speaking and writing tests) (Report RRI 2011-7-1). Seoul: KICE.

Lee, M. B., Hwang, J. B., Jeon, J. H., Choi, Y. H., Kim, J. Y. & Chang, E. K (2013). Cho-jungdeung-yeongeo gyoyuk hweoynhwang bunseok yeongu (Analysis of the current primary and second school English education in 2013) (Research Report CRE 2013-7-1). Seoul: KICE.

Leki, I., Cumming, A. & Silva, T. (2008). *A Synthesis of Research on Second Language Writing in English*. New York: Routledge.

Lillis, T. & Curry, M. J. (2006). Professional academic writing by multilingual scholars: Interactions with literacy brokers in the production of English-medium texts. *Written Communication, 23*, 3-35.

Matsuda, P. K. (2003). Second language writing in the twentieth century: A situated historical perspective. In B. Kroll (Ed.), *Exploring the Dynamics of Second Language Writing* (pp. 15-34). Cambridge: Cambridge University Press.

Matsuda, P. K. & Silva, T. (2010). Writing. In N. Schmitt (Ed.), *An Introduction to Applied Linguistics* (pp. 232-246). London: Hodder Education.

Min, C. (1994). Yeongeo-gyoyuk-gwa sseuy-gi-gyoyuk (English education and teaching writing). *English Teaching, 48*, 171-187.

MEST (Ministry of Education, Science & Technology). (2009). *Yeongeo-gwa gyoyuk-gawjeong (English Language Curriculum)*. Seoul: MEST.

MEST. (2011). *Yeongeo- gwa gyoyuk-gawjeong (English Language Curriculum)*. Seoul: MEST.

MOE (Ministry of Education). (1986). *Gyoyuk-gwajeong (1946-1981) Oegukeogwa [Curriculum (1946-1981): Foreign Languages]*. Seoul: MOE.

MOE. (1988). *Godeung-hakgyo Oegukeo-gwa gyoyuk-gwajeong (yeongeo I, II) (The Guidelines of the High School Foreign Languages Curriculum: English I and II)*. Seoul: MOE.

MOE. (1995). *Godeung-hakgyo Oegukeo-gwa gyoyuk-gwajeong haeseol (I): Gongtong yeongeo, yeongeo I, II, yeongeo dokhae, yeongeo hoehwa, silmu yeongeo (The Guidelines of the High School Foreign Languages Curriculum: High School English, English I and II, English Reading, English Conversation, and Business English)*. Seoul: MOE.

MOE. (1997). *Oegukeogwa gyoyukgwajeong (I) (Foreign Languages Curriculum I)*. Seoul: MOE.

MOE & HRD (The Ministry of Education and Human Resources Development). (2000). *The Guidelines of the High School Curriculum: Foreign Languages (English)*. Seoul: MOE & HRD.

MOE & HRD. (2006). *Cho-jungdeung hakgyo gyoyuk-gwajeong bubun sujeong gosi (Partial Revision of Elementary School English).* Seoul: MOE & HRD.

MOE & HRD. (2007). *Woygukeo gyeyyeoyl gyogwa gyoyuk-gwajeong (Foreign Languages Curriculum).* Seoul: MOE & HRD.

Moon, Y. (1976). Gu-han-al-euy yeongeo-gyoyuk-go (A review of English education at the end of Yi Dynasty). *English Teaching,* 12, 1-12.

Pae, D. B. (1999). Historical development of English language curriculum. In H. S. Lee (Ed.), *Foreign Language Acquisition and Curriculum* (pp. 241-260). Seoul: Hanguk Publisher.

Pae, D. B. (2000). *Foreign Languages Curriculum.* Seoul: Hanguk Publisher.

Pae, D. B. (2002). *English Language Education.* Seoul: Hanguk Publisher.

Park, J. S. (2008). Yeongeo sseuy-gi-ey gwanhan yeongu hweoynhwang-gwa banghyang-seong mosaek (A review of studies on writing in Korean EFL context). Unpublished master's thesis. Konkuk University, Seoul, South Korea.

Raimes, A. (1991). Out of the woods: Emerging traditions in the teaching of writing. *TESOL Quarterly,* 25, 407-430.

Reichelt, M. (1999). Toward a more comprehensive view of L2 writing: Foreign language writing in the U.S. *Journal of Second Language Writing,* 8, 181-204.

Reichelt, M. (2001). A critical review of foreign language writing research on pedagogical practices. *The Modern Language Journal,* 85, 578-598.

Silva, T. (1990). Second language composition instruction: Developments, issues, and directions in ESL. In B. Kroll (Ed.), *Second Language Writing: Research Insights for the Classroom* (pp. 11-23). Cambridge: Cambridge University Press.

Silva, T. & Brice, C. (2004). Research in teaching writing. *ARAL (Annual Review of Applied Linguistics),* 24, 70-106.

Silva, T., Brice, C., Kapper, J., Matsuda, P. K. & Reichelt, M. (2001). Twenty-five years of scholarship on second language composing process: 1976-2000. *International Journal of English Studies,* 1(2), 211-240.

Silva, T. & Leki, I. (2004). Family matters: The influence of applied linguistics
and composition studies on second language writing studies: Past, present,
and future. *The Modern Language Journal,* 88, 1-13.

Silva, T. & Matsuda, P. K. (2002). Writing. In N. Schmitt (Ed.), *An Introduction
to Applied Linguistics* (pp. 251-266). London: Arnold.

Silva, T. & Matsuda, P. K. (Eds.) (2010). *Practicing Theory and Second Language
Writing.* West Lafayette, IN: Parlor Press.

Song, M. & Lim, J. (2010). Hyeondae-yeongeo-gyoyuk haksulji 10-nyeon: Ilg-gi
mit sseuy-gi gwanryoen hwoygo (A critical review of reading-and-writing-
related studies in the *Modern English Education* journal). *Modern English
Education,* 11(2), 60-81.

Swales, J. (2004). *Research Genres: Exploration and Analysis.* Cambridge:
Cambridge University Press.

Chapter 7
The Status of ESL/EFL Writing in Lebanon

Fatima Esseili

University of Dayton

Introduction

Research on writing in a second or foreign language has been growing rapidly, with around 2600 articles published in the past 15 years, an average of 170 per year (Silva, McMartin-Miller, Jayne & Pelaez-Morales, 2011). While Lebanese scholars authored only about two percent of those publications, L2 writing research in Lebanon goes back to the 1960s, primarily in the form of MA theses. Since then, only one synthesis article had been published (cf. Bacha, 2007), but it remained narrow in its coverage. Thus, the aim of this chapter is to provide an overview and synthesis of scholarship on L2 writing[1] in Lebanon. It presents findings based on a total of 72 sources from three major universities in Lebanon. The types of publications reviewed are categorized based on their focus, and they include journal articles, book chapters, and MA theses.

The chapter provides a brief description of the context for and history of second language writing (SLW) studies in Lebanon and the infrastructure supporting L2 writing. Then, trends in scholarship with regard to teaching and

---

1 I will be using the terms L2 writing, SLW, and ESL/EFL writing interchangeably.

learning challenges, characteristics of students' writing, curricular and instructional developments and methods, error correction and types of feedback, WAC/WID studies, assessment practices, and writing centers are discussed. Finally, recommendations for future research are offered.

Background and Description of the Context

Lebanese scholars have often celebrated Lebanon as a "multicultural" and "multilingual" country (e.g., Bacha, 2000; Bacha & Bahous, 2011, 2013; Diab, 2004, 2009; Shaaban & Ghaith, 2000, 2002). Multilingualism is certainly present in Lebanese society though in various levels and degrees. This richness in languages is partly due to Lebanon's trilingual policy where in addition to Arabic, the native language, students in Lebanese schools get to learn and use a foreign language (either French or English) as a medium of instruction in math and sciences in grade one and learn a second foreign language in grade seven or even four.

The extent to which students are proficient in the languages they presumably speak, however, is yet to be investigated (Esseili, 2011, 2014). To elaborate, some students may have learned English for twelve years in schools, but their English proficiency turns out to be basic at the university level. In addition, the majority of the aforementioned studies that are related to aspects of English language teaching and learning in Lebanon have been generally conducted in the capital's most prestigious and affluent private universities where the total student population does not exceed 9,000 per university. Such universities are representative of only one portion of Lebanese society. Lebanon has 31 private universities, 10 university institutes and colleges, and only one public university (Ministry of Education, 2014). Table 1 shows the ranking of the major universities, which I refer to in this paper, in terms of the number of students enrolled for the academic year 2012-2013.

Table 1   Number of Students for the Academic Year 2012-2013

University	Student Population
The Lebanese University (LU)	75,000
The Lebanese American University (LAU)	8,138
The American University of Beirut (AUB)	7,982
The University of Balamand (UOB)	5,316

Bilingual or trilingual students on Lebanese campuses come from a variety of backgrounds. They include students who were born, raised, and educated in Lebanon—these constitute the majority of the student body, and they could be either French educated or English educated; Arab students; international and exchange students; and first or second generation Lebanese immigrants who are native speakers of English (or other languages). These groups of students have different needs when it comes to writing in a second language. Some students may sound like native speakers of English, but their writing skills might need improvement. Others may have studied English as a second or third language and might need slight or extensive skill development depending on the nature of the contact level they have had with English at their schools. For the academic year 2011-2012, for example, 60% of the total number of schools in Lebanon used French as a medium of instruction while only 27% used English. The rest of the schools used both French and English. When we look at the student population, we find that around 60% of the student body learned French as a first foreign language, and 40% learned English as a first foreign language (Ministry of Education, 2013). A great number of these 60% of students choose to enroll in English-medium universities and are forced to function in English as a third language. Many of them attend universities where English is not used much outside of the classroom or even in the classroom where code switching might occur. Some of these universities are outside the capital, where English is mostly used as a foreign language (EFL) even though it would be used as a second language in the university itself. In other instances, English is used both inside and outside of the classroom in daily interaction.

This can be seen in American universities and schools and in their surrounding neighborhoods in the capital, Beirut. English in this context is used as a second language (ESL). Many researchers in Lebanon often use the terms ESL and EFL interchangeably even when referring to the same institution (e.g., Diab 2005a, 2005b). Such a situation puts Lebanon in a unique place where, following the Kachruvian paradigm, the country is an Expanding Circle country but has some of the characteristics of an Outer Circle country (Esseili, 2011). In fact, the boundary between circles is not clear-cut, as the circles may overlap and might exist within circles (Berns, 1995, 2005); they could be described as "dynamic and changing" (Kachru 2008, p. 364). Thus, it could be argued that while multilingualism exists in such American universities, surrounding neighborhoods, and other areas (e.g. Armenian neighborhoods), this is not entirely the case for students in other universities and Lebanese residents in other geographic areas, such as in the North or South.

Like other contexts in the world that are witnessing a rise in the teaching of ESL or EFL, the teaching of writing in Lebanon is one of the most important topics at the tertiary level. In this paper, writing in a second language could be defined as any "writing done in a language other than the writer's native language or languages" (Silva, forthcoming). Silva's definition of SLW is inclusive of "writing done in both second language contexts where the language being learned is dominant, for example, learning Chinese in China, and in foreign language contexts where the language is not dominant, for example, learning Chinese in Brazil" (forthcoming). Based on this definition and on the above discussion of ESL/EFL, writing in English in Lebanon could be classified as writing in a second language.

In order to address the different needs of the aforementioned groups of second language writers, almost all of the universities in Lebanon have adopted a system whereby, depending on students, scores on the SAT, TOEFL, or locally designed placement tests (e.g., the English Entrance Exam in LAU), they get placed in intensive English programs or test immediately into "the Communication Skills Program" (e.g., at AUB & NDU), or "the Composition and Rhetoric Sequence" (e.g., at UOB). The names of such programs differ, but in essence they are supposedly similar in what they cover. All students are required to take first year composition (equivalent to Freshman composition) and an advanced writing course. Such programs do not only focus on developing language related skills; they also develop students' critical thinking skills and initiate them into practices related to academic integrity, among other learning outcomes. The writings of students in these programs and the teaching practices used have been the focus of a number of studies conducted by Lebanese scholars. The next sections will present major findings from these studies. First, the infrastructure supporting SLW in Lebanon is presented, followed by the methodology utilized in selecting data for this review.

Infrastructure

While prominent SLW scholars in the USA have worked hard to create the necessary infrastructure for SLW to flourish (such as the *Journal on Second Language Writing*, the Symposium on Second Language Writing, listservs, and various special interest groups at the CCCC and TESOL), a fraction of such a support system is still lacking in Lebanon for various reasons that are beyond the scope of this paper. Suffice it to say that the civil war which lasted for more than 15 years and which arguably finished in the early 1990s is an important contributor to this shortage. The country has been limping from one conflict to another for the past 25 years. Such conflicts, with all their ensuing corruption and lack of stability, have not only affected the education system and its infrastructure, but also Lebanese students (cf., Abu-Saba, 1999; Oweini, 1998).

Professional organizations, committees or interest groups, conferences, and scholarly journals that are specifically dedicated to writing are still lacking. This lack of infrastructure seems to be slowly changing. In late 2013, the first symposium on the teaching of writing was launched by AUB. Professors and lecturers from a number of universities across Lebanon were invited for a one-day session where they discussed three pressing issues: program needs, visions, and future plans. A listserv and a group on LinkedIn (Symposium on the Teaching of Writing) were created with occasional posts related to language learning in general. In addition to the symposium, AUB's 4th International Conference on Effective Teaching and Learning in Higher Education dedicated a strand on writing instruction and research in higher education for the first time. They maintained this strand in their 5th international conference. Workshops on developing writing assignments for the college classroom and on assessing student writing across disciplines were conducted. Such venues are indispensable for the constructive exchange of ideas and the development of the field, and it is important that they are maintained.

Concerning graduate programs, all major universities in Lebanon have departments of English that house undergraduate and graduate programs in English language and literature. Some universities have certificates in TEFL (e.g., AUB) or in ELT (e.g., UOB). The past ten years have also witnessed a rising interest in writing centers or language centers. Thus, AUB, LAU, UOB, and NDU have all created such centers to support their students.

Methodology

For this chapter, MA theses supervised by ELT scholars in three universities in Lebanon were examined. These universities included AUB, LAU, and UOB. In addition, the *Journal of Second Language Writing,* which is considered the leading journal in the field, was surveyed for publications related to writing in Lebanon. The search, however, yielded no results. In fact, with the exception of two recent articles published in *Writing and Pedagogy* and *Assessing Writing* in 2010 and 2011 respectively, the majority of the articles on writing in Lebanon were published in venues related to teaching English in general such as in the *TESL Reporter, English Language Teaching Forum, ESP Journal, Journal of English for Academic Purposes, Asian Journal of ELT, the Asian ESP Journal, International Journal of Arabic-English Studies, TESOL Quarterly,* and *TESOL Journal;* or in venues dedicated to issues related to other disciplines, such as *The International Journal of Business and Social Science, Research Papers in Education, The Linguistics Journal,* and *Business Communication Quarterly.* Table 2 summarizes the major findings by university.

Table 2   Types of Publications by University

	Book Chapters	Articles	MA Theses	Total
AUB	0	2	31	33
LAU	2	22	7	31
UOB	1	3	4	8
Total	3	27	42	72

It is worth mentioning that professors in the Education Department supervised the majority of the MA theses at AUB, and that a researcher who is now affiliated with LAU published the only two articles that are listed under AUB. The next section offers a description of major trends in L2 research in Lebanon.

Challenges

The challenges that teachers and students face in writing courses both in schools and universities in Lebanon was the topic of at least one book chapter, six articles, and five MA theses. Subthemes included the existence of different learning cultures (Bacha & Bahous, 2013; Bhuyian, 2012), issues of plagiarism and academic integrity (Bacha & Bahous, 2010; Bacha, Bahous & Nabhani, 2010; Esseili, 2012), transfer from other languages (Bacha, 2000; Diab, N., 1998; Esseili, 2012; Hawrani, 1974), difficulty in motivating students (Bahous, Bacha & Nabhani, 2011), and students' writing anxiety and apprehension (Kishli, 2007; Nazzal, 2008; Zghir, 2007).

Transitioning from a high school to a university is often challenging to students on many levels but especially in regard to writing courses. Bhuyian (2012) used a case study to investigate this issue, and based on students' perspectives, she found that two out of four students felt they were unprepared, which might be the result of differences in background. This was further supported by the existence of differences in cultures of learning within the same educational system, which played a significant role in students' academic achievement at the university level (Bacha & Bahous, 2013). Those differences were manifested in three factors that students faced when they transitioned from schools to universities. According to the authors, schools in Lebanon do not emphasize "critical thinking, classroom interaction, and student centeredness" whereas universities that follow the American model do (p. 117). Another factor that posed a challenge to students is the conflict between their "social identity" that is tied to their native language, Arabic, and their "academic identity" which is related to the second language they have to use as a medium of communication in academia. A third factor is the conflict between the learners' collectivist spirit that is nourished in their culture and at school, and the individualistic spirit that is characteristic of the American university model.

This collectivist versus individualistic perspective prompted studies that investigated, among other issues, whether students cheat, or "help each other", because of their collectivist culture. One of these studies was conducted in high school (Bacha, Bahous & Nabhani, 2010), and the other two were related to the university level. A common theme among all three studies was that most students did not believe that there was anything wrong with helping a friend in need. Students in high school admitted to helping their friends during exams by allowing them to copy. Such a practice is "reflective of the society that accepts this type of 'helping friends' type of relationship even if it is on exams, where if help is not offered it might mean negative consequences for the friendship or [even] a breakup," the authors argued (p. 372). When it came to the university level, students admitted that, while they had been instructed about plagiarism and referencing styles, they were not provided with the necessary tools to avoid plagiarism, a claim which was of course not supported by teachers (Bacha & Bahous, 2010). Students' justifications for cheating and plagiarizing varied from "because it was permitted in high school" and "I won't get caught" (Bacha &

Bahous, 2010), to lack of knowledge about referencing, lack of confidence in expressing ideas in students' own voices and words, and the difficulty for students to write academic research papers (Esseili, 2012).

The third challenge, one that is often overlooked, and unfortunately, sometimes even dismissed by teachers as a mere "excuse" (Esseili, 2012), is the effect of other languages on students' writing in English. As mentioned earlier, slightly more than half of high school students who choose to continue their undergraduate studies in an English medium university have studied French as a second language and English as a third language. Not only do such students face challenges in communicating fluently and accurately in English, but also their writing in English is affected. No wonder these students attributed their weak English skills to being "French educated" (Bacha, 2000; Esseili, 2012). This means that teachers have to deal with transfer in students' communication skills from two sources: their native language, Arabic, and their second language, French (Esseili, 2012). Transfer could be positive, especially with cognate words, or negative when students, for example, think that the word has a similar meaning in the target language, but ends up being incorrect. When it comes to the Lebanese context, a number of studies concluded that errors in the use of connectives in particular may be the result of learners' lack of knowledge or training rather than interference from their first language, Arabic (Bacha, 1979; Bacha & Hanania, 1980; Carthy, 1978; Hawrani, 1974; Shalhoub, 1981). Diab, N. (1998) examined transfer from Arabic to English in students' writings. In her study, she focused in particular on syntactic, semantic, lexical, and grammatical errors, and excluded learners' use of connectives. The study attributed almost all errors to transferring from L1. Such an attribution, however, is often hard to pinpoint because it could be the result of learners' restricted knowledge in the area as the abovementioned studies had shown. It also could be due to the fact that, in the Lebanese context, the shift in the language of instruction makes it harder for teachers to identify the "factors contributing to student language problems" (Bacha, 2000, p. 241). While proficiency in other languages could definitely be an advantage for students when learning other languages, there's no doubt that such students have different needs than students who learned English as a second language.

Motivation is a fourth area that affects students' writing skills. A number of studies focused on the role of motivation in learning foreign languages in general (e.g., Al-Asmar, 2008; Ghaith, 2003; Salem, 2006; Shaaban & Ghaith, 2000). When it comes to writing, it was found that the fact that first year composition classes are mandatory is demotivating to students (Esseili, 2012). Bacha (2000, 2002) concluded that students' lack of motivation to write was the main cause that hindered their skill development in such courses. Many learners found the English courses inadequate simply because they were unable to see how such courses could cater to their own needs in their disciplines (Bahous, Bacha & Nabhani, 2011; Esseili, 2012). As a result, students might resort to plagiarism and cheating. Lack of motivation could also be attributed to uninteresting reading materials, in-class writing (rather than having students follow the writing process and write their papers outside class), and the inability to choose their own topics (Esseili, 2012). Another reason was that little to no writing was done in their disciplines (Bahous, Bacha & Nabhani, 2011; Nicolas & Annous, 2013). Bahous, Bacha & Nabhani (2011) questioned the use of first year composition when students end up writing technical reports, for example, in their future jobs. They also suggested that teachers might not be taking learners' individual differences into account, and concluded that "there is a clear need for selecting content that is more relevant to the learners' lives and also on an international level" (p. 39).

Other challenges included writing anxiety and apprehension. One study examined the relationship between writing anxiety and students' major (Zghir, 2007). Findings revealed that nursing students were much more likely to suffer from writing anxiety (fear of writing, evaluation, and of showing their own writings to others) than business students who showed higher levels of writing enjoyment. In another case study that looked at the relationship between SLW apprehension, writing self-efficacy beliefs, and the writing performance of EFL students, it was found that students' attitudes towards writing and their motivation to write, as well as their self-efficacy beliefs, were positively affected by a teacher's type of writing instruction, feedback, and assigned topics (Nazzal, 2008). Finally, a third study examined the effect of prewriting techniques on writing quality and writing apprehension among high school students. The study found that while such techniques improved the quality of students' papers, they increased learners' writing apprehension (Kishli, 2007).

Characteristic of Students' Writing

In the Lebanese context, there are at least seven studies or sections of studies that describe different aspects of Lebanese students' writing. Studies on the use of connectives in the Lebanese context revealed that learners have difficulty in using connectives along with correct punctuation, which might be the result of their restricted exposure to the use and variety of transition words (Bacha, 1979; Bacha & Hanania, 1980; Shalhoub, 1981). Carthy (1978) analyzed the use of transitional devices in the writings of native and non-native speakers of English. While no significant difference was found in the frequency of usage among the groups, Arabic-speaking students used coordinating transitions more frequently than native speakers. Bacha, Cortazzi and Nakhle (2002) investigated cohesive patterns manifested in Lebanese students' essays, and found that such students used coordination, parallelism, repetition, and exaggeration excessively, and that they had limited academic vocabulary. The authors compared the lexical cohesive patterns in academic expository essays in 40 high and low-rated academic texts written by students in the EFL program, and they compared the results with Hoey's (1991) study on cohesive devices employed by native speakers. It was found that "both the high and low-rated texts were not quality texts by native standards as the high percentage of simple repetition indicated, especially in the low-texts at short distances" (p. 144). However, comparing the low- and high-rated texts revealed that the latter employed more lexical variation and sophisticated types of lexical cohesion (e.g., complex paraphrases, complex repetition, etc.), which is indicative of "good writing" (p. 144).

In a case study, students' writing at the secondary level exhibited an awareness of the topic they were developing, but their writing did not reflect "a level of thinking relevant to their class and age level" (Fakhreddine, 2007, p. 4). Students found difficulty in developing their ideas and using evidence to support their claims. The author listed a number of other characteristics such as inability to write specific titles that reflect the nature of their essays, absence of voice, and presence of errors in mechanics.

At the university level, and through the analysis of a corpus consisting of 1158 expository and argumentative essays, Bacha (2005) investigated the lexis that students used in order to identify the most frequent content and function words and the degree of repetition that occurred in students' writing. The author compared students' text with the model academic texts they read in class. Results indicated that the word "the" is the most frequent word in both the model passages and students' essays. However, students' essays had fewer content words, and their vocabulary range, irrespective of genre or topic, was very limited with lots of repetition of the same word (synonyms were rarely used). The most repeated content words were "war", "parents", and "teenager", which might be due to the assigned topics. The average letters per word was found to be four letters, which the author attributed to students' limited lexicons. The author also examined sample writing from one class at the beginning of the semester and at the end of the semester. Analysis revealed that "words appearing only once [were] not that 'sophisticated' indicating that between the first writing and the second there [was] very little improvement in lexical sophistication" (p. 133). This suggests that little development in terms of students' vocabulary has taken place over the semester.

Muhammad (1968), El Mufti (1997), and Farhat (2008) identified the most common errors that students in a high school and the IEP at LAU make. Results from Muhammad's (1968) quantitative analysis indicated that when it came to errors in function words, students tended to overuse prepositions, which constituted the highest percentage of the total number of errors. Errors in prepositions were followed by errors in articles, pronouns, and conjunctions. As far as content words were concerned, errors in the use of verbs (e.g., subject verb agreement) and nouns (e.g., omission of subjects or objects) ranked first. El Mufti (1997) and Farhat (2008), on the other hand, found that irrespective of genre, students were consistent in the errors they made and that such errors were of a morphological and syntactic nature and included errors in prepositions, verb tenses, word choice, and subject verb agreement. Findings also showed that students often translated from their L1 and were afraid to use the target language in class. The authors suggested ways that could enable teachers to help their students improve their writing skills.

Curricular and Instructional Developments

This area of research has received extensive attention. Ten studies were restricted to the university level, while 16 studies were dedicated to examining effective teaching strategies in schools. At the university and school levels, studies examined a variety of techniques and approaches to teach specific writing skills or genres.

To begin with, Bacha (1979), Bacha and Hanania (1980), and Shalhoub (1981) explored the use of transitional words by learners and whether such skill could be taught effectively. They found that using appropriate instructional materials to instruct students was effective in improving learners' use of connectives. Moving to a more macro level approach, Bacha (2002) examined the use of task-based learning in order to develop students' general academic writing skills and considered its effect on motivating students to write and to develop their skills. She found that "practical research writing may be a motivating basis in helping lower-proficient learners to improve" (p. 169).

Four studies examined the use of certain approaches and techniques to teach specific genres such as argumentative essays and critique writing. Bacha (2010) offered an instructional approach to teach the academic argument where students have to argue on an issue by using different sources. Using qualitative analysis of students' papers, the author found that students showed improvement in their argumentative structures and were able to transfer the skill to new topics. Annous (1997) conducted an experiment in which he examined how role-playing can enhance students' argumentative writing. Results of the post-test revealed that the quality of students' written texts who used role playing was much better, and their texts had significantly improved as opposed to the ones who received deductive formal instruction in the control group. In another study, Bacha (2011) used a scaffolded approach to teach critique writing. Inspired by Systemic Functional Linguistics, the author followed Feeze's (1991) model that emphasized peer and teacher collaboration to scaffold learning. Results revealed that by getting involved in interactive collaboration, students became more sensitive to other points of view and reassessed their original opinions in regard to a particular topic, an approach which develops their critical thinking skills and increases their "threshold of tolerance" (p. 175). Another approach to teaching critique writing was offered by Diab and Balaa (2009, 2011). The authors designed rubrics and assessed their effectiveness in improving students' critique writing based on students' perceptions and grades. Rubrics were found beneficial in locating students' strengths and weaknesses. Although students' grades on their second drafts improved, the authors were cautious in their interpretation of the results since improvement might have been due to other factors. Overall, students believed that grading was fair and they had a positive attitude toward rubrics. The students felt motivated and "empowered" because they were involved in designing the rubrics.

At the school level, using innovative techniques or strategies to teach writing was the focus of one journal article and 16 MA theses, 13 of which were experimental studies and three of which were descriptive in nature. The findings are summarized below:

- Deeb (1972) provided a description of a number of methods for teachers to use in order to foster creative thinking and creativity in students' writing. In addition, Abboud (1992) confirmed that selecting readings and other stimuli that were relevant to students' lives improved the practice of teaching writing, made students more interested in reading, and decreased their writing frustration. Along the same descriptive lines, Jabbour (2011) offered a writing kit, which consisted of ideas and strategies to teach writing for grade eight learners.

- Shalhub (1991) investigated the effectiveness of using process writing with high-intermediate, pre-university EFL students in order to prepare them for university level writing courses. Results showed that using process writing was successful in preparing students for the university, but more time was needed.

- Fakhreddine (2007) found that using reading-writing activities played a significant role in students' overall ability to understand texts and improved their skills and the quality of their essays.

- Fidaoui (2008) and Fidaoui, Bahous and Bacha (2010) discussed the use of computer-assisted language learning (CALL) to motivate fourth graders to write and develop their ESL writing skills. Both students and teachers had favorable attitudes towards using CALL and agreed that it was both motivational and beneficial. "It enabled them to have fun, while at the same time attempting to produce creative, neat, organized, error-free written products. It helped them express their feelings and gather relevant information to fulfill the requirements" of the assignment (p. 164).

- The use of rubrics as an instructional tool was investigated by two studies. Houssami (2005) conducted a comparative study in which she examined the effect of gender and student-generated versus teacher-provided instructional rubrics on writing achievement among eighth grade ESL students. Results showed no significant difference between students who used their own generated rubric and those who used their teacher's rubric. A significant difference, however, was found between females and males where the former performed better than the latter, and between students who used teacher-generated feedback versus ones who used the traditional teacher feedback in favor of the former. Shehab (2011), on the other hand, examined third grade students' and teachers' perceptions regarding the efficacy of using rubrics, and found that the two groups believed that such a tool was effective. It enabled students to identify their strengths and weaknesses, a finding echoed by Diab and Balaa (2009, 2011) at the university level.

- Obeid (2011) used a case study to investigate the use of fairy tales to improve third graders' writing skills and vocabulary repertoire. She found the careful selection of fairy tales and their accompanying activities to be effective in developing the intended skills and in creating a positive classroom atmosphere.

- By using action research, Zailaa (2011) found that the use of drama (role play and visualization exercises) in teaching process writing at the high school level was an effective tool to motivate students to write.

- At least two studies investigated the use of the writing workshop approach to improve learners' writing skills. Hachem (2005) investigated the way in which writing instruction was differentiated through the use of the writing workshop and found that the model served as a motivational tool to increase students' interest in writing and develop their skills. Likewise, Shami (2010) examined the effect of using writer's workshop as an instruction model to develop fifth graders' writing. The study also attempted to find out which proficiency level (below average, average, and above average) benefited the most from such a model. Results indicated that using this model was effective with regard to the writing progress of all groups, but the above average group benefited the most.

- The topic of the effect of journal writing or dialogue journal writing as techniques used to improve students' essay was the focus of four studies (Bazih, 1996; Idriss, 2002; Kadi, 2004; Obeid, H., 2001). Bazih (1996) and Obeid, H. (2001) examined the effect of journal writing in improving student writing fluency, complexity, and accuracy. While the first study revealed that students' writing had improved after nine weeks of journal writing with the exception of accuracy, which regressed, the second study found no significant difference. Kadi (2004) also examined the effect of journal writing on students' achievement and found that the technique improved students' fluency and overall communicative purposes. Finally, Idriss (2002) investigated the effect of journal writing on reading comprehension, writing quality, and writing apprehension. Findings revealed that journal writing did increase reading comprehension and improve their writing quality, but it did not reduce writing apprehension.

Writing Across the Curriculum (WAC)/Writing in the Disciplines (WID)

A total of six studies were located on this topic, four of which are from scholars at LAU and two from UOB (Bacha, 2003; Bacha, 2012; Bacha, 2013; Bacha & Bahous, 2008; Nicolas & Annous, 2013; Nicolas & Annous, 2014). Although AUB implemented WAC requirements in their General Education Program, LAU and UOB have been the leading institutions in research related to WAC and WID. The next section presents research on writing needs of students from different disciplines at LAU, followed by those from UOB.

In a study that examined the perceptions of 1658 students and 48 faculty members in different disciplines in regard to the English for Academic Purposes (EAP) and English for Professional Purposes (EPP) skills and tasks they find most important and useful in their majors and future jobs, Bacha (2003) found that the perceptions of students and faculty differed in regard to a number of issues. Faculty and students did not agree on which language skill and individual tasks were more important and which type of English to be taught. Both faculty and students, however, indicated that the English courses helped in students' EAP and EPP and improved their skills. The author concluded that the university's English program should play a better role in helping across the curriculum in various ways including "team teaching with other departments, helping underachievers, initiating students into the English type academic culture, and preparing them for work later where they will have to communicate in the medium of English" (p. 53).

In another study, Bacha (2012) surveyed teachers (n=40) and students' (n=257) perspectives on writing in the disciplines hoping that such knowledge would improve learning of disciplinary writing. Results revealed a discrepancy between students and teachers' perceptions. While students believed that they learned to write best when they were provided with models and explanation, teachers believed that students learned best through explanation and Internet sources. Also, students thought that their writing had developed over the course of the semester, in contrast to teachers who did not think that students were improving. Moreover, students considered their major problems in writing to be related to grammar and organization, in contrast to teachers who believed that students had problems in all writing aspects. Finally, students believed that they were not receiving enough help from the English and discipline teachers, but teachers disagreed. Students stated that help should come from their disciplinary teachers, but the latter disagreed and thought that help should come from the English teacher. Despite such a discrepancy in their views, the two groups considered reports and lecture note-taking to be the most frequent tasks required in their discipline, and that there should be a collaboration between the disciplinary teachers and the English teachers. The author concluded by stating that disciplinary teachers are neither qualified nor willing to teach English writing skills.

While Bacha (2003, 2012) focused on the general language needs of students from different disciplines and compared teachers' and students' perspectives, Bacha & Bahous (2008) examined business students' writing needs and proficiency levels. Students complained that their English courses did not address their needs in their major, and faculty members complained that students had poor writing skills. Main areas of inquiry included importance of language skills, student language ability, student writing ability, frequency of writing tasks (essay writing, essay tests, letters, reports, research papers, summaries of lectures, and note taking), rate of writing improvement, and role of faculty in developing students' writing. A product rather than a process approach seemed to be followed by teachers in the discipline. Both students and faculty ranked listening and reading as the most important skills, followed by speaking and writing. In fact, students in business ranked writing as the least important skill. In addition, the two groups agreed that the major problems in students' writings were related to sentence structure and vocabulary. Similar to findings of previous studies, students rated their proficiency level higher than their instructors did. Business faculty believed that students' unsatisfactory language abilities did not enable them to perform "the business required writing tasks" (p. 82).

In more recent studies that examined WAC elements in Business syllabi at UOB, Nicolas and Annous (2013) found that little to no writing was being incorporated in the business courses. Through content analysis (review of 30 syllabi), it was found that only 30% of the syllabi required some sort of writing assignments, almost all of which were not well described (e.g., did not identify genre, length, or nature of assignment). Only six syllabi mentioned "essay" and "report writing", but with no clarity as to other requirements. In fact, a reference to any sort of "written communicative competence" and to assessment of students' writing was almost nonexistent in the learning outcomes of all 30 courses. As a follow up on this content analysis study, the authors (2014) examined Business professors' views on students' writing abilities and the instructors' willingness to focus on the writing skill and found that such professors were neither willing nor expert enough to focus on writing. None of the 6 professors interviewed was able to explain what WAC referred to, and none of them "encouraged any drafting process" due to time constraints. All professors agreed that the heavy content in business encouraged minimal writing. Two out of six professors admitted to using Arabic in the classroom, and one of them allowed students to do the same when it came to asking questions. All professors agreed that students writing skills were weak and one described their skills as "catastrophic"! Some of the factors that contributed to such a state of affairs, the authors concluded, included the lack of preparation programs for teachers' in the disciplines to provide feedback on language related issues, teachers' belief that it was not their job to teach language skills, the lack of time to cover business content, the lack of emphasis on reading in the country, and the fact that English is being taught as a foreign language.

The previous studies examined how much writing was being done in the disciplines and looked at teachers and students' perceptions in regard to students' needs in the discipline and to what extent those needs were being met. Bacha (2013), on the other hand, surveyed 35 discipline teachers (Engineering and Architecture, Business, Pharmacy and Computer Science) and 289 students in order to have a better understanding of the type of feedback (local/mechanical and global/content) given and received, respectively. Results indicated that there is a discrepancy between teachers and students' self-assessments with the former believing that they give "more local language feedback than their students' perceived receiving" (p. 249). The two groups agreed that the final grade on their assignments was based on global language considerations with little or no feedback.

Error Correction and Type of Feedback

Error correction is a controversial topic in L2 writing in general. In Lebanon, there are at least 14 studies published on the topics of error correction, students' and teachers' preferences, type of feedback, and the effect of type of feedback on students' development of writing skills both at the university and school levels.

R. Diab's (2005a, 2006) studies compared and contrasted students and teachers' preferences for error correction and teacher feedback on writing at

AUB. While the two articles are published in two different venues, they complement each other in the sense that they essentially deal with the same data and rely on the same survey instrument, which is a modified version of Leki's (1991) survey. The first article is restricted to students' preferences. The second article (Diab, R. 2006) deals with the other half of the data, teachers, and it compares and contrasts students' and teachers' preferences. In line with some of the L2 literature on students' preferences, the majority of learners in Diab's studies were concerned about accuracy, and they seemed to believe that organization, grammar, and mechanics were of equal importance to content. The students also believed that their instructor should point out errors in grammar on their first draft and give a clue about it (86%) and should correct their errors on the final paper (82%). Students ranked grammar slightly higher than other features. As far as students' preferences for paper-marking techniques (proofreading symbols, red-colored pen), they were neutral. Diab, R. (2006) compared students' preferences to that of teachers and found that there was a great discrepancy in the groups' responses, even among teachers themselves. Students and teachers had different views when it came to the importance of different writing features, feedback on first draft versus final paper, and the number of errors a teacher should respond to, among many other issues. In a similar study, Diab, R. (2005b) examined teachers' and students' beliefs about responding to L2 writing. By using think-aloud protocols and semi-structured interviews with two students and one instructor, Diab found that both the instructor and the students preferred surface-level correction even though the former was familiar with research on L2 writing concerning the efficacy of error correction. In addition, there was a discrepancy between students' and teachers' beliefs when it came to responding to first drafts as opposed to final papers.

While R. Diab's studies were conducted in Beirut, Hadla (2006) examined teachers' and students' preferences in three universities in Bekaa, and El Joukhadar (2013) offered the perspective of students from a third region in Lebanon, the North. Hadla (2006) examined teacher practices and student preferences for error correction in three universities in the Bekaa region: The American University of Science and Technology (AUST), The Lebanese International University (LIU), and the Culture and Education American University Institute (C & E). Hadla, like Diab, adapted his student questionnaire from Leki's (1991) study. Similar to the aforementioned studies, students preferred all of their errors to be marked by showing where the error was and giving a clue about how to correct it, a practice that was preferred by teachers as well. In contrast to Diab's study, however, Hadla's research revealed that students did not equate grammar, organization, and mechanics with ideas. Content and organization were not as important as grammar. Such findings are reasonable since the students who participated in this study were all in the intensive English program, whereas the participants in Diab's studies were students enrolled in English language courses, including students from Intensive English Programs. Student background is one variable that should be taken into consideration in future studies. In a study that examined students' perceptions of the effect of grammar correction in an English language course at UOB in North Lebanon, El Joukhadar's (2013) findings were somewhat inconsistent with previous studies where students were found to be divided in regard to direct and indirect error correction during their interviews. However, survey results indicated that students preferred direct feedback. In addition, slightly more than half of students preferred to receive feedback on both content and grammar. Students reported that conferences with teachers increased their ability to understand their teachers' comments and their ability to self-edit their papers.

Six studies dealt with type of feedback explicitly at the university level and an additional two at the school level. Hamzeh (1996) examined the effect of diagnostic and non-diagnostic feedback on the development of the expository writing proficiency of L2 learners in the IEP at LAU. Her findings suggested no difference between the effect of diagnostic and non-diagnostic feedback on the development of students' writing. In addition, no interaction was found in regard to the type of feedback and the level of student achievement. On the other hand, by using action research, Shatila (2010) investigated the effectiveness of trained peer response on students' writing quality and revision types. The author found that peer editing enabled students to do more meaning-related changes than surface level changes in their second drafts, thus improving the quality of their papers. Similarly, Diab, N. (2009) examined whether the use of peer-editing was effective in making students become more aware of the criteria required for writing quality essays, hence enabling students to write better revised essays. Results indicated that students were able to perform better in the final paper without receiving any feedback, which might suggest that students have internalized the criteria needed to write essays. Like Shatila's study, students in this study gave favorable opinions about peer editing and thought it helped them improve their overall editing skills and the content and organization of their essays. In two more articles that complement each other and that were based on action research, Diab, N. (2010) examined whether peer editing or self-editing were more effective in reducing the percentage of rule-based (e.g., SVA + pronoun agreement) and nonrule-based errors (e.g., wrong word choice and awkward sentences) in revised essays. Results indicated that the group that used peer editing was able to reduce rule-based errors significantly because their attention was drawn to the forms that needed improvement during form focused instruction sessions. It was found that "student collaboration during the editing sessions seemed to have increased student awareness of these errors [meaning and form], allowed them to negotiate possible alternatives, and to arrive together at correct linguistic forms, thus constructing new knowledge and reducing language errors in their essays" (p. 91). Students were also more "actively engaged in the writing process" (Diab, N., 2011, p. 286). The two groups, however, did not improve in non-rule based errors despite the fact that they received form-focused instruction. Training students in both peer editing and self-editing was effective in allowing learners to "revise their writing because the two techniques involve practice of cognitive and meta-cognitive strategies that have been noted to bring writing development" (Diab, N., 2011, p. 286). Finally, Akouri (2011) conducted an action research study where she examined the effect of using collaborative e-portfolios (peer review and wiki use for e-portfolios postings) on students' writing. Overall, students were highly motivated as a result of using technology and peer interaction in the classroom. However, they were divided as to the usefulness of e-portfolios, which the author attributed to students' lack of "technical knowledge". In contrast to Shatila (2010), Akouri's students provided feedback primarily on grammar and mechanics rather than content and organization.

At the school level, rather than merely looking at students' and teachers' perceptions in terms of error correction, Kazem (2005) used a quantitative approach to investigate whether teachers' use of error feedback was actually helping students improve their writing accuracy. She found that there was a significant difference between the coded and no feedback groups in their ability to self-edit their errors primarily in errors related to sentence structure and noun-endings. Kazem also found no significant relationship between the students' explicit grammar knowledge and their ability to edit their errors, but the author was cautious in interpreting this finding. The author suggested that "using a consistent system of marking and coding errors throughout a learning class, paired with mini lessons which built students' knowledge base about the error types being marked, might yield more long-term growth in students' linguistic accuracy" (p. 50). This suggestion is especially important because it relates to El Joukhadar's (2013) context where a similar suggestion was proposed. In investigating the effect of collaborative learning versus teacher's feedback on the writing progress of grade ten students, Shaaban (2001) found that students who received the former type of feedback scored much higher than the group that received feedback from the teachers. Peer interaction enabled students to improve their content and organization, but not accuracy.

Assessment and Evaluation

Many of the above reviewed articles dealt with the topic of evaluation in one way or another. However, there are only three articles that are strictly related to assessment and evaluation. One article focused on students' expectations of grades compared to their actual final grades in introductory writing courses (Bacha, 2002). The other two articles dealt with using different tools to assess students' achievement in writing courses (Bacha, 2001; Khachan & Bacha, 2012). Results from the first study (Bacha, 2002) revealed that there was a discrepancy between students' expectations and the reality of the grades they earned.. While students did not expect to fail in their essays and while they were overly confident, results showed that about 13% failed their two essays, and scores were generally lower than expected. Learners did not seem to be aware of or did not fully understand their teachers' expectations in regard to what they were being tested on. In another study, Bacha (2001) adopted two types of scoring instruments, analytic and holistic, for the purpose of checking which one was more effective in decisions related to promoting students from one level to another. Results indicated that holistic scoring uncovered little information about students' performance in regard to individual language components. The author recommended that a combination of both analytic and holistic scoring is needed. Finally, Khachan and Bacha (2012) used corpus analysis to evaluate whether students' scores on the English Entrance Exam (EEE), a locally developed university English proficiency test, were adequate measures of their active vocabulary, and were on par with other international tests such as TOEFL and IELTS. Results showed that the academic vocabulary used in EEE "[was] not as challenging as the international writing exams, indicating lower writing quality" (p. 69).

Writing Centers

A total of three MA theses were written on the topic of writing centers. Honein-Shehadi (2007) investigated teachers' perceptions regarding writing needs and writing centers in four schools in Lebanon while Khater (2009) examined the need for a writing center at the Lebanese American University. The majority of teachers indicated that their students were in a great need of additional support from tutors in writing centers. Based on identifying the needs and expectations of students and faculty from different disciplines, Khater (2009) offered recommendations for establishing a writing center at the university. Geha (2008), on the other hand, investigated the perceptions of tutors and tutees regarding the effectiveness of tutoring services in writing centers in a university and in a school that already had writing centers. The majority of tutors in the two centers believed that their services played a positive role in students' writing development, and the tutees perceived that their writing had developed as a result of their sessions with the tutors.

Conclusion and Recommendations for Future Research

This chapter reviewed L2 writing scholarship produced by researchers and graduate students in three major universities in Lebanon. Excluded from this review were publications by scholars from other universities in Lebanon and abroad. This limitation is primarily due to feasibility and lack of accessibility of materials available in other universities at the time this article was written. In addition to examining research done by scholars abroad, future research should consider the work of scholars in the Lebanese University, which has a student body of more than 75,000, for a better representation of the status of English in general and second language writing in particular. Such scholars might publish their work either online as conference proceedings (e.g., the ELT conference organized by the Association of Teachers of English in Lebanon) or in Arabic.

Some of the above reviewed studies were either repetitive in nature (e.g., Diab, R. & Balaa) or did not take previous findings in the same context into consideration (e.g., MA studies on type of feedback). This review should help future researchers to extend on previous findings and to identify gaps in the literature for future studies. In addition, this review shows the great need for research on how L2 writers are representing their identity and voice in their writing; how writing programs are, or are not, giving students the freedom to do so. Such studies with their pedagogical implications could have the potential to influence another under researched area, which is ways to motivate students to write in order to make writing their own, rather than imposed (e.g. imposing topics, genres, responses to uninteresting reading materials, etc.), and ways to make writing programs localized rather than imported models with superficial adaptations. The student population in Lebanon might seem to be homogenous, but they are not. Thus far, studies have been restricted to particular assignments or genres, but none has examined the efficacy of a holistic approach to teaching first year composition.

WAC and WID studies suggest that teachers in the disciplines should be aware of their role in improving students' communicative skills. So far, none of the studies presented success stories. In other words, how are the teachers in English Departments helping, if at all, students' writing in their disciplines?

A common theme that runs through most of the above studies is that students often perceive their writing to be better than it actually is as compared to teachers' perceptions. This suggests that programs need to rethink their instruction strategies. Teachers and students should be on the same page when it comes to many writing issues including the importance of language components and providing feedback. Also, while perceptions, preferences, or beliefs of students are important, mixed methods research that examines the actual writings of these learners is needed. Such research can provide a more in-depth look into students' needs and their development as writers.

References

Abboud, P. (1992). Reading selections and other stimuli for the teaching of writing. Unpublished master's thesis, The American University of Beirut.

Abboud, S. (1969). A survey of reading and writing assignments of the freshman and sophomore at the American University of Beirut. Unpublished master's thesis, The American University of Beirut.

Akouri, L. (2011). Impact of collaborative e-portfolios on students' writing. Unpublished master's thesis, The University of Balamand.

Al-Asmar, L. (2008). The effect of teacher corrective feedback on the student intrinsic motivation, time on-task, and achievement. Unpublished master's thesis, The American University of Beirut.

Annous, S. (1997). Using role playing to teach argumentative writing. Unpublished master's thesis, Bilkent University.

Annous, S. & Nicolas, M. O. (2014). Academic territorial borders: A look at the writing ethos in business courses in an environment in which English is a foreign language. *The Journal of Business and Technical Communication,* *29*(1), 93-111.

Bacha, N. (1979). Teaching the use of transitional words to advanced students of English as a foreign language. Unpublished master's thesis, the American University of Beirut, Lebanon.

Bacha, N. (2012). Disciplinary writing in an EFL context from teachers' and students' perspectives. *International Journal of Business and Social Science,* *3*(2), 233-256.

Bacha, N. & Hanania, F. (1980). Difficulty in learning and effectiveness of teaching transitional words: A study on Arabic-speaking university students. *TESOL Quarterly, 14*(2), 251-254.

Bacha, N. N. (2000). Academic writing in a multilingual context: A study of learner difficulties. *International Journal of Arabic-English Studies, 2*(2), 239-268.

Bacha, N. N. (2001). Writing evaluation: What can analytic versus holistic scoring tell us? *System, An International Journal of Educational Technology and Applied Linguistics. 29*(3), 371-383.

Bacha, N, N. (2002). Testing writing in the EFL classroom: A study of student expectations. *English Language Teaching Forum,* USAID Information Service, Washington, U.S.A., April Issue, 14-19, 27.

Bacha, N. N. (2002). Developing learners' academic writing skills in higher education: A study for educational reform. *Language and Education International Journal, (16)*3, 161-177.

Bacha, N. N. (2003). English across academic and professional communities. A study of EFL learners' needs at the Lebanese American University, *The Official Journal of the Association of American International Colleges and Universities, 2,* 16-62.

Bacha, N. N. (2005). Academic vocabulary: A corpus analysis approach. *International Journal of Arabic-English Studies (IJAES), 6*(1), 123-146.

Bacha, N. N. (2007). Research of EFL students writing at two Lebanese universities. *Asian Journal of English Language Teaching, 17,* 129-135.

Bacha, N. N. (2010). Teaching the academic argument in an EFL environment. *Journal of English for Academic Purposes 9*(3), 229-241.

Bacha, N. N. (2011). Teaching critique writing: A scaffolded approach. In M. Pennington & P. Burton (Eds.), *The College Writing Toolkit: Tried and Tested Ideas for Teaching College Writing* (pp. 251-280). London: Equinox Publishers.

Bacha, N. N. (2013). Teacher corrective feedback on EFL writing in the disciplines: An exploratory study. *The Linguistics Journal, 7*(1), 294-319.

Bacha, N. N. & Bahous, R. (2008). Contrasting views of business students' writing needs in an EFL environment. *English for Specific Purposes, 27,* 74-93.

Bacha, N. N. & Bahous, R. (2010) Student and teacher perceptions on plagiarism in academic writing. *Writing and Pedagogy 2*(2), 251-280.

Bacha, N. N. & Bahous, R. (2013). Cultures of learning in academia: A Lebanese case study. In M. Cortazzi & L. Jin (Eds.) *Researching Cultures of Learning* (pp. 116-135). Houndmills, Basingstoke, Hampshire, UK: Palgrave, Macmillan

Bacha, N. N., Cortazzi, M. & Nakhle F. (2002). Academic lexical literacy: Investigating the cohesion of Arabic speakers' essays in English. *International Journal of Arabic-English Studies, 3,* 119-152.

Bacha, N. N., Nabhani, M. & Bahous, R. (2011) High Schoolers' perceptions of academic integrity. *Research Papers in Education,* 1-17.

Bazih, O. (1996). Effect of journal writing on ESL students. Unpublished master's thesis, The American University of Beirut.

Bhuiyan, N. (2012). High school-to-college writing transition: Student perspectives in Lebanon. Unpublished master's thesis, The American University of Beirut.

Bohsali, L. (2010). Research based design for assessment techniques. Unpublished master's thesis, The Lebanese American University.

Carthy, V. (1978). An analysis of the use of transitional devices in descriptive composition of native and non-native speakers of English. Unpublished master's thesis, the American University of Beirut, Lebanon.

Deeb, N. (1972). Methods for developing creative writing abilities among English speaking elementary school children. Unpublished master's thesis, The American University of Beirut.

Diab, N. (1998). Interference of Arabic in the English writings of Lebanese students, *ESPecialist Journal, 1*(1).

Diab, N. (2009). Assessment of a constructivist approach to teaching writing. *Proceedings of the Regional Conference on Program and Learning Assessment,* 38-50.

Diab, N. (2010). Effects of peer- versus self-editing on students' revision on language errors in revised drafts. *System, 38,* 85-95.

Diab, N. (2011). Assessing the relationship between different types of student feedback and the quality of revised writing. *Assessing Writing, 16*(4), 274 -292.

Diab, R. & Balaa, L. (2009). Case study: The use of rubrics in assessing critique writing, *Proceedings of the Regional Conference on Program and Learning Assessment,* 51-59.

Diab, R. & Balaa, L. (2011). Developing detailed rubrics for assessing critique writing: Impact on EFL university students' performance and attitudes. *TESOL Journal, 2(1),* 52-72.

Diab, R. (2005a). Teachers' and students' beliefs about responding to ESL writing: A case study. *TESL Canada Journal, 23*(1), 28-43.

Diab, R. (2005b). EFL university students' preferences for error correction and teacher feedback to writing. *TESL Reporter, 38*(1), 27-51.

Diab, R. (2006). Error correction and feedback in the EFL writing classroom: Comparing instructor and student preferences. *English Teaching Forum*, 44(3), 2-13.

El Joukhadar, N. (2013). Students' perceptions of the effect of grammar correction in an English language course at a Lebanese university. Unpublished master's thesis, The University of Balamand.

El Mufti, N. (1997). Error analysis of intensive English students' written compositions at the Lebanese American University: A case study. Unpublished master's thesis, The American University of Beirut.

Esseili, F. (2011). English in Lebanon: Implications for national identity and language policy. Unpublished doctoral dissertation: Purdue University.

Esseili, F. (2012). Faculty and EFL student perceptions of L2 writing at the University of Balamand. Unpublished survey results, Beirut, Lebanon.

Esseili, F. (2014). English language teaching in Lebanon: Trends and challenges. In K. M. Bailey &. R. M. Damerow (Eds.), *The Teaching and Learning of English in the Arabic-speaking World* (pp. 101-114). New York: Routledge.

Fakhreddine, J. (2007). The reading-writing connection: Effect on students' skills acquisition. Unpublished master's thesis, The Lebanese American University.

Farhat, R. (2008). EFL learners' errors at a higher education institution. Unpublished master's thesis, The Lebanese American University

Fidaoui, D. (2008). The effect of computer-assisted language learning on motivating students to write. Unpublished master's thesis, The Lebanese American University.

Fidaoui, D., Bahous, R. & Bacha, N. N. (2010). CALL in Lebanese elementary ESL writing classrooms. *Computer Assisted Language Learning* 23(2), 151-168.

Geha, N. (2008). The perceptions of tutors and tutees regarding the effectiveness of tutoring in writing centers on second/foreign language learners' writing proficiency. Unpublished master's thesis, The American University of Beirut.

Hachem, A. (2005). Implementing the writing workshop: An approach to differentiating writing instruction in a second grade mixed-ability classroom to help students demonstrate improved writing skills. Unpublished master's thesis, The Lebanese American University.

Hadla, Z. (2006). Teacher practices and student preferences for error correction in intensive English instruction. Unpublished master's thesis, The American University of Beirut.

Hamzeh, S. (1996). Effect of diagnostic & nondiagnostic feedback on the development of the expository writing proficiency of second language (L2) learning. Unpublished master's thesis, The American University of Beirut.

Hawrani, Sh. (1974). Contrastive analysis of meaning relationships and linking devices in English and Arabic. Unpublished master's thesis, the American University of Beirut.

Honein-Shehadi, N. (2007). Writing needs and writing centers in Lebanese secondary schools: A survey of teachers' perceptions. Unpublished master's thesis, The American University of Beirut.

Houssami, M. (2005). A comparative study of the effect of student-generated and teacher-provided instructional rubrics on writing achievement. Unpublished master's thesis, The American University of Beirut.

Idriss, B. (2002). The effect of dialogue journal writing on reading comprehension, writing quality and writing apprehension of Lebanese third intermediate students. Unpublished master's thesis, The American University of Beirut.

Jabbour, V. (2011). My classroom writing kit. Unpublished master's thesis, The Lebanese American University.

Kachan, V. & Bacha, N. N. (2012). A lexical corpus based analysis of L2 academic vocabulary: A case study. *The Asian ESP Journal, 8*(1), 53-74.

Kadi, S. (2004). The effect of journal writing on the achievement of second elementary Lebanese students in English as a foreign language. Unpublished master's thesis, The American University of Beirut.

Kazem, R. (2005). The effect of teachers' feedback on the students' ability to self-editing L2 writing classes. Unpublished master's thesis, The American University of Beirut.

Khater, C. (2009). Towards establishing a writing center. Unpublished master's thesis, The Lebanese American University.

Kishli, R. (2007). The effect of prewriting techniques on writing quality and writing apprehension. Unpublished master's thesis, The American University of Beirut.

Nazzal, N. (2008). The relationship of second language writing apprehension, writing self-efficacy beliefs, and the writing performance of EFL AUB students. Unpublished master's thesis, The American University of Beirut.

Nicolas, M. & Annous, S. (2013). Assessing WAC elements in business syllabi. *Business Communication Quarterly, 76*(2), 172-187.

Muhammad, H. (1968). A quantitative analysis of grammatical errors in written English. Unpublished master's thesis, The American University of Beirut.

Obeid, H. (2001). The relative effectiveness of journal writing and sentence combining practice in promoting the writing development of EFL students. Unpublished master's thesis, The American University of Beirut.

Obeid, O. (2013). Using fairy tales to improve students' writing skills: A case study. Unpublished master's thesis, The University of Balamand.

Ministry of Education and Higher Education. (2014). Private universities and institutions in Lebanon. Retrieved from http://www.higher-edu.gov.lb/english/Private_Univ.htm

Shaaban, Th. (2001). The effect of collaborative learning on the writing progress of 10th grade students. Unpublished master's thesis, The American University of Beirut.

Shaaban, K. & Ghaith, G. (2000). Student motivation to learn English as a foreign language. *Foreign Language Annals, 33*, 632-644.

Shalhoub, N. (1981). The use of connectives in English writing by second language learners. Unpublished master's thesis, The American University of Beirut.

Shalhub, L. (1991). Process writing with high-intermediate, pre-university students: A teaching/learning experience. Unpublished master's thesis, The American University of Beirut.

Shami, Gh. (2010). The effect of the writer's workshop on the writing progress of EFL fifth grade students. Unpublished master's thesis, The American University of Beirut.

Shatila, S. (2010). The effectiveness of trained peer response on ESL students' writing quality and revision types. Unpublished master's thesis, The Lebanese American University.

Shehab, M. (2011). Teachers' and students' perspectives on using rubrics in the writing classroom. Unpublished master's thesis, The Lebanese American University.

Schleifer, A. (1972). A model for teaching the writing of vocabulary and sentence structure with slides and audio tape. Unpublished master's thesis, The American University of Beirut.

Silva, T., McMartin-Miller, C, Jayne, V. & Pelaez-Morales, C. (2011). Scholarship on L2 writing in 2010: The year in review. Retrieved from http://newsmanager.commpartners.com/tesolslwis/issues/2011-11-30/9.html

Scott, M. (1973). Error analysis: A study of Arab students' written and oral production in English. Unpublished master's thesis, The American University of Beirut.

Yaqub, D. (1970). A proposed method for teaching the writing of expository paragraphs to university level non-native speakers of English according to traditional rhetorical principles. Unpublished master's thesis, The American University of Beirut.

Zailaa, N. (2011). Using drama in teaching writing at grade 11 in a private school English course: An action research project. Unpublished master's thesis, The University of Balamand.

Zghir, R. (2007). Writing anxiety among sophomore students: A survey in a private university in Beirut. Unpublished master's thesis, The American University of Beirut.

Chapter 8
Small Components: Some Big Contributions
—L2 Writing Research in New Zealand

John Bitchener

AUT University, Auckland

Introduction

The focus of L2 writing research in New Zealand and the extent to which it has been a priority of researchers compared with L2 research in other areas of L2 teaching and learning have largely been determined by (a) the educational contexts (primary/secondary schools and tertiary institutions) in which L2 writing is taught and (b) by the interests of teachers, researchers and research students in these contexts. Compared with countries that have populations in excess of New Zealand's 4.3 million, the range and number of institutions catering to the needs of L2 writers is relatively limited. This means, of course, that the number of teachers and researchers working in the field of L2 writing as teachers and researchers is also limited. In spite of this, I believe that the contribution of New Zealand L2 writing research is relatively extensive and that many of the prominent areas of international L2 writing research are ones that have been contributed to by New Zealand researchers. Thus, the title of this paper: Small components, some big contributions.

It is the aim of this article (a) to background the contexts in which L2 writing is taught and researched, (b) to outline some of the main areas of L2 writing research that have been addressed and are currently being researched and published by New Zealand researchers (including doctoral students) and (c) to assess the contribution of this work to the field as a whole. The New Zealand L2 writing research that is covered in this paper is that which has been undertaken by New Zealand teachers and researchers as well as students completing doctorates at New Zealand universities. Data informing the research are most often from the New Zealand context, but sometimes they have been collected overseas.

The Contexts in Which L2 Writing Is Taught and Researched in New Zealand

All educational institutions in New Zealand (from primary schools through secondary schools to tertiary institutions like universities, polytechnics and private training establishments) are seeing an increase in the number of migrant and international students studying as L2 learners and writers. While the majority of them are either English as a second language (ESL) or English as a foreign language (EFL) learners and writers, languages other than English (for example, Japanese, Mandarin, German and so on) are sometimes also offered by these institutions. Because these languages are typically not spoken in communities where L1 speakers live and work, they are categorized as foreign languages (FL). Students who learn either English or another language as a second or foreign language are typically placed in classes that focus on grammar, vocabulary, and the four language learning skills (reading, writing, speaking and listening).

The School Sector: Primary and Secondary

In school contexts, ESL learners are mainstreamed and offered L2 classes as part of their learning program. FL learners have usually chosen their additional language as part of an option program from their school's curriculum. Irrespective of whether the language being learned is a second or foreign language, the development of writing skills in the language is most often given lesser prominence in the curriculum than are the other three skills. Not surprisingly, therefore, less attention has been given to L2 writing research by teachers and researchers within school contexts. One has only to peruse the table of contents of the two New Zealand language teaching journals to see that far more research is undertaken and published on other areas of language learning than is the case on L2 writing and its development. The first journal, *The TESOLANZ Journal,* published by TESOL Aotearoa New Zealand (the New Zealand TESOL affiliate) produces one issue a year. Articles are broadly focused on language teaching issues in New Zealand and therefore are primarily of interest to New Zealand TESOL teachers and researchers. The second journal, *The New Zealand Language Teacher,* is published once a year by the New Zealand Association of Language Teachers (NZALT) and publishes research on the teaching and learning of foreign languages. As well as providing teachers and researchers with opportunities to disseminate L2 writing research in these national journals, opportunities are also available for dissemination at the two associations' conferences. However, while L2 writing research conducted in the school contexts is not prominent in either of these journals or at either association's conferences, the situation is different in the tertiary sector.

The Tertiary Sector: Universities, Polytechnics and Private Training Establishments

The New Zealand tertiary sector comprises universities, polytechnics and private training establishments (PTEs), and each of these offers L2 teaching and learning programs for migrant and international students. The PTEs (including private language schools) offer a wide range of training programs and some of these include ESL and EFL courses. Those that do, offer (1) general English courses for beginners to advanced learners of English and (2) courses in English language development that focus on preparation for particular examinations like IELTS and Cambridge certificates or on English for specific purposes, for example, English for business purposes. General English courses at lower proficiency levels focus on the teaching and learning of grammar and vocabulary as well as skills in reading, writing, speaking and listening. It is most often the case that writing activities at these levels are seen more in terms of opportunities for learners to develop knowledge of linguistic forms, structures and vocabulary than in terms of opportunities for developing knowledge and skills in discourse development. In other words, the focus is more on *writing-to-learn-language* than on *learning-to-write* discourse (Manchon, 2009, 2011). On the other hand, more advanced language learners, while continuing to focus on developing their linguistic competence, are provided with opportunities to develop discourse in a range of genres and for an increasing range of purposes.

Universities and polytechnics in New Zealand often have language-focused pre-degree courses within foundation programs (e.g. International House at AUT University and the English Language Academy at University of Auckland) and these offer similar types of classes and courses to those provided by private language schools. In addition to those preparing students for external examinations, many provide English for Academic Purposes (EAP) courses where there is a focus on the writing of discourse for a wide range of academic purposes and in a wide range of genres. Teachers of these courses are more likely to be interested in L2 writing research, especially that which focuses on pedagogical questions and concerns. Those who are teaching in a university or polytechnic context find themselves working in a research culture and environment that is better able to provide them with time and resources to undertake and publish research than is the case in smaller, less publicly funded institutions.

Undergraduate programs at tertiary institutions offer qualifications in a wide range of discipline areas, and this means that generic and discipline-specific knowledge of discourse and genre expectations are required. Consequently, institutions offer discipline-specific seminars, workshops and sometimes credit-bearing courses in the first year as well as one-on-one tutorial advice for all students across all years of enrolment. These opportunities are available to both L1 and L2 students so the focus is not on what might be categorized as typically L2 writing issues. However, support for L2 writers is available within institution-wide learning support centers.

At the graduate/postgraduate level, similar support can be found in schools and departments as well as in university-wide postgraduate centers where a wide range of optional thesis-research and thesis-writing seminars and workshops are available for all students. Some programs within tertiary institutions offer credit-bearing generic and discipline-specific academic writing courses, but they are not specifically designed for L2 writers. Some institutions offer bridging courses for students seeking entry to higher qualifications (e.g. reading papers with a writing focus) but again these are not specifically for L2 writers. New Zealand tertiary institutions, unlike those in many other parts of the world, do not offer programs and qualifications in L2 writing as such. L2 writing occupies a relatively minor place within qualifications offered by departments or schools of General and Applied Linguistics or Education. L2 writing research becomes increasingly prominent at the graduate/postgraduate level when thesis/dissertation students undertake research for Masters and Doctoral degrees. Most L2 *writing* research students can be found in departments/schools where supervisors are committed to L2 writing research. However, the number of supervisors undertaking L2 writing research at New Zealand universities is small. The six universities that house departments where general and applied linguistics is taught usually have no more than 2-3 members of staff/faculty engaged in L2 writing research. Other departments and schools sometimes have staff/faculty investigating writing-related questions/topics but they tend to not be L2-oriented. Some L2 writing research staff/faculty may supervise up to 10 PhD or Master's students, but not all of them are necessarily working in the field of L2 writing.

From this background, then, it can be seen that more students than academics/supervisors are likely to be engaged in areas of L2 writing research.

However, this does not mean that research topics/questions are necessarily more related to writing issues at graduate and postgraduate levels. The next section of this paper outlines some of the main areas of L2 writing research that have been published by New Zealand researchers in New Zealand and international publications.

Some of the Main Areas of L2 Writing Research Published by New Zealand Researchers

L2 writing research in New Zealand can best be categorized, as indeed it can be internationally, according to whether its primary focus is on *learning-to-write* (Hyland, 2011) or on *writing-to-learn-language* or *writing-to-learn-content* (Manchon, 2009, 2011). In low proficiency language learning classes, it is more often the case that writing activities are undertaken as exercises for learners to practice and consolidate the learning of L2 linguistic features, whereas in higher proficiency language classes, more attention is given to the *learning-to-write* discourse for a range of purposes and audiences in multiple genres. In tertiary institutions (and I include here pre-degree programs offering EAP courses), *learning-to-write* is not surprisingly the perspective of focus. This overview of New Zealand L2 writing research is divided into two parts: Part One looks at the *writing-to-learn-language* research and Part Two at the *learning-to-write* research.

Part One: *Writing-to-Learn-Language* Research in New Zealand

New Zealand L2 writing research that has been situated within the *writing-to-learn-language* perspective has been dominated by a focus on the value of written corrective feedback for second language learning and acquisition, especially with respect to the development of grammatical form and structure. This body of research has been led by Bitchener, Bitchener's colleagues, Ellis,

Ellis' colleagues, and added to most recently by contributions from a number of doctoral students at AUT University, Otago University and Auckland University. Other areas of research with a *writing-to-learn-language* focus include studies by Coxhead and colleagues on academic vocabulary development, especially that required for academic writing contexts, and those on the mediating effect of planning time on the development of written complexity by Adams and colleagues and by doctoral student, M. Frear.

New Zealand L2 writing research on the role of written CF for L2 development. In response to the call by Truscott (1996) for the abandonment of written CF on the grounds that research had shown it to not be effective, a steadily growing number of studies have been published in recent years to show that this claim was both premature and not necessarily valid. Leading the research contribution from New Zealand, Bitchener, Ellis and colleagues have published a range of studies that were designed to investigate several of the key claims made by Truscott.

The first question about whether or not written CF can be expected to facilitate the development of L2 form and structure has been considered in a number of New Zealand studies (Bitchener, 2008; Bitchener & Knoch, 2008, 2009a, 2009b, 2010a, 2010b; Ellis et al, 2008), drawing mainly on elementary and intermediate international and migrant students in New Zealand and one advanced group in the USA. These studies have shown consistently that written CF can be effective under certain conditions at least, with treatment groups outperforming control groups.

The second question about the durability of immediate effects from written CF was also considered by the same studies referred to above. In each case, the gains in accuracy revealed in the immediate post-tests were retained over time in the delayed post-tests. The effects were seen over one to two month periods and in one study (Bitchener & Knoch, 2010a) over a ten-month period.

The third question about whether written CF is more effective for targeting certain linguistic forms and structures has received less attention in both the New Zealand and international research. The studies referred to above found that written CF can be effective in developing an accurate use of certain rule-based grammatical forms like the two main functional uses of the English article system (first and anaphoric mentions of people, places and things, for example) and the simple past tense. Item-based features of the L2 have received less research attention internationally, but one New Zealand study by Bitchener, Young and Cameron (2005) found written CF to be less effective for developing accuracy in the use of prepositions. Until further research examines the effectiveness of written CF for targeting other rule-based and item-based forms and structures, care needs to be taken with any tendency to overgeneralize its effectiveness.

The fourth question about whether one type of written CF (for example, direct, indirect and meta-linguistic) is more effective than another type has been studied to some extent by Bitchener, Ellis and colleagues. While the studies referred to above have shown no difference in effect for these three types, one reason for this might be the fact that the studies were not designed to specifically test the relative effectiveness of separate variables. They had been designed to test the effectiveness of different types of typical classroom practice involving a combination of feedback approaches. Studies by Ellis with Sheen and colleagues (2009) and by Shintani and Ellis (2013) have found that meta-linguistic feedback was more effective than direct feedback for learners in these studies, but clearly there is a need for further research on this in a wider range of contexts and for studies that test the interacting effect of different proficiency levels. Another area of written CF research that had focused on different types of feedback is that which compares focused feedback (or feedback targeting one or a couple of linguistic features) and unfocused feedback (that is, comprehensive feedback). However, this has not been the focus of New Zealand studies; New Zealand studies have only investigated targeted, focused feedback.

The fifth question about whether a single provision of written CF is sufficient feedback for learners has been and is continuing to be investigated in

New Zealand research because it is not clear whether learners who fail to uptake and/or retain knowledge provided by this limited "treatment" would have benefited from more than one provision or a different type of feedback. Several studies in other countries, for example, case studies by Storch and Wigglesworth (see Wigglesworth & Stroch, 2012) have suggested that a more mediated, scaffolded approach may be more helpful for learners who have fewer partially acquired forms or structures than others within the same proficiency level. At the moment, two doctoral students are completing studies on the effectiveness of scaffolded written CF for language learning. At AUT University, Guo Qi's thesis comprises two studies. In the first of these, participants were given written CF on one piece of writing and, in the second study, those who did not uptake in the first study were scaffolded with additional feedback. The long-term effect was examined in a new piece of writing after nine weeks. Preliminary findings have shown that the participants were able to correct their errors over time with less explicit written CF and that the effects were retained. The second doctoral study, by Sobhani from Otago University, is investigating the efficacy of providing graduated written CF to L2 learners with a view to understanding how individual learners perceive their use of and success with self-regulatory strategies, how such strategies are influenced by the provision of graduated feedback, how the uptake of written CF is mediated by learners' beliefs about L2 learning, and how those beliefs are influenced by the provision of graduated feedback.

New Zealand written CF research has also made a contribution to exploring the mediating effect of individual and contextual factors on learners' use of written CF. At a macro-contextual level, Bitchener & Knoch (2009b) have investigated the effect of the educational and L2 learning background of learners on their receptiveness to written CF and found no difference between those who had had greater exposure to explicit forms of instruction, including exposure to written CF. More recently, AUT University doctoral student, Rummel, investigated the effects of written CF and learner beliefs for L2 learners of English from Laos and Kuwait. In terms of facilitating uptake and retention over time, written CF was found to be effective for all Lao learners of English, irrespective of the type of feedback they were given, but only for Kuwaiti learners who received direct written CF. The biodata showed that many Lao learners had been exposed to various types of written CF and for a longer period of time than the Kuwaiti students who had only recently been exposed to types of feedback other than direct feedback. It could be that, although they believe these other types of feedback are beneficial, they are not as skilled at using them. A new study by Bitchener (forthcoming), on the mediating effect of different individual factors and micro-contextual factors on whether learners respond positively or negatively to written CF suggests that a plethora interacting factors can explain why learners respond the way they do and that these factors then have an effect on uptake of written CF.

For an overview of this research within the context of that undertaken elsewhere, see Bitchener and Ferris (2012), the special issue of *Journal of Second Language Writing* (2012) and the forthcoming book by Bitchener and Storch (2014) on Written CF theories and research.

New Zealand L2 writing research on learning academic vocabulary. The second body of research within the *writing-to-learn language* perspective could arguably be categorized as research about *learning-to-write* academic prose. However, Coxhead and I believe that the primary focus of the research is the learning of vocabulary. Her first article with Byrd (Coxhead & Byrd, 2007) explains that (a) knowledge of the literature on what constitutes the language of academic discourse and (b) the development of skills for analyzing particular examples of academic writing can help teachers identify the language that their students need for different types of academic writing. Against this background, Coxhead's doctoral research reported in several articles (Coxhead, 2011a, 2012) investigated the use of vocabulary from input texts and found both negative and positive effects from the instructed use of target vocabulary in writing. Negative effects included anxiety, whereas positive effects included higher levels of awareness of target words. The study also found that in learning and using vocabulary appropriately, teachers and learners need knowledge about (a) how to actually use words when writing, (b) the academic context of the writing, (c) the writing topic itself and (d) the role of learners' attitudes towards the use of academic vocabulary. Two particular recommendations stand out at the end of this research: (a) that direct instruction is effective in teaching vocabulary even though many teachers adopt approaches that are more centered on meaning-focused input and incidental learning and (b) that teachers should consider a range of approaches to create an environment that fosters vocabulary use. Another article (Coxhead, 2011b) reported on what students felt about the importance and learning of academic vocabulary. Interviews revealed that they (a) had an overall sense of the importance of academic vocabulary for the writing of academic texts, (b) had a high level of awareness of the academic audience and its impact on their choice of vocabulary and (c) used a variety of techniques to incorporate academic and technical words into their essays. Coxhead's focus on the learning and importance of academic vocabulary complements decades of New Zealand research and publications by Nation on vocabulary teaching and learning. Together, their contribution has been internationally noteworthy.

New Zealand L2 writing research on the effect of planning time on L2 writing. Over the years, a growing body of research has investigated the effect of different types of planning time on oral production, but less attention has been given to its effect on written accuracy, fluency and complexity. Adding to the insights from international research, New Zealand researcher, M. Frear, a doctoral student at AUT University, has investigated the effects of task complexity on written complexity, of pre-task planning time combined with task complexity on written complexity, of post-task editing combined with task complexity on written complexity, and the nature of the relationship between learners' attitudes and complex written output. The study found that increases in task complexity produce fewer dependent clauses (though the addition of pre-task planning time appeared to reverse this trend), while post-task editing has no apparent effect. Findings also suggest that increases in task complexity increase lexical variety (though the addition of pre-task planning time rendered the findings non-significant), while post-task editing has no apparent effect.

A recently published study by Adams and colleagues (2013) also considered the effects of planning time on written communication. It investigated the effect of planning on the task-based writing of Malaysian civil engineering majors who were asked to write a proposal via a wiki for the best type of equipment to use. The study had three experimental conditions: pre-task planning, on-line planning and no planning. As well as analyzing complexity of writing, the researchers examined the writing for fluency and accuracy. The findings suggest that planning time, rather than mitigating the effects of attentional capacity limitations, may in this context push learners to direct their attentional resources either toward complexity or toward accuracy. Thus, both studies by New Zealand researchers have added to our understanding of conditions that a wider international research base has shown and continues to show can facilitate L2 writing capabilities.

Part Two: *Learning-to-Write* Research in New Zealand

Much of the New Zealand *learning-to-write* research has focused on identifying and articulating issues associated with helping students develop academic literacy appropriate to a new academic environment. While it is not possible to place all the research into either pre-degree, undergraduate and post-graduate categories, a framework that is organized around the three different levels does provide a useful one for understanding the particular concerns and interests of teachers and researchers at these levels.

Research situated at the pre-degree and undergraduate levels. At pre-degree level, and sometimes spreading into the first year of under-graduate study, EAP programs seek to prepare students from a range of L2 backgrounds for the types of teaching, learning and assessment they will encounter as tertiary students. The need for such courses in New Zealand is clear when one considers the number of international students choosing New Zealand for their study: 30,555 students at universities and polytechnics and 30,505 at PTEs, including private language schools (NZ Ministry of Education, 2013). In offering EAP courses, the question of their effectiveness in preparing students for tertiary study is an important one to ask not only the providers and teachers of these courses but, arguably and more importantly, the students themselves as they often come from learning backgrounds characterized by very different epistemologies, values and expectations.

One recent New Zealand study (Wette & Lessels, 2010) has reported that students can sometimes feel under-prepared even when they have taken EAP courses. Commenting, for example, on the value of the writing components of their course, the participants in this study identified four key differences between the writing demands of their EAP courses and those of their university courses: they said they found their EAP writing tasks focused on more general and less conceptually-demanding content, that they were shorter and more leniently marked/assessed, and that they received more feedback on language elements than on the quality of their ideas and argumentation. On the other hand, they emphasized that many aspects of the course were valuable: instruction in research skills, in the use of sources, in how to construct a coherent academic argument; the focus on language development (including, for example, prefabricated chunks for signposting and making transitions, hedging options, tone and register) and the writing of a 1500-word researched essay. Wette and Lessels conclude by explaining that EAP curricula need to include (a) instructional tasks that approximate as closely as possible to the task demands, (b) conceptual complexity and types of real-world data and evidence that characterize writing in subject disciplines and (c) writing activities and assessments that are pitched at the same level they will be assessed at in tertiary institutions.

Related to the focus of this study are two new studies by Wette (in press a and b). The first of these studies, to be published in the New Zealand journal *TESOLANZ Journal*, investigated process-oriented and product-oriented components of a New Zealand EAP writing curriculum and teachers' instructional priorities. It found that most of the courses were genre-based and process-focused and that teachers' main priorities centred around the developmental needs of the students vis-a-vis the academic literacy demands of undergraduate disciplinary courses. The second study investigated the kinds of instructional strategies that EAP teachers employ and how they account for their choices. Drawing upon data from seven experienced teachers in five New Zealand tertiary institutions (10-12 class hours through observations supported by post-lesson interviews and study of teaching materials and course documents), the findings revealed repeated use of a number of instructional strategies referred to as modelling. It found that teachers "modelled" flawed and exemplary text products for analysis and discussion, focused on the processes involved in creating a particular text by demonstrating and discussing cognitive processes with the class, leading whole-class collaborations that produced jointly constructed texts, and facilitating cooperative pair or group composing and editing activities. The study is noteworthy for its focus on practices that blend textual, cognitive and interactional components in order to advance students' skills across a range of academic text types.

The third piece of research by Wette (2010) on the role and use of sources in academic writing and the question of what constitutes "plagiarism" makes a valuable contribution to an ever-increasing body of international research on the subject. In this article, Wette focuses on instructional interventions that might be employed to help students master this complex aspect of academic literacy. The study recruited 78 undergraduate students from six strands of credit-bearing L2 writing courses. A pre-unit quiz and guided writing task were used to determine the current level of knowledge and skill. After eight hours of instruction and practice on technical and discourse skill components, students completed a post-unit task and wrote reflective comments. Added to this data were the texts of out-of-class assignments. The study found that instances of direct copying from the sources decreased in post-tasks and assignments and that, even though there was a modest overall improvement, the students were not yet proficient with more sophisticated and subtle aspects of source use (e.g.

integrating citations with their own voices and positions).

Also focusing on the issue of source use and plagiarism is the research of Henderson, a final year doctoral student at the University of Otago. As a case study of an undergraduate EAP class, the study draws upon data from surveys, qualitative analyses of reflective journal entries and interviews, and text analyses to examine students' knowledge of source use and plagiarism from a socio-cultural perspective. Adopting this approach, Henderson seeks a fuller understanding of the varied contexts in which writing takes place and the impact that these contexts have on the students' writing processes. Findings suggest that a number of the students were very aware of the cultural, institutional and disciplinary contexts in which they were writing but, as an examination of the text data revealed, even a nuanced understanding of plagiarism did not guarantee the students' abilities to use sources successfully in their writing. For instance, they employed a number of non-standard textual borrowing strategies in their work.

While many international students entering undergraduate programs at tertiary institutions in New Zealand have completed some form of transitional study to prepare them for the academic writing demands of higher education, a large number have not. Consequently, this can present enormous difficulties for both students and teachers. Understanding the expectations and conventions of English academic writing and developing academic writing skills appropriate to a new academic context, including a discipline-specific academic context, can create all sorts of issues of both an academic and personal (including inter-personal) nature. Research by Skyrme (2013), for example, has highlighted the nature of these issues for undergraduate Chinese students learning to write in a business and informational sciences program at a New Zealand university. While her doctoral study looked at a range of personal, interpersonal and intercultural issues that the students were coming to terms with, including those more directly concerned with understanding similarities and differences in what the academic communities of China and New Zealand expect, Skyrme (2013) reveals that in spite of their growing understanding and, even in some cases, alignment with the values of the university, there were matters where the Chinese students did not adopt ways of writing favored within the new culture of learning. Sometimes, this was a result of inability; other times it was their strategic choice. Some of the key issues included understanding what is meant by the invitation to be creative or original, understanding what it means to borrow text appropriately, understanding the importance of engaging critically with the thinking and research of others, and unravelling what seemed to be conflicting demands in understanding different disciplinary discourses. Skyrme reports that she is now involved in a new study of undergraduate L2 students who have completed a first semester course in Academic Writing in English for Speakers of Other Languages to understand whether learning about writing continues throughout the undergraduate years of study and if so, what helps students become better writers.

Another New Zealand doctoral student, Walker (2012), recently completed her doctoral study at Otago University in a similar area of interest—the self-perceptions of Malaysian ESL learners about academic writing in Malaysian higher educational institutions. Using a mixed methods approach, comprising an initial survey of 170 students, followed by two semi-structured interviews with eight student participants, the study found that the students' self-concepts in academic writing and engagement were dynamic constructs in that they were influenced by multiple internal and external factors from their past and present contexts. Both self-concept in academic writing and engagement were found to play an important role in helping them adapt to their new academic context and learning demands. Corroborating the findings of international research, the study also found that students may benefit from writing support and a writing curriculum that is discipline-specific to help enhance their self-concept, academic identity and academic legitimacy. The issues identified in the work of both Skyrme and Walker are not only confined to undergraduate L2 writers. Similar themes emerge in the L2 writing research situated at graduate or post-graduate level.

Research Situated at the Undergraduate and Postgraduate Levels

It would be fair to say that the greater proportion of the New Zealand L2 writing research has focused on issues related to students undertaking research for a thesis or dissertation. However, some attention has also been given to developing general academic writing skills for undergraduate and graduate students enrolled in course-work papers.

Research on the Process of Developing General Undergraduate and Graduate Academic Writing Skills

Informed by socio-cultural theory, Wall, a doctoral student at Otago University, is investigating the socially situated nature of human cognition in her study of how five tertiary students apply their knowledge and skills after four weeks of explicit instruction on self-questioning and self-instruction strategies, textual coherence, and argumentation structure. The study adopts an activity theory framework, using systemic theoretical instruction and microgenetic analysis. Materialization and verbalization are seen as a key for participants' self-regulation as they read multiple texts in order to compose an argument essay. Pre-task questionnaire self-reported strategy use and post-task written self-reflection data, together with video-recorded data during a reading-to-write task and interview data are triangulated to examine how reading-to-write activities are mediated and regulated. According to Wall, the findings provide evidence of participants' developmental stages in concept formation and task completion indicates purposeful mediated learning with a strong orientation towards task, based on conceptual understanding and specific goals. She adds that the findings highlight the need (a) to re-mediate the concept of writing and (b) to investigate not only how learners' reading-to-write performance can be promoted but also how socio-cultural obstacles impeding academic development may be addressed so that L2 learners may benefit from using writing as a psychological tool to regulate their own thoughts and those of others.

Also looking at generic writing skills required for argumentative and expository writing are new studies by Basturkmen (forthcoming) and Tarawhiti (forthcoming). The first of these is investigating similarities and differences in the coherence and cohesion-related discourse features employed by L1 and L2 students in the creation of argument. Drawing upon 30 samples of postgraduate writing from an English language diagnostic needs assessment (DELNA at the University of Auckland), the aim of this exploratory, descriptive study is (a) to identify the range of features used in writing at postgraduate level and (b) to explore raters' conceptualizations of cohesion and coherence when grading writing samples. Although these investigations are being undertaken to provide understanding of generic knowledge and skill issues related specifically to L2 writers at postgraduate level, they are not necessarily seen as issues of relevance to L2 students and their teachers; they are often issues that teachers and L1 students identify with as well. The second study by Tarawhiti, an AUT University doctoral student, is investigating the writing difficulties that L2 learners in a freshman program experience when preparing to study at an English-speaking university. The study is comparing the perceptions of students and the difficulties revealed in pieces of expository text before evaluating the effectiveness of a strategy-oriented approach to resolving the identified issues.

The importance of providing student writers with feedback on their academic writing has also been seen in New Zealand and internationally as a necessary part of the process of helping student writers develop appropriate academic writing skills. In her doctoral thesis at Otago University, Kumar (2008) was interested in adding to a steadily growing international research on feedback by investigating the thought processes of L2 student writers as they attend to written feedback. Using a case study approach that included the verbal protocols of eight postgraduate students as they attended to teacher feedback on their essays, their written texts, teacher comments, and a questionnaire survey, the study found that students attended to written feedback recursively, that the act of thinking aloud led to noticing the disparities highlighted in the feedback, and that engagement with the feedback is a social activity that encompasses a complex and dynamic interpersonal process between student writers and the feedback provider. A report on the cognitive processes and reactions of an L2 writer of Confucian Cultural heritage from the data-set that later appeared in M. Kumar, V. Kumar and Feryok (2009) revealed that although cultural attributes are often mentioned in relation to Confucian Heritage Culture learners, they did not seem to play a strong role in this case.

Further feedback research is currently being undertaken by Bian, a doctoral student at AUT University, into how a Chinese EFL teacher makes his/ her decisions about what to focus on when giving feedback on expository writing, how to word the feedback and how the students make their decisions about (a) what to act on and (b) how to act on feedback when processing what the teacher has provided. Particular attention is being given to understanding the extent to which a collaborative relationship between teacher and student is formed over time and to the extent to which students develop self-regulation over time. Thus, a process-centred socio-cultural approach informs the methodology. Viewing feedback in this light directs attention to the core of feedback—the development of student self-regulation—and encourages a focus on the interactive and collaborative feedback process leading to such a development. Thus, the study is expected to extend existing international research that has tended to focus on feedback as a more unidirectional activity.

Research on the development of thesis-writing skills. The growing number of studies emerging in the literature from New Zealand supervisors and doctoral students on topics related to the writing of a thesis or dissertation by L2 students is not altogether surprising given the large number of international students coming to New Zealand for this part of their postgraduate study and given the range of issues encountered by L2 students in a new academic environment that need to be understood and investigated by those most responsible for their success—the supervisors. As a result, supervisors interested in exploring such issues often attract doctoral students (both L1 and L2 students) who are also interested in understanding and developing L2 writing capabilities. The studies that have been published, or are in the process of being completed, can be grouped according to three broad categories: (a) those that focus on general supervision issues; (b) those that focus on the nature of supervisory feedback; and (c) those that focus on understanding what characterizes the discourse and part-genre expectations of thesis writing.

General issues related to thesis supervision. Leading much of the L2 writing research on issues to do with authorship, voice, agency, supervisor-supervisee relationships, and the nature of academic English accepted by the academy, Strauss, with colleagues and research students, has published several thought-provoking research articles in recent years. A theme running through each of these works is the question of what variety of English is acceptable to the academy. Strauss and Walton (2005) describe some of the language proficiency issues that supervisors and L2 students find it necessary to resolve during the supervisory process, including, for example, issues about authorship and voice. In doing so, the article discusses some of the dilemmas confronting both the supervisor and the student as they attempt to find a way forward. As the researchers explain, the status imbalance between the novice L2 student writer and the experienced supervisor can become an issue if the student does not feel empowered and does not feel s/he has an equal voice in decisions that are made. The extent to which linguistic difficulties can impact negatively on the relationship between supervisor and L2 student is also focused on in Strauss (2012) where the added issue of different assumptions and expectations by both parties, especially with regard to which variety of English is acceptable, can be seen as a factor in further exacerbating disharmony. Further exploring this issue, Chang and Strauss (2010) examined the issue of learner agency in the supervisory relationship through a small scale study of supervisors and Chinese-speaking international students. Rather than focusing on the voice of the supervisor alone, the study examined data from the point of view of students in order to capture their voices. From these insights into issues that can hinder the progress of L2 thesis writers, Strauss calls for further investigations into ways in which student and supervisor issues can be addressed and for an inclusion of the less powerful (student) voices in such discussions.

The nature and focus of supervisory feedback. Feedback on thesis-writing has been the focus of several researchers and research teams in New Zealand over the last decade and continues to be so. Perhaps the most extensive investigation into feedback at this level has been a national study of the feedback practices of New Zealand supervisors and the extent to which both L1 and L2 students find the feedback effective and helpful. Undertaken by Bitchener, Basturkmen, and East with funding from the Ako Aotrearoa (an agency of the Tertiary Education Commission), the study investigated what supervisors and students in New Zealand universities identified as effective practice in the feedback that is typically given on drafts of thesis chapters in three main disciplines: humanities, sciences/mathematics, and commerce. The team was interested in seeing whether or not there were similarities and differences in supervisor and student perspectives within and across disciplines and whether any differences were typical of the focus and delivery of feedback to L1 and L2 students. The study adopted a multi-method approach to data collection in order to triangulate the self-report data of questionnaire responses and interview comments with evidence of feedback from samples of draft texts.

The findings of the study have been reported extensively in journal articles (Bitchener, Basturkmen & East, 2010, 2011; East, Bitchener & Basturkmen, 2012; Basturkmen, East & Bitchener, 2012) and at conferences and seminars in New Zealand, Australia, USA, UK, South East Asia and selected European countries. Of particular interest for this article are some of the overall findings on feedback given to L2 thesis writers. The study found that in the early stages of receiving feedback, students expected to receive feedback on the extent to which their writing aligned with supervisors' expectations of what is appropriate for the genre. On the other hand, it found that their supervisors were often more concerned to provide feedback on the effectiveness of argumentation (that is, structure, organization, cohesion and coherence). With regard to linguistic accuracy and appropriateness, not all supervisors agreed that attention should be given to these aspects in the early stages given that redrafting would normally be required. Those who said they provided this type of feedback did so because they wanted to stress the importance at the outset of linguistic accuracy and precision with regard to tone, register and word choice. In terms of how feedback was delivered, many L2 students felt that direct feedback was more helpful than indirect feedback, but their supervisors, while not always disagreeing with them, felt it was more important to select direct or indirect feedback strategies according to the focus or topic of the feedback and that, by engaging the students in the thinking process through the provision of indirect feedback, they would develop a relationship in which they were self-regulated agents in a partnership of equals rather than as passive members of a relationship that was essentially unidirectional. The study was particularly interested in looking at the extent to which the feedback supervisors said they provided their students with was also present in feedback on chapter samples. Thus, the analysis of sample texts was an important part of the study. The team was not only interested in categorizing the focus or content of the feedback but also interested in seeing whether there was any relationship between the focus of the feedback and the way in which it was framed and delivered. Informing the analysis of pragmatic characteristics of the feedback were frameworks previously used by Kumar and Stracke (2007) and Ferris (1997). While the approach reported by Ferris is applicable to genres other than the thesis, that which Kumar and Stracke used was specifically relevant to the thesis. The national study did not find any differences in the way feedback was delivered to L1 and L2 students. The interview data revealed that this may have been a result of L2 writers at postgraduate level not needing to be treated in any way different to L1 writers. Any observed differences were more a factor of individual differences in the confidence expressed by students and of the nature of the relationship established between them and their supervisor.

Because this was an exploratory study into a range of perspectives, the extent to which practices and perspectives were held by supervisors and students was not a goal of the project. What the study produced was a wide range of practices and reasons for their adoption with a view to mounting a more quantitative investigation of the key questions. As a result, the team is currently collecting data in New Zealand, Australia, the USA and the UK and hopes to publish the results of this global study in 2016.

While the focus of feedback on thesis writing has tended to give more attention to written feedback, some attention was given in the national study to oral feedback practices. No distinction was made between the oral feedback practices of supervisors with L1 and L2 students even though some said that they encouraged their L2 students to record oral feedback meetings so they could clarify any details they may have missed, or not followed during the oral feedback session, by replaying the recording in their own time. L2 students said they appreciated this practice. The importance of oral feedback to L2 writers has also been discussed in an article by New Zealand researchers, Strauss, Sachtleben and Turner (2008) who investigated its value for L2 thesis writers in the faculty of Business at AUT University. Referred to as "talkback", the practice was found to be particularly useful for teaching and empowering L2 students to express their voice with their supervisors and other postgraduate stakeholders.

While it is most often the supervisor or supervisors' feedback that students receive when writing a thesis, another source of feedback can also be available to students, namely, that which is provided by advisors in learning support centers. Centers such as these are available at all New Zealand tertiary institutions so students can make appointments to visit advisors for one-on-one advice on the writing of theses, essays and assignments. The focus of this service is more directed at teaching the learner to become self-regulated rather than at providing a proofreading service. However, the value of the service has been reported by some to not have the status they feel it should have. In a forthcoming article, Strauss (in press) investigated the perspectives of postgraduate learning advisors at universities around New Zealand concerning the status they believe they have in their institutions. While the article reports that the advisors themselves feel that they are not held in high esteem by their institutions, it suggests a range of ways in which their position could be strengthened and recognition gained. The key recommendation is for the establishment of a formal networking structure that regularly brings learning advisors and supervisors into the same conversation and that it be conducted on a basis of mutual respect. Other recommendations, involving the learning advisors themselves, include finding a champion, uniting to form a strong unified representative body, attending and presenting at educational conferences and inviting discipline staff to lead research projects. Thus, the development of personal relationships and networks is seen as critical to benefiting what all stakeholders have to offer.

Understanding the discourse and part-genre expectations of thesis-writing. Much of the advice that supervisors provide in their feedback to L1 and L2 thesis students is that which helps their students understand the discourse requirements and expectations of the academy for the various part genres of the thesis. While this kind of advice is available in books like *Writing an Applied Linguistics Thesis or Dissertation* by Bitchener (2010) and *How to Write a Better Thesis* by Evans, Gruba and Zobel (2011), L2 students, in the national study referred to above, often said that they find it more helpful to attend classes and seminars on this type of material. Bitchener (2012), in a volume of reports on writing programs worldwide, describes and evaluates a seminar series on writing the different parts of a thesis that he offers at AUT university for L1 and L2 students across the disciplines. He explains that the majority of thesis students who attend the seminars are in fact L2 writers. In one study of 37 thesis writers (of which 18 were L2 writers), Bitchener and Banda (2007) investigated the level and depth of knowledge that the students had of the various functions of a literature review before receiving instruction and found that the L2 writers had a more limited understanding of (a) the role of theoretical perspectives underpinning research, (b) the need to critically assess the validity and reliability of claims and conclusions reported in research articles, and (c) the argumentation characteristics valued in Western academic institutions. Focusing on the skills required for writing an effective argument as part of a wider literature review, Turner and Bitchener (2006) reported on an evaluation of the effectiveness of an approach to teaching eight L2 students how to write an effective argument as part of a short literature review section. Employing a pre-test/instruction/post-test (immediate and delayed) design, the study found clear evidence of improvement in all areas that were targeted, including, for example, a logical and effective rhetorical organization of ideas and an appropriate use of meta-discourse.

Concluding Remarks

In terms of the amount of L2 writing research that has been produced by many countries with a much larger population than New Zealand's, this article has shown that even though the total outputs are relatively small, the contribution of the small components has, nevertheless, made a significant contribution to the wider literature on L2 writing research in a number of areas: the efficacy of written corrective feedback for L2 development, the nature and focus of supervisory feedback for L2 thesis writers and of general academic literacy development. Leading much of this research over the last decade, the contributions from Bitchener, Ellis, Wette, Strauss and Coxhead have been prominent and show every sign of continuing in the years to come. What is particularly noteworthy is the emergence of L2 writing research by a very able group of doctoral students dedicated to testing and developing a range of theoretical perspectives. L2 writing research in New Zealand has consistently been published in the leading international journals, including, for example, *Applied Linguistics, TESOL Quarterly, Language Learning, Modern Language Journal, Journal of Second Language Writing, Journal of English for Academic Purposes* and *Teaching in Higher Education*. Against this background, the future of L2 writing research in New Zealand looks bright with a plethora of publications from doctoral students about to emerge. Given the dearth of teaching vacancies in New Zealand institutions, many of these upcoming scholars may head overseas and contribute to the contributions of other countries. While it will be difficult to limit such an exodus of young talent, it should not be impossible to foster more L2 writing research from teachers across the sectors who are currently not involved in any research activities.

References

Adams, R., Amani, S., Newton, J. & Aloesnita, N. (2013). Planning and production in CMC writing. In H. Byrnes & R. Manchon (Eds.), *Task-based Language Learning: Insights from and for L2 Writing* (pp. 137-162). Amsterdam: John Benjamins.

Basturkmen, H. (forthcoming). Similarities and differences in the coherence and cohesion-related discourse features of L1 and L2 students in the creation of argument.

Basturkmen, H., Bitchener, J. & East, M. (2012). Supervisors' on-script feedback comments on drafts of dissertations: Socialising students into the Academic Discourse Community. *Teaching in Higher Education*, http://dx.doi/10.1080/13562517.2012.752728

Bian, M. (forthcoming). Chinese EFL teachers' written feedback on expository argumentation: A process-oriented approach. Unpublished PhD thesis, AUT University, Auckland, New Zealand.

Bitchener, J. (forthcoming). Mediating individual and micro-contextual factors on uptake from written corrective feedback.

Bitchener, J. (2012). Teaching writing at the Auckland University of Technology: A model of a seminar series for postgraduate students writing their first thesis or dissertation. In C. Thaiss (Ed.), *Writing Programs Worldwide: Profiles of Academic Writing in Many Places* (pp. 301-311). New York: Parlor Press.

Bitchener, J. (2012). The potential of written corrective feedback for SLA. *Journal of Second Language Writing, 21,* 348-363.

Bitchener, J. (2012). Written corrective feedback for L2 development: Current knowledge and future research. *TESOL Quarterly, 46 (4)*, 855-860.

Bitchener, J. (2010). A genre approach to understanding empirically-based thesis writing expectations. *Good Practice Publication Grants Ako Aotearoa E-Book* (pp.1-11).Wellington, NZ: Ako Aotearoa. www.akoaotearoa.ac.nz/gppg-ebook

Bitchener, J. (2010). *Writing an Applied Linguistics Thesis or Dissertation: A Guide to Presenting Empirical Research*. Houndsmill, UK: Palgrave Macmillan.

Bitchener, J. (2008). Evidence in support of written corrective feedback. *Journal of Second Language Writing, 17* (2), 69-124.

Bitchener, J. & Banda, M. (2007). Postgraduate students' understanding of the functions of thesis sub-genres: the case of the literature review. *New Zealand Studies in Applied Linguistics, 13*(2), 61-68.

Bitchener, J., Basturkmen, H. & East, M. (2011). Best practice in supervisor feedback to thesis students. Report on Ako Aotearoa website.

Bitchener, J., Basturkmen, H. & East, M. (2010). The focus of supervisor feedback to thesis/dissertation students. *International Journal of English Studies, 11*, 79-97.

Bitchener, J. & Ferris, D. (2012). *Written Corrective Feedback in Second Language Acquisition and Second Language Writing*. New York: Routledge.

Bitchener, J. & Knoch, U. (2008). The value of a focused approach to written corrective feedback. *ELT Journal, 63* (3), 204-211.

Bitchener, J. & Knoch, U. (2009a). The relative effectiveness of different types of direct written corrective feedback. *System, 37*(2), 322-329.

Bitchener, J. & Knoch, U. (2009b). The receptiveness of international and migrant ESL students to written corrective feedback. *Language Teaching Research Journal, 12* (2), 409-431.

Bitchener, J. & Knoch, U. (2010a). The contribution of written corrective feedback to language development: A ten month investigation. *Applied Linguistics, 31* (2), 193-214.

Bitchener, J. & Knoch, U. (2010b). Written corrective feedback and advanced ESL learners. *Journal of Second Language Writing, 19,* 207-217.

Bitchener, J. & Storch, N. (2013/2014). *Written Corrective Feedback for SLA: Theoretical Perspectives and Empirical Research.* Clevedon, UK: Multi-Lingual Matters.

Bitchener, J. & Turner, E. (2011). Assessing the effectiveness of one approach to the teaching of thematic unit construction of literature reviews. *Assessing Writing, 16,* 123-136.

Bitchener, J., Young, S. & Cameron, D. (2005). The effect of different types of corrective feedback on ESL students. *Journal of Second Language Writing, 12*(3): 191-205.

Chang, C. & Strauss, P. (2010). "Active agents for change?" Mandarin students in New Zealand and the thesis writing process. *Language and Education, 24,* 415-429.

Coxhead, A. (2011). Student perspectives on writing frames for EAP. *Tertiary Writing Network Colloquium Proceedings,* Wellington, December 2-3, 2010 (pp. 1-10). Available on CD.

Coxhead, A. (2011). What is the exactly word in English?: Investigating second language vocabulary use in writing. *English Australia, 27,* 3-17.

Coxhcad, A. (2012). Academic vocabulary, writing and English for academic purposes: Perspectives from second language learners. *RELC Journal, 43,* 137-145.

Coxhead A. & Byrd, P. (2007). Preparing writing teachers to teach the vocabulary and grammar of academic prose. *Journal of Second Language Writing, 16,* 129-147.

East, M., Bitchener, J. & Basturkmen, H. (2012). What constitutes effective feedback on postgraduate students' writing? The students' perspective. *Journal of University Teaching and Learning Practice, 9*(2), 1-16. Article 7. http://ro.uow.edu.au/jutlp/vol9/iss2/7

Ellis, R., Sheen, Y., Murakami, M. & Takashima, H. (2008). The effects of focused and unfocused written corrective feedback in an English as a foreign language context. *System, 36,* 353-371.

Evans, D., Gruba, P. & Zobel, J. (2011). *How to Write a Better Thesis*. Melbourne: Melbourne University Press.

Ferris, D. (1997). The influence of teacher commentary on student revision. *TESOL Quarterly, 31,* 315-339.

Frear, M. (forthcoming). The effects of cognitive task complexity on writing. Unpublished PhD thesis, AUT University, Auckland, New Zealand.

Guo, Qi. (forthcoming). The extent to which written corrective feedback facilitates EFL learners' acquisition of certain grammatical forms and structures. Unpublished PhD thesis, AUT University, Auckland, New Zealand.

Henderson, S. (forthcoming). Source use and authorship in second language academic writing. Unpublished PhD thesis, University of Otago, Dunedin, New Zealand.

Hyland, K. (2011). Learning to write: Issues in theory, research and pedagogy. In R. Manchon (Ed.), *Learning-to-write and Writing-to-learn in an Additional Language* (pp. 17-35). *Journal of Second Language Writing (Special Issue), 21(2012).* Amsterdam: John Benjamins.

Kumar, M. (2008). Feedback and revision: A protocol analysis. Unpublished PhD thesis, University of Otago, Dunedin, New Zealand.

Kumar, M., Kumar, V. & Feryok, A. (2009). Recursiveness in written feedback. *New Zealand Studies in Applied Linguistics, 15,* 26-37.

Kumar, V. & Stracke, E. (2007). An analysis of written feedback on a PhD thesis. *Teaching in Higher Education, 12,* 461-470.

Manchon, R. (2009). Broadening the perspective of L2 writing scholarship: The contribution of research on foreign language writing. In R. Manchon (Ed.), *Writing in Foreign Language Contexts: Learning, Teaching, and Research* (pp. 1-19). Bristol: Multilingual Matters.

Manchon, R. (2011). Writing to learn the language: Issues in theory and research. In R. Manchon (Ed.), *Learning-to-write and Writing-to-learn in an Additional Language* (pp. 61-82). Amsterdam: John Benjamins.

NZ Ministry of Education. (2013). *International Student Enrolments in New Zealand 2006-2012.* Wellington, NZ: International division of Ministry of Education.

Rummel, S. (forthcoming). The effects of L2 learners' beliefs on their response to written corrective feedback. Unpublished PhD thesis, AUT University, Auckland, New Zealand.

Shintani, N. & Ellis, R. (2013). The comparative effect of direct written corrective feedback and metalinguistic explanation on learners' explicit and implicit knowledge of the English indefinite article. *Journal of Second Language Writing, 22,* 286-306.

Skyrme, G. (2013). "It's totally different": Undergraduate Chinese students learning to write in a New Zealand university. In L. Jin & M. Cortazzi (Eds.), *Researching Intercultural Learning: Investigations in Language and Education* (pp. 152-170). Houndsmill, UK: Palgrave Macmillan.

Sobhani, A. (forthcoming). Investigating the effectiveness of providing second language writers with written corrective feedback: Self-regulation in uptake of correct forms. Unpublished PhD thesis, University of Otago, Dunedin, New Zealand.

Strauss, P. (in press). "I don't think we're seen as a nuisance"—the positioning of postgraduate learning advisors in New Zealand universities. *Text Journal of Writing and Writing Courses.*

Strauss, P. (2012). "The English is not the same"—Challenges in thesis writing for second language speakers of English. *Teaching in Higher Education, 17,* 283-293.

Strauss, P. & Walton, J. (2005). Authorship, voice and the EAL thesis. In E. Manalo & G. Wong-Toi (Eds.), *Communication Skills in University Education: The International Dimension* (pp. 51-61). Auckland: Pearson Education.

Strauss, P., Sachtleben, A. & Turner, E. (2008). Talkback: Empowering EAL thesis writers. In J. van Rij-Heyligers (Ed.), *Intercultural Communication Across University Settings—Myths and Realities* (174-188). Auckland: Pearson Education.

Tarawhiti, N. (forthcoming). The effect of a strategies instructional approach to second language writing difficulties encountered in text construction. Unpublished PhD thesis, AUT University, Auckland, New Zealand.

Turner, E. & Bitchener, J. (2008). An approach to teaching the writing of literature reviews. www.zeitschrift-schreiben.eu 11.6.2008 pp.1-10.

Turner, E. & Bitchener, J. (2006). Literature reviews and the concept of argument: Evaluating an EAL teaching approach. *New Zealand Studies in Applied Linguistics, 12* (2), 17-36.

Walker, I. (2012). An investigation of Malaysian ESL learners' self-perceptions about academic writing in English in higher learning institutions. Unpublished PhD thesis, University of Otago, Dunedin, New Zealand.

Wette, R. (2013). Teachers' practices and priorities in EAP writing instruction: Case studies from the New Zealand context. *The TESOLANZ Journal,* (21, 45-46).

Wette, R. (2014). Teachers' practices in EAP writing instruction: Use of models and modeling. *System.*

Wette, R. (2010). Evaluating student learning in a university-level EAP unit on writing using sources. *Journal of Second Language Writing, 19,* 158-177.

Wette, R. & Lessels, S. (2010). Completely different worlds? Writing in an EAP course and the transition to mainstream study. *The TESOLANZ Journal, 18,* 15-30.

Wigglesworth, G. & Storch, N. (2012). What role for collaboration in writing and writing feedback. *Journal of Second Language Writing, 21,* 364-37.

Chapter 9

EFL Writing in Poland, Where Traditional Does not Mean Current, but Current Means Traditional

Łukasz Salski

University of Łódź

Introduction

Poland's rich literary heritage includes four Nobel Prizes, which reflects the nation's 20th century history. In 1905, Henryk Sienkiewicz was awarded the Nobel Prize for his literary output in Polish. Such recognition must have been an important accomplishment for the author, who had written his historical novels "to uplift the hearts" of the oppressed compatriots, as well as a reason to be proud of for the whole nation. Then, Władysław Reymont's positivist portrayal of Polish rural and urban societies, earned him a Nobel in 1924. The poet Czesław Miłosz emigrated to the U.S. after World War II, where he taught Slavic languages and literatures at the University of California; so, you could say he got his Nobel as a representative of the generations of Polish emigrants. Finally, in 1996 Wisława Szymborska won a Nobel for poetry showing her "joy of writing" and uncommon "ability to preserve" common things in common language. Among accomplished Polish authors there is also Joseph Conrad, one of the world's best-known writers whose output was created in English as a second language. To me, it remains a mystery why a nation of such a rich literary tradition pays so little systematic attention to teaching writing—especially in its mother tongue, and has virtually no tradition of writing research. On the other hand, it has to be admitted that, relatively, much is being done in terms of instruction and research of writing in English as a foreign language in the Polish context; undoubtedly, this has been influenced by the tradition of teaching and researching writing in the English-speaking world.

In this paper, I sketch out the present day situation, as well as perspectives, of EFL writing practice and research in Poland. To delineate the immediate background, I start by characterizing the context of writing in Polish as L1. Then, I outline the status of EFL writing instruction. Finally, I refer to earlier EFL writing research, and discuss the most recent publications and studies in progress. The information for this report comes from my own observations and firsthand experience, as well as from an informal survey, which I carried out among colleagues researching EFL writing in Poland.

Teaching Writing in Polish

The attitude toward writing instruction has always been relatively loose and unregulated in Poland. Generally speaking, it seems to be assumed that development of native language writing skills at Polish schools should take care of itself. Some teachers apparently believe that it is not necessary to teach writing, that students can develop writing skills simply by being exposed to texts, so they rely on the learners' ability to pick up writing skills by osmosis. Generally, how much effort an individual student devotes to writing practice depends to a large extent on the teacher: on her individual beliefs and attitude. It is not surprising, then, that there are considerable differences between individual teachers' approaches. At one elementary or middle school some students may have hardly any writing practice in Polish, while others not only receive regular classroom assignments, but are also involved in writing for editing and publishing a school newsletter. The situation seems to call for a third category to be added to Hinds' (1987) division into reader- and writer-responsible languages, or cultures—unclear curricular goals with regard to writing skills development make writing in Polish clearly teacher-responsible.

In 1999 a major reform of the Polish education system was introduced. One of the important changes it brought about was in the format of the final school-leaving examination, which students take at the end of grade twelve, roughly at the age of nineteen. In the old format, the written examination in Polish required students to write a several-page-long essay on a topic typically based on obligatory readings from Polish literature and within the time limit of five hours. Preparation for such an examination required extensive writing practice throughout the years spent at school. The new system, on the other hand, requires students to take an examination in Polish at the end of each stage of education: elementary, middle, and high school. The examinations are similar in format and consist of a set of multiple choice questions and a short written assignment: a descriptive or narrative essay, or—in higher grades—a short literary analysis/critique. Since the examinations are administered and rated centrally, open tasks are kept to the absolute minimum, and rating them is regulated by a detailed key. As a result, students are openly told how to meet the requirements of the answer key, rather than to respond to the given topic, and definitely not to think critically or to make an argument. It is easy to imagine how eighteen-or nineteen-year-olds feel about having to write what they are supposed to write, instead of what they really think. On the other hand, preparation for the old exam format involved extensive practice, even if students were not taught about writing explicitly, and creating an extensive piece of text was challenging, both as a mental exercise and in terms of developing writing skills. Today, to be fair with their students, teachers tell them that being original is risky and does not pay, as it is an easy way to lose your points at the exam. It is not surprising, then, that some students report that even though they did enjoy writing at elementary school, when it was still at least a little creative, during high school they lost interest and motivation to write. This seems to be a high price to pay for a fairly objective centralized test.

Added to this is the way writing is taught. Polish education never took to the process approach in teaching writing. A typical classroom procedure consists in assigning and collecting a paper, and then grading and giving it back with little feedback. The common excuse for neglecting writing instruction is that it takes up precious class time as well as teachers' free time out of school. Also, the current core curriculum does oblige teachers to teach their students to write, other than for the respective school-final tests. Overall, it is not surprising that the general attitude toward writing is far from encouraging or even positive. With the advent of the new examination system, featuring numerous genres, more attention has been paid to genre-specific characteristics and requirements, possibly analyzing model texts, but typically writing instruction follows the current-traditional model, with most attention paid to content and orthographical accuracy.

EFL Writing in Poland

In Poland, English language instruction, and by the same token, English language writing is done in the foreign language mode. That is, English is not used for everyday communication outside the classroom. Apart from the obviously limited exposure to the target language input, this bears other consequences. Figure 1 shows a model of foreign language writing based on Matsuda's (1997) dynamic model of second language writing. I (Salski, 2011) call this model quasi-dynamic because, as can be seen, text production and reception are placed within the L1 speech community, and even though the L2 speech community typically provides genre characteristics, the audience and purpose are artificially provided by the task, rather than being inherent to the process of written communication and thus subject to negotiation. This characteristic of the EFL writing context is inevitable—except, perhaps, for those cases when EFL writers are taught by L2 native speaker instructors—and adds to the challenge of both learning and teaching to write in a foreign language.

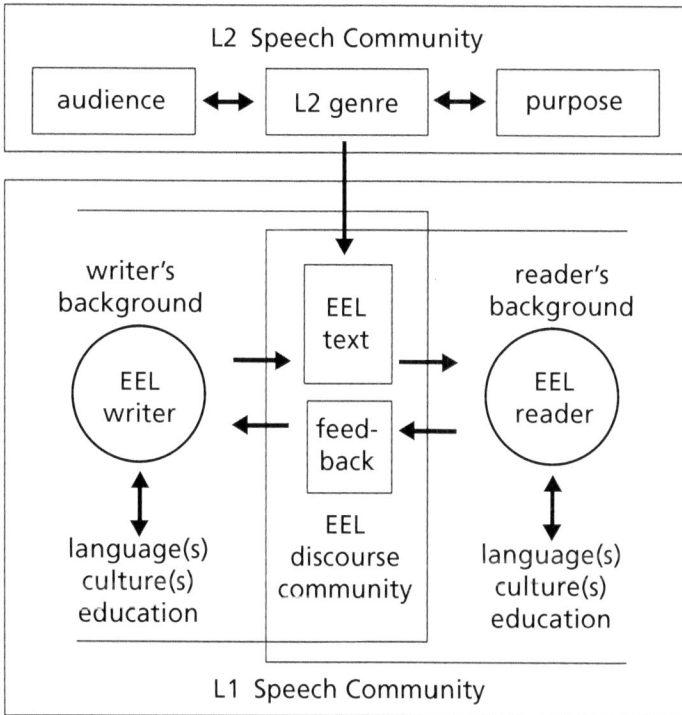

Figure 1. A quasi-dynamic model of EFL writing. Adapted from "The dynamic model of writing and its implications for the FL classroom" by Ł. Salski (2011), p. 58.

By law, all Polish children start learning a foreign language in grade one; for a vast majority of them, this language is English. The second foreign language begins obligatorily in grade seven, the first year of middle school, but some elementary schools introduce it in grade four or five. Teenagers continue to learn two foreign languages through high school, and all students take a school-final examination in one of them. Over ninety-five per cent of high school students study English, as an obligatory first or second foreign language, and most of them take the obligatory school-leaving foreign language exam in

English. The exam requires them, apart from other tasks, to write in English—depending on the level—a shorter or longer functional text (a note, email, letter), or a narrative, description or review. Nevertheless, writing in a foreign language—although formally required—is typically not taught systematically in Polish schools, either. Each teacher's approach is the effect of her or his own individual convictions, beliefs, attitude, or simply willingness to devote time to reading students' papers. On the other hand, university students majoring in English often admit that the first overt writing instruction they received was not in Polish, their native language, but in EFL. By saying this, at least some of them mean additional language courses rather than regular school classes. This can be partly attributed to the fact that these courses, run by private language schools, prepare students for English-language examinations, typically the Certificate in Advanced English, Certificate of Proficiency in English, and less often Cambridge First Certificate, which all include a writing section. It can also be assumed that increased attention paid to writing in EFL classes may partly result from English teachers' education and exposure to the attitude to writing characteristic of the English-language speech community. However, at this point I must mention being asked to give a workshop presentation on teaching foreign language writing to a group of school teachers. The host—an English-language teaching advisor from the local board of education—introduced me by telling the audience, "Dr. Salski will share with us a couple of ideas which can help keep students motivated to write. Well, this is a hard nut to crack because, as we all know, writing is boring." I do not think she was joking; certainly, the teachers in the audience just nodded with understanding.

At Polish colleges and universities there is typically no equivalent of the American freshman composition or first year writing course, neither is there any other class that focuses on the development of L1 writing skills. Even students of law, who—it would seem—should be able to write legal documents, are expected to pick up writing skills, rather than develop them in any systematic process. On the other hand, to be honest, it is unlikely that they will need to write much in their workplace, as they can now easily get electronic templates of all sorts of documents, which require only entering specific information in the otherwise complete text of the document. Still, for many Polish scholars in various disciplines, English is lingua franca which allows them to join international professional discourse communities (c.f. Duszak & Lewkowicz, 2008). So, while writing instruction in Polish may be lacking, courses in English academic writing are sometimes offered as electives to non-English majors (Sobejko, 2012).

In this system, university programs for foreign language majors are an exception, as they do get students to write; however, writing classes are typically treated there mainly as part of general language development programs. Yet, courses in academic writing are generally seen as necessary to prepare students to write their B.A. and M.A. theses in a foreign language, especially that their L1 writing skills are limited. What is more, inadequate writing skills may not be the only problem: having researched both Polish and American student writers and their writing, I have noticed that it is not only writing skills per se, but also attitudes and beliefs that are crucial for students' written performance. To help both with writing skills and attitudes, a completely new writing course was created at the Institute of English, University of Łódź, which aims at creating a positive attitude toward writing as well as at introducing basic academic writing skills (Reichelt, 2013).

The culture-specific beliefs and attitudes to writing seem to influence both instructors' and researchers' approaches. With little local interest in developing writing skills, it is not a coincidence that the first thorough and comprehensive report on the situation of teaching EFL writing in Poland was written by an American researcher, Melinda Reichelt (2005). Although the situation has changed since her article was published, it is still true that while teachers of Polish tend to focus on the content of the students' papers, Polish EFL teachers usually pay more attention to all aspects of language accuracy, as writing is seen mainly as a means of language practice. Also, the product approach still dominates at all levels of education, possibly with the exception of some university instructors and high school teachers—because of their experience of learning or teaching writing, or because they are familiar with and believe in a more process-oriented approach, and try to make a difference.

Writing Research in Poland

It seems that dominance of the product approach in EFL writing instruction in Polish schools and universities has shaped both students' attitudes and research directions. There is relatively little interest in Poland in teaching and researching writing, which may be caused by the fact that traditionally, at English departments, EFL writing has been taught by faculty specializing in literature, for whom literature remains the main academic interest. While a "literary approach to writing classes" (Majer, 2011) has its advantages, all aspects of language development have been traditionally associated with linguistics. Still, also among linguists, or even applied linguists, there are relatively few Polish scholars who see EFL writing as their main area of research. Also, it seems that the fact that the product remains the center of attention of writing students and instructors exerts its influence also on the way writing is researched, making text analysis, and hard-evidence quantitative research, appreciated more than elusive writing processes or intangible qualitative data.

In her 1996 book on contrastive rhetoric, Ulla Connor refers to only one Polish name—Jacek Fisiak. Professor Fisiak is, indeed, well-known in Poland for his studies in Polish-English contrastive linguistics, but his work has focused mainly on grammatical features of the languages rather than "thought patterns" or text analysis. However, a number of Polish-English contrastive rhetoric studies were carried out later. Anna Duszak of the University of Warsaw, has been interested in comparing Polish and English academic genres (Duszak, 1998); she has also (Duszak, 1997) supplemented Kaplan's (1966) set of "doodles" by adding a diagram illustrating typical development of argument in Polish (see Fig. 2). She finds Polish academic writing digressive, but she has also added "thematic detours and reformulations" that advance the flow of discourse only superficially by extending metacomments on contents that already stand in focus" (p. 329). She differentiates between:

- digressions proper, or text fragments less relevant to the main idea of the text, and
- elaborations, or explanations or reformulations of the subject matter, marked by the loops between individual moves of text.

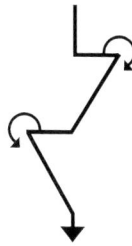

Figure 2. Digressive patterns in Polish. Adapted from *Culture and Styles of Academic Discourse* by A. Duszak (1997), p. 329.

Another name associated with Polish-English contrastive studies is Zosia Golebiowski of Deakin University, Australia. She has been involved in Polish-English contrastive rhetoric studies (Golebiowski, 1998, 2006, 2007), for which she has developed the Framework for the Analysis of the Rhetorical Structure of Text (FARS). FARS facilitates tracing relations between propositions and organizing them in functional categories. Each of the categories contains a number of specific types of relations, which complement the meaning of the text conveyed in the semantic load of the individual propositions. Using FARS, Golebiowski (2006) analyzed introductory paragraphs of Polish, English, and EFL academic journal articles in the field of sociology, and found a considerably higher level of complexity in texts written by Poles compared to their English counterparts.

My own research of personal narrative writing (Salski, 2012a) was inspired by readings of Duszak and Golebiowski. Having taught EFL writing for years, I expected contrastive rhetoric to provide me with an explanation of and solution to the problems I encountered in my students' writing. However, my study showed that students writing in Polish as L1 did not digress significantly more than Americans writing in English as L1; on the other hand, texts written by Poles in EFL contained more instances of digression of different kinds, and their digressive passages were on the average considerably longer than those in L1 texts. This led me to the conclusion that what accounts for the differences between how texts are written in English and in Polish is not so much prescriptive—at least to some extent—rhetoric, but incongruent attitudes to text, audience, and writing in general. In my further research I intend to pursue this theme. Naturally, additional difficulty also lies in the foreign language assignment itself—it requires student writers to focus not only the content and form of the text, but they also associate it with language practice and assessment.

Still, other rhetoric-related studies have been carried out. For example, Ola Majchrzak, a doctoral student and writing center tutor at University of Łódź has published an article (Majchrzak, 2012) on the influence of L2 writing experience on organizing formal letters in L1. Additionally, she has been interested in intercultural text features. Also, Iga Lehman of Academy of Sciences in Warsaw, has been interested in intercultural rhetoric—she has published on the topic of Polish-English contrastive rhetoric (Lehman, 2012a, 2012b, 2013), and her recent PhD "Co-Construction of authorial identity in student writing in Polish and English academic texts" has been one of the few dissertations within the area of composition studies in the country.

Other text-based studies have looked into problems of broadly understood language competence of Polish EFL writers. Ewa Witalisz of the Jagiellonian University of Cracow investigated L2 transfer (Witalisz, 2006). Findings of two other studies (Salski, 2007; Salski & Majer, 2006) point to considerable differences between Polish and English with regard to reader vs. writer responsibility. Moreover, Agata Klimczak (Warsaw University) analyzed the application of the genre approach in the Polish context (Klimczak, 2011). At this point it should be also acknowledged that the University of Opole Press has published two editions of an English-language academic writing textbook co-authored by Małgorzata Adams-Tukiendorf and Danuta Rydzak (2003, 2012).

Another area of text-oriented research is connected with the use of language corpora. For some years now the University of Łódź has been involved in a project called PELCRA (Polish and English Language Corpora for Research and Applications). While this project aims at research in linguistics, and relies on the British National Corpus and the Corpus of the Polish Language, it has recently branched out to create PLEC (PELCRA Learner English Corpus), which comprises spoken and written texts produced by Polish learners of English (Pęzik, 2012). Students majoring in English, and specializing in linguistics and TEFL, are not only involved in compiling the corpus, but also encouraged to use the material for their B.A. and M.A. projects. For example, Wodarczyk (2013), for his M.A., analyzed the use of linking expressions in academic texts written by Poles in English as a foreign language.

Clearly less research has been done in Poland into writing processes. The best-recognized name in this area is Jan Zalewski of the University of Opole, who has written articles on writing processes (Zalewski, 2001, 2002) and a book, *Epistemology of EFL Writing Processes* (Zalewski, 2004). Zalewski has also published on teaching academic writing (2009), the importance of the M.A. thesis requirement (2012), and the general condition of writing instruction in Poland (2011). Earlier, in the mid-1980s, two reports on studies investigating writing processes were published, both acknowledged by Tony Silva (1993) in his article on SL writing research. Skibniewski and Skibniewska (1986) analyzed composing processes of Polish intermediate and advanced learners of English writing in English and in Polish, and Skibniewski (1988) used behavior protocols to compare writing processes of advanced EFL writers writing in English and in Polish. More recently (Salski, 2012b), I used think-aloud protocols to look into individual student differences within their writing processes.

Other areas Polish researchers have looked into include creativity in writing, investigated as an individual difference by Małgorzata Adams-Tukiendorf of the University of Opole (Adams-Tukiendorf, 2011, 2012). On the other hand, Justyna Leśniewska and Ewa Witalisz of the Jagiellonian University in Cracow have been involved in a European project titled "Creative writing as a tool in second language teaching." In cooperation with Strathclyde University in Glasgow and Institut Supérieur des Sciences Humaines in Tunis, they investigate the effectiveness of including elements of creative writing into FL writing programs at the university level. As part of the project, a corpus of student written language is being created, with the view to allowing a number of different text-based studies, including L1 influence on FL written performance.

There are also EFL researchers who do not commit themselves specifically to the study of writing, but do not avoid it as they deal with teaching of all areas of language. For example, Olga Trendak (University of Łódź) is interested in language learning strategies, writing strategies among them (Trendak, 2013). Mirosław Pawlak's (Adam Mickiewicz University, Kalisz) wide scope of academic interests includes feedback on written work (Pawlak, 2014). Paweł Scheffler and Marcin Cinciała (Adam Mickiewicz University, Poznań) have contributed to the discussion on written error correction (Scheffler & Cinciała, 2011). Marcin Gliński (University of Silesia) has been interested in motivation and peer-assessment (Gliński, 2012a, 2012b).

It is particularly pleasing to acknowledge the growing interest with writing among university and high school EFL teachers. Determined to improve their classroom practice, they undertake their own EFL writing research, and pursue their PhDs. For instance, Barbara Gęsicka, a language teacher at a private high school in Łódź, provides her students with additional writing practice by encouraging them to write a blog and correspond by email. Monika Sobejko, an EFL instructor at the Jagiellonian University in Cracow, teaches an academic writing course for PhD students (Sobejko, 2012). Agnieszka Turzańska, a middle school teacher and a doctoral student at the University of Silesia, has just started researching learner journals.

Finally, it must be noted that with the realization of the fact that the profile of students at English departments has changed over the last ten years or so, writing centers started appearing. At the moment there are two writing centers operating at Polish universities. In the academic year 2011/2012 ERIC (English Writing Improvement Center) was created at the Institute of English, University of Łódź (Reichelt et al., 2013). With very limited resources, it operates mainly thanks to volunteer peer-tutors recruited from among graduate as well as strong undergraduate students, who can easily provide readership as well as advice to peers with weaker language and writing skills. In the following year, the writing center of the University of Silesia was created. Both owe a lot to scholars and English Teaching Assistants of the Fulbright program. At the moment, inspired by reports on English-language writing centers, the Institute of Romance Philology at the University of Wrocław, has started its own "centre d'écriture francaise." Being academic enterprises, writing centers strive not only to offer tutorials and writing workshops, but also promote the field of foreign language writing as an academic discipline among young and prospective researchers, who take active part in conferences and become members of professional organizations, such as the European Writing Centers Association.

Perspectives

Arguably, the main problem of FL/EFL writing in Poland is that it is not generally recognized as a unified field of study. Among Polish (applied) linguists, also those specializing in EFL, there are grammarians, phoneticians, contrastivists, even experts on computer applications in learning and teaching—but there are few researchers identifying with the field of writing research, or instruction. We are individuals scattered around the country, often not knowing about each other's research.

For this reason, the present report on the current state of EFL writing research in Poland cannot be complete, as some of the work is done locally, not only as Ph.D., but also M.A. projects with which scholars from other universities may be unfamiliar. Therefore, one of the priorities is to ensure a better sense of community of FL, or at least EFL, writing researchers. With this idea in mind, the Department of Psycholinguistics and English Language Teaching, University of Łódź, started a conference devoted to foreign language writing theory, research, and practice. The biannual conference is called FLOW (Foreign Language Opportunities in Writing), and so far it has had three editions with such distinguished guests as (in order of appearance) Tatyana Yakhontova (Ivan Franko University of Lviv, Ukraine), Ann Mott (American University of Paris, France; then chair of the European Writing Centers Association), Jan Zalewski (University of Opole, Poland), Mirosław Pawlak (Adam Mickiewicz University, Kalisz, Poland), Melinda Reichelt (University of Toledo, USA), Tony Silva, Margie Berns and Linda Bergmann (Purdue University, USA). We hope that a specific-theme conference may serve integrating a small and dispersed community better than bigger events, such as the annual Conference on Second/Foreign Language Acquisition and Learning at the University of Silesia, which usually feature some presentations devoted to writing anyway, plus cover other areas of language studies. However, scholars not limiting themselves to writing may prefer the latter, as they give a better picture of the development of the vast fields of EFL instruction and research. Needless to say, Polish researchers also take part in international conferences, the Symposium on Second Language Writing, the European Association for the Teaching of Academic Writing, the European Writing Centers Association, and the Teaching English Academic Writing, Writing SIG.

To get a better understanding of the needs and perspectives of the field, I asked my colleagues what they saw as priorities and goals of EFL research in Poland. My respondents suggested continuing intercultural rhetoric studies, mutual L1 and L2 influences in writing, writer identity in academic writing, analyzing L2 writer needs, as well as—more practically—propagating the process approach to FL writing and investigating writing processes, raising students' awareness of differences in academic conventions, and improving EFL teacher education to give novice teachers a better understanding of and confidence in teaching writing. All these directions seem very appropriate, and reflect not only individual interests of the respondents, but also their understanding of the specific needs of Polish EFL student writers.

Conclusion

It seems that the rich Polish literary tradition has had little influence on how writing in Polish as L1 is currently taught. Yet, in spite of the fact that writing instruction in Polish is often neglected and typically relies on outdated current-traditional methodology, EFL writing in Poland is a growing field. Because of the differences in rhetorical patterns and reader/writer roles between Polish and English, and clearly thanks to the contact with the English-language tradition, EFL writing in Poland is a developing field, with devoted practitioners and researchers, with a wide range of interests, and representing numerous academic centers. The field has a clear agenda for the nearest future, based on solid understanding of its peculiarity, as well as on good international contacts and models. It is particularly rewarding to see that English-language writing instruction and studies have started influencing other foreign language writing practices.

What EFL writing in Poland needs most now is recognition of the general academic community that it is a fully legitimate area not only of specialized language instruction, but also of interdisciplinary research. Some time ago, I met with a colleague, also a graduate of an English department, whom I had not seen for some time. Inevitably, we started talking about what we did professionally,

"So you are at the university. Interesting. What's your field?"

"Writing," I said.

"Oh, you are a writer! What do you write? Novels? Poetry?"

"Well, not exactly. I look into how Poles learn to write in English."

"So you write text books, is that right?"

"No, no. I mean I research how people write in English."

"Oh, now I got you. English spelling can be tricky."

My hope is that, with the constant, or even growing, need for writing skills in the modern international community, composition studies will strengthen its position as a well-established field of study; and that Polish EFL writing research will become a recognized area of current academic research, as it can give a nation with a strong literary tradition means of efficient intercultural communication.

References

Adams-Tukiendorf, M. (2011). Why do less creative writers write longer texts? In J. Majer & Ł. Salski (Eds.), *Foreign Language Opportunities in Writing* (pp. 125-144). Łódź: Łódź University Press.

Adams-Tukiendorf, M. (2012). Students' creative potential and their academic writing: Stable aspect in variable context. In E. Piechurska-Kuciel & L. Piasecka (Eds.), *Variability and Stability in Foreign and Second Language Learning Contexts,* Vol. 2. (pp. 160-186). Newcastle upon Tyne: Cambridge Scholars Publishing.

Adams-Tukiendorf, M. & Rydzak, D. (2003). *Developing Writing Skills. Manual for EFL Students.* Opole: Wydawnictwo Uniwersytetu Opolskiego.

Adams-Tukiendorf, M. & Rydzak, D. (2012). *Developing Writing Skills. Manual for EFL Students* (2nd Edition). Opole: Wydawnictwo Uniwersytetu Opolskiego.

Duszak, A. (1997). Cross-cultural academic communication: a discourse-community view. In A. Duszak (Ed.), *Culture and Styles of Academic Discourse* (pp. 11-39). Berlin: Mouton de Gruyter.

Duszak, A. (1998). Academic writing in English and Polish: Comparing and subverting genres. *International Journal of Applied Linguistics, 8*(2), 191-213.

Duszak, A. & Lewkowicz, J. (2008). Publishing academic texts in English: A Polish perspective. *Journal of English for Academic Purposes, 7*(2), 108-120.

Gliński, M. (2012a). The affective role of peer review in the development of autonomous writing skills. *The Teacher, 10*(102), n.p.

Gliński, M. (2012b). Teaching writing to young students: changing theory into practice. *The Teacher, 12*(104), n.p.

Golebiowski, Z. (2006). Globalisation of academic communities and the style of research reporting: the case of a sociology research article. *Transcultural Studies: A Series in Interdisciplinary Research* (Vol. 1), pp. 57-72.

Golebiowski, Z. (2007). What organising strategies do academic writers use? A Polish-English study. In J. Arabski (Ed.), *On Foreign Language Acquisition and Effective Learning* (pp. 171-182). Katowice: Wydawnictwo Uniwersytetu Śląskiego.

Golebiowski, Z. (1998). Rhetorical approaches to scientific writing: An English-Polish contrastive study. *Text-interdisciplinary Journal for the Study of Discourse, 18*(1), 67-102.

Hinds, J. (1987). Reader vs. writer responsibility: A new typology. In U. Connor & R. B. Kaplan (Eds.), *Writing Across Languages: Analysis of L2 Text* (pp. 141-152). Reading, MA: Addison-Wesley.

Klimczak, A. (2011). Genre approach to teaching formal letter writing. In J. Majer & Ł. Salski (Eds.), *Foreign Language Opportunities in Writing* (pp. 205-212). Łódź: Łódź University Press.

Lehman, I. M. (2012a). Patterns of cultural differences that affect second-language writing. *Kwartalnik Neofilologiczny*, 1/12. Warszawa: Polish Academy of Sciences.

Lehman, I. M. (2012b). Discourse in a culturally diverse classroom. *Kwartalnik Neofilologiczny*, 4 /12. Warszawa: Polish Academy of Sciences.

Lehman, I. M. (2013). From contrastive rhetoric to intercultural rhetoric: Why intercultural rhetoric needs to reframe the concept of culture. In Ł. Salski & W. Szubko-Sitarek (Eds.), *Perspectives on Foreign Language Learning* (pp. 31-47). Łódź: Wydawnictwo Uniwersytetu Łódzkiego.

Majchrzak, O. (2012). Wpływ języka drugiego na redagowanie listów formalnych w języku ojczystym—element strukturalne listu. *Rozprawy Humanistyczne* (Vol. 14). Włocławek: Wydawnictwo Naukowe PWSZ we Włocławku.

Majer, K. (2011). In the beginning there was the sentence: A few remarks on a literary approach to writing classes. In J. Majer & Ł. Salski (Eds.), *Foreign Language Opportunities in Writing* (pp. 197-204). Łódź: Łódź University Press.

Majer, J. & Salski, Ł. (2011). *Foreign Language Opportunities in Writing*. Łódź: Łódź University Press.

Matsuda, P. K. (1997). Contrastive rhetoric in context: A dynamic model of L2 writing. *Journal of Second Language Writing, 6*(1), 45-60.

Pawlak, M. (2014). The role of written corrective feedback in promoting language development: An overview. In W. Szubko-Sitarek, Ł. Salski & P. Stalmaszczyk (Eds.), *Language, Discourse and Communication: Studies in Honor of Jan Majer* (pp. 3-21). Cham: Springer International Publishing.

Pęzik, P. (2012). Towards the PELCRA learner English corpus. In P. Pęzik (Ed.), *Corpus Data Across Languages and Disciplines, Łódź Studies in Language* (Vol. 28). Frankfurt am Main: Peter Lang.

Reichelt, M. (2005). English-language writing instruction in Poland. *Journal of Second Language Writing, 4*, 215-232.

Reichelt, M. (2013). English-language writing instruction in Poland: Adapting to the local EFL context. In O. Majchrzak (Ed.), *PLEJ_2 czyli Psycholingwistyczne Eksploracje Językowe* (pp. 25-42). Łódź: Łódź University Press.

Reichelt, M., Salski, Ł., Andres, J., Lowczowski, E., Majchrzak, O., Molenda, M., Parr-Modrzejewska, A., Reddington, E. & Wiśniewska-Steciuk, E. (2013). A table and two chairs: Starting a writing center in Łódź, Poland. *Journal of Second Language Writing, 22*(3), 277-285.

Salski, Ł. (2007). Reader and writer responsibility: Relevance for teaching English composition to Polish EFL students. In P. Stalmaszczyk & I. Witczak-Plisiecka (Eds.), *PASE Studies in Linguistics* (pp. 255-261). Łódź: Łódź University Press.

Salski, Ł. (2011). The dynamic model of writing and its implications for the FL classroom. In J. Majer & Ł. Salski (Eds.), *Foreign Language Opportunities in Writing* (pp. 53-60). Łódź: Łódź University Press.

Salski, Ł. (2012a). *Contrastive Rhetoric in Teaching English Composition Skills.* Łódź: Łódź University Press.

Salski, Ł. (2012b). Głosy w procesie pisania. *Rozprawy Humanistyczne* (*Vol. 13*). (pp. 141-157). Włocławek: Wydawnictwo Naukowe PWSZ we Włocławku.

Salski, Ł. & Majer, J. (2006). The role of formal schemata in teaching English composition to Polish learners. *Rozprawy Humanistyczne* (Vol. 6. pp. 55-67). Włocławek: Wydawnictwo Naukowe PWSZ we Włocławku.

Scheffler, P. & Cinciała, M. (2011). Explicit vs. implicit grammar knowledge in written grammar correction. In J. Majer & Ł. Salski (Eds.), *Foreign Language Opportunities in Writing* (pp. 61-77). Łódź: Łódź University Press.

Silva, T. (1993). Toward an understanding of the distinct nature of L2 writing: The ESL research and its implications. *TESOL Quarterly, 27*(4), 657-675.

Skibniewski, L. (1988). The writing processes of advanced foreign language learners in their native and foreign languages: Evidence from think-aloud and behavior protocols. *Studia Anglica Posnaniensia, 21*, 177-186.

Skibniewski, L. & Skibniewska M. (1986). Experimental study: The writing processes of intermediate/advanced foreign language learners in their foreign and native languages. *Studia Anglica Posnaniensia, 19,* 143-163.

Sobejko, M. (2012). English for research paper writing: Some practical aspects of teaching writing to doctoral students. *Zeszyty Glottodydaktyczne, 4,* 11-17.

Trendak, O. (2013). Writing strategies employed by advanced learners of English—a questionnaire study. In Ł. Salski & W. Szubko-Sitarek (Eds.), *Perspectives on Foreign Language Learning* (pp. 49-67). Łódź: Wydawnictwo Uniwersytetu Łódzkiego.

Witalisz, E. (2006). Transfer in L2 writing: Linguistic competence vs. composing skills. *Studia Linguistica Universitatis Iagiellonicae Cracoviensis, 123,* 169-178.

Wodarczyk, Ł. (2013). A quantitative corpus-based analysis of linking adverbials in students' academic writing. In Ł. Salski & W. Szubko-Sitarek (Eds.), *Perspectives on Foreign Language Learning* (pp. 69-86). Łódź: Wydawnictwo Uniwersytetu Łódzkiego.

Zalewski, J. (2001). Teaching and learning to revise: A rationale for a process-oriented writing assignment. In J. Arabski (Ed.), *Research on Foreign Language Acquisition* (pp. 33-39). Katowice: Wydawnictwo Uniwersytetu Śląskiego.

Zalewski, J. (2002). Peer-respondent and reviser roles in EFL composition: A case study of two university students. In A. Niżegorodcew (Ed.), *Beyond L2 Teaching: Research Studies in Second Language Acquisition* (pp. 53-61). Kraków: Wydawnictwo Uniwersytetu Jagiellońskiego.

Zalewski, J. (2004). *Epistemology of the Composing Process: Writing in English for General Academic Purposes*. Opole: Wydawnictwo Uniwersytetu Opolskiego.

Zalewski, J. (2009). Beyond surface mannerisms in teaching and learning academic discourse. In J. Zalewski (Ed.), *Language, Cognition and Society* (pp. 147-155). Opole: Wydawnictwo Uniwersytetu Opolskiego.

Zalewski, J. (2011). Beyond foreign language writing instruction: The need for literacy pedagogy. In J. Majer & Ł. Salski (Eds.), *Foreign Language Opportunities in Writing* (pp. 5-19). Łódź: Łódź University Press.

Zalewski, J, (2012). Why have our students write master's theses: Variable academic environment versus stable literacy goals. In E. Piechurska-Kuciel & L. Piasecka (Eds.), *Variability and Stability in Foreign and Second Language Learning Contexts Vol. 2.* (pp. 266-282). Newcastle: Cambridge Scholars Publishing.

Chapter 10

The Hole in the Donut: The Shape of Second-Language Writing Studies in Sweden

Diane Pecorari

Linnaeus University

Introduction

In many parts of the world, second-language (L2) writing is a well-established research area, as other contributions to this volume have demonstrated. In Sweden,[1] by contrast, the situation is rather different. Indeed, as the title of this chapter suggests, the status of L2 writing studies in Sweden is easier to describe in terms of what is absent rather than what is present. In this chapter the basis for this claim is first presented, followed by some of the reasons for it. The chapter concludes with comments on future directions.

Metrics of Engagement

Two metrics are good indicators of the extent of Swedish activity in L2 writing research. The first of these is the level of published research output

---

1 Although this chapter is concerned with Sweden, the situation in the rest of the Nordic region is broadly similar.

from Sweden. The flagship publication in the field is the *Journal of Second Language Writing* (*JSLW*). Volumes 1 through 22 of *JSLW* contained 303 research articles with 401 authors.[1] Of those, three articles had authors with institutional affiliations in Sweden. One—the earliest—had a single author, while the other two had two co-authors each, one of whom was the author of the first article, for a total of five authorship credits to four individual researchers.

An examination of other journals in which L2 writing research is published yields a similar figure. A search on the archives of *Applied Linguistics,* and on Science Direct, which catalogues journals such as *Journal of English for Academic Purposes* and *Assessing Writing*, returns 49 research articles which have "second-language writing" as a keyword, excluding articles which appeared in *JSLW*. Just one article has authors—two—with institutional affiliations in Sweden, one of whom is an author of one of the *JSLW* articles. To judge by internationally published research output, research in L2 writing is conducted in Sweden by a small number of individuals.

It is of course true that Sweden is a relatively small country, with a population of fewer than 10 million. The fact that there are relatively few individuals working in L2 writing studies in the country could be an artefact of the small population. However, by way of comparison, New Zealand, with a population of approximately 4.4 million, is represented by fourteen authorship credits in these outlets.

Another indication of research activity is a national database of research output from Swedish universities. In principle there is an expectation from university administration that all research works, ranging from the undergraduate dissertation to the doctoral thesis to the publications and

---

1 Some authors, naturally, have contributed more than one article to *JSLW*. This figure is the number of authorship credits on research articles rather than the number of discrete individuals. This method of calculating research output has limitations, one of which is that it overlooks mobility. All of the Swedish researchers included in these numbers have other output which has resulted from research conducted at universities outside Sweden. Authors' affiliation is however the best (if imperfect) indication of research activity in a given geographical area.

conference papers of university teaching staff, will be included in the DiVA database. However, like journal tables of contents, DiVA shows little activity in this research area. A search for L2 writing as a keyword, using all reasonable permutations of spelling and language (e.g., *second language writing, L2 writing*, the Swedish term *andraspråksskrivande*) produces only eight hits; that is, eight research publications that give L2 writing as a keyword.

This measure, too, is imperfect, in part because authors can fail to include potentially relevant keywords. In addition, DiVA's coverage is not complete. The database has existed since the beginning of the 21st century but some researchers have entered their earlier publications, while others have not, and some are more meticulous than others about entering newly published work. However, if the raw numbers are likely to underestimate the number of publications on the topic, the reasons for that underrepresentation affect all research topics, and presumably in approximately equal measure, so it is once again possible to gain a sense of the relative strength of L2 writing studies in Sweden by comparing it to other research areas. Repeating the same keyword search, "sociolinguistics" generates 129 hits and "discourse analysis" 1,476.

It is thus evident that Swedish researchers are not conspicuous by their numbers in the international L2 writing community, and that L2 writing does not occupy a prominent position as a research area within the language studies community in Sweden. It is therefore necessary to conclude that L2 writing research does not thrive in Sweden as it does in, for example, the United States. The reasons for this state of affairs are instructive and have significant implications for the future of the research area, within Sweden and without.

Different Landscapes

One reason for the relatively low degree of activity in L2 writing studies lies in the fact that the academic climate is very different in Sweden than in the places where L2 writing research emerged and has thrived historically. A "parent discipline" of the field is the North American composition studies tradition. This tradition is closely implicated in the English for Academic Purposes (EAP) movement (Silva & Leki, 2004), which is prominent in the UK and in countries, like Australia and New Zealand, which have been influenced by the UK. In this sense, L2 writing studies is very much a child of the Anglophone university.

University education in the United States is characterized by the liberal arts curriculum, one feature of which is the widespread use of writing tasks for assessment purposes. The ability to write is an inescapable necessity for all students, and the composition classroom, equipping students with writing skills, developed as the logical concomitant. When international students arrived at US universities in significant numbers, it eventually became clear that their needs were not adequately met by the first-year writing courses provided for domestic students and the teaching of second-language writing emerged (Matsuda, 1999).

Although the first-year writing classroom is not a standard feature of university education in most of the rest of the English-speaking inner circle, international students are, and their need for English language support resulted in English for Academic Purposes programs. The absence of the liberal arts curriculum in countries like the United Kingdom means that assessment of writing is done in "content" courses, giving rise to the concern with disciplinary and generic differences which is so prominent in EAP research, but the basic objective of preparing students for writing assessment tasks is present.

A difference therefore among the English-speaking countries with a significant L2 writing research community is the status of writing instruction more generally: in the US, L2 writing instruction sprang up to provide international students with something equivalent to that which their domestic student counterparts already had, while elsewhere it was an "extra" offered to international students to level the playing field by supporting them in tasks which domestic students were presumed to be equipped to do. The common element across these contexts is that the presence of international students created a demand for instruction, and the teaching of academic writing produced a corollary supply of practice-based research questions to investigate.

As a result of this development, L2 writing studies has inherited two biases. The first is that it is primarily concerned with academic writing. By way of illustrating this point, the program of the 2013 Symposium on Second Language Writing included 134 papers apart from the plenary addresses, and in only five cases do the abstracts specify that the presentation would report a study with a focus on non-university-level or non-academic writing. Academic writing is thus the mainstay of L2 writing studies, and this is the case because, as noted above, the research field has its origins in a particular language-learning context.

However, the Swedish context is very different. The liberal arts curriculum is not a feature of Swedish higher education. Nor is there an equivalent of freshman composition or, more generally, any widespread practice of teaching students to write in their disciplines. Instruction in how to write academic texts is provided unevenly across the university, and when present is frequently perfunctory, often presented in the form of handbooks providing declarative rules for formatting rather than structured, process-oriented instruction in the skills of academic writing. This is as true for Swedish L1 speakers studying in their first language as it is for second language users.

Nor has Sweden traditionally received large numbers of international students, although this situation is rapidly changing. Thus, the factors which created a void for L2 writing studies to fill in the English-speaking world have not obtained in Sweden.

A second bias in L2 writing research is that English is, overwhelmingly, the L2. Returning to the program for the 2013 Symposium on Second Language Writing, only one abstract deals with a second language other than English.[1]

---

1 Ninety-two of the 132 papers explicitly identified English as the target language. A number of the other 39 papers dealt with topics such as theoretical issues rather than any specific L2. It is possible that some of the remainder dealt with an L2 other than English but did not explicitly say so in the abstract. However, in most cases all indications are that English was indeed the L2 under investigation.

This is a natural result given the origins of the field as outlined above, which have been very much in the English-speaking world. The linguistic situation in Sweden is, however, more complex.

Accepting for the moment the emphasis on academic writing, it is worth noting that English is the global lingua franca for academia as for all else. As a result, English is prominent in academic life in Sweden, and academics in Sweden, from the postgraduate level upward, need to write a wide range of texts in English. Academic researchers publish almost exclusively in English (apart from rare exceptions such as Scandinavian studies; see Fredrickson & Swales, 1992), for the same reason which causes academics all over the world to do so: impact depends on visibility. In addition, a large number of master's and PhD programs, and a small but increasing number of undergraduate[s] courses, are taught entirely or partially through the medium of English, meaning that a significant and growing number of assessment genres, including the high-stakes thesis, are done in English.

This situation is one which might be expected to lead naturally to a demand for L2 writing instruction, and indeed there are indications that that will be a growing trend in the future. For example, the Centre for Academic English at Stockholm University offers courses on writing theses and research articles. However, it is a minority of the university's postgraduates who enroll in such courses. The Centre is unique in Sweden and is less than ten years old at time of writing. The provision of L2 writing instruction is thus a relatively recent and still not widespread phenomenon in Sweden despite the fact that there is a growing need for it.

One reason for this apparently contradictory situation has to do with the special status of English in Sweden. As a small country with aspirations of a presence on the international stage, Sweden has long prioritized the teaching of English. It is a compulsory subject from the early primary school years and a prerequisite for admission to any university course. As a result, there is a widespread expectation of English competence, encapsulated in the commonplace phrase *alla kan ju engelska*—"after all, everyone knows English."

In most vocational and professional sectors, job-related competence involves the ability to perform key activities in English if circumstances dictate. Because English is both a mandatory part of the national school curriculum and a requirement for university admissions, there is an administrative assumption that university students can cope with performing academic tasks, including writing, in English. Somewhat paradoxically, then, the strong status of English in Sweden has worked to stunt the development of EAP instruction at Swedish universities. If *alla kan ju engelska,* then what necessity is there to take subject-related content out of the curriculum in order to teach that which everyone is expected to be able to do?

It is important to note that the expectation that university students have the required English skills to perform academic tasks in English is optimistic rather than realistic. Recent research (e.g., Airey, 2009; Björkman, 2010; Pecorari, Shaw, Malmström & Irvine, 2011; Shaw & McMillion, 2008) has demonstrated limitations on the abilities of Swedish university students to perform in English as easily as they could in Swedish, and/or on their perceptions of their ability to do so. A particularly vulnerable group are immigrants and Generation 1.5 students. Sixteen percent of Sweden's population was born abroad (Statistikcentralbyrån, 2014). They, and their children born in Sweden, are at a disadvantage in several respects compared to their native Swedish counterparts. First and most obviously is that for non-native speakers of Swedish, all writing tasks—whether in Swedish or in English—are done in an L2, and given that Swedish speakers have comparatively strong skills in English, from an international perspective, the use of English—which is an L2 for everyone—does not necessarily level the playing field for immigrants. In addition, a significant proportion of immigrants are refugees, from countries such as Iraq and Afghanistan, and may have limited literacy in their L1. While these groups are unlikely to study at university level, their children may, and they may well lack the academic advantages that growing up in a household which emphasizes literacy can confer.

There is therefore clearly a large constituency which could benefit from L2 writing instruction in English, and a smaller but significant group which could additionally benefit from L2 writing instruction in Swedish. However, the lack of a tradition in first-language writing instruction has stunted the development of L2 writing as a pedagogical field, and has therefore not yielded a need for an applications-based companion research field. As a result, the trajectory which resulted in a community of L2 writing researchers in the US and elsewhere has not been matched in Sweden. That offers a partial explanation for the relative underrepresentation of L2 writing studies in Sweden. Another powerful factor is described in the next section.

Is This Our Kind of Place?

Having described the field of L2 writing studies as sparsely populated in Sweden, I would like to emphasize that it is not a population of zero. This demonstrates that L2 writing research can be meaningfully done in the Swedish context. In the previous section I advanced one explanation for the paucity of research, namely that the context was not conducive to the development of the Anglophone L2 writing research agenda. An additional reason lies in perceptions of disciplinary affiliations. That is, there are in fact researchers investigating questions with a very real and close relationship to L2 writing, but who do not perceive themselves as members of the L2 writing community—or indeed are possibly not aware that there *is* an L2 writing community.

For example, Sundberg (2006) is a discussion of the problem of assessing texts produced by writers who have learned Swedish as an L2 as adults, and who have, as a result, an organization and rhetorical structure that outstrips their lexico-syntactic accuracy. Forsberg and Bartning (2010) is a study of formulaic language in the written production of L1 Swedish speakers learning French as L2. Nelson's (2010) doctoral thesis, *Second language speakers at work: A sociolinguistic study of communication in a major Swedish company* is an articulate and insightful report of a study of five second-language users of Swedish in the workplace. Both their oral and their written communication is studied and the conclusions from this research provide valuable indications for ways in which education and introduction to the workplace can improve the conditions for L2 users.

Yet none of these works is identified with "second language writing" as a keyword, which can be taken as an indication that the authors do not see their work as being situated in the field. Nor do they cite any articles from *JSLW*, which is an indication that they do not see the potential for L2 writing research to inform their work. Nor would it be easy to claim that they are wrong. Although all three of these works—along with others which could be named— are investigations of aspects of writing in a second language, they have foci which differ from the "mainstream" L2 writing research concern with academic writing in English.

As noted above, L2 writing studies has had a heavy emphasis on academic writing, and Belcher (2012; 2013) points out that this emphasis has been at the expense of areas, such as young learners and adult learners outside of academic contexts, which are worthy of investigation. Researchers whose work is set in those or other contexts will find little in the pages of *JSLW* or in the program of the Symposium on Second Language Writing which they would find directly citable, or which would make them identify themselves as part of that research community.

It is not of course my contention that the L2 writing community has actively sought to exclude any of these interests; however, by exploring a rather tight range of research topics, the field has constructed for itself a homogeneous identity. Researchers with interests from outside of this narrow area may perceive that their work does not fit the profile of L2 writing research, and consequently may not identify themselves with this field.

It is now possible to observe that the metaphor in the title of this paper is to some extent an example of hyperbole rather than literal truth. There is *not* the absolute absence of L2 writing in Sweden which the image of the hole in the donut suggests. There is, however, an absence of a sense of an L2 writing community, and that is due to two factors: the researchers working in the area are relatively few in number; and many of them do not identify themselves as part of the research community.

Does It Matter?

Of course, it would be possible to argue that in a research area which has sprung from the practical needs of a community of language users, a narrow focus is an asset, or at least a sign of an appropriate degree of specialization. If Swedish applied linguists—apart from a few—see their work as having a natural home elsewhere, perhaps they are the best judges of an unproblematic situation. From the manifest success of L2 writing research, as evidenced in signs such as a successful journal and a symposium, both of longstanding, and large numbers of PhDs in the area, it is tempting to conclude that it doesn't matter to the field of L2 writing studies very much; the research area is managing to get along quite nicely without significant Swedish involvement in quantitative terms.

There are, however, several problematic aspects to this situation. For the reasons described above, it is clear how Sweden avoided developing a significant body of teaching on L2 writing in academic circles, and thus avoided developing a pool of researchers working in the area, but it is not at all clear that that focus is not needed. The fact that the situation is additionally complex, with a significant proportion of university students writing in Swedish as L2 and another writing in English as L2, suggests that the need to understand the issues these constituencies face and effective strategies for addressing them is pressing. It would be beneficial both in research and in teaching if the traditional, core interests of L2 writing research were more prominent in Sweden.

However, I've also argued that part of the issue is that researchers working outside of the traditional mainstream do not perceive themselves as part of an L2 writing community. This is symptomatic of a wider problem: in focusing on a relatively narrow set of core concerns, many topics have been left unresearched. By expanding from the traditional focus on academic English, the L2 writing community could significantly expand its impact. At the same time, if L2 writing researchers create a wider space, it will allow new members to move into it more comfortably. The result then could be that the hole in the donut turns into a rich, nourishing stew simmering in a cauldron of activity.

References

Airey, J. (2009). *Science, Language & Literacy Case Studies of Learning Swedish University Physics.* Uppsala: Uppsala Universitet.

Björkman, B. (2010). Spoken lingua franca English at a Swedish technical university: An investigation of form and communicative effectiveness. Doctoral Thesis. Stockholm: Stockholm Studies in English.

Forsberg, F. & Bartning, I. (2010). Can linguistic features discriminate between the communicative CEFR-levels?—A pilot study of written L2 French. In I. Bartning, M. Martin & I. Vedder (Eds.), *Eurosla Monograph Series 1* (pp. 133-158). European Second Language Association.

Fredrickson, K. M. & Swales, J. M. (1992). Competition and discourse community: Introductions from Nysvenska Studier. In B-L Gunnarsson, P. Linell & B. Nordberg (Eds.), *Text and Talk in Professional Contexts: Selected Papers from the International Conference "Discourse and the Professions",* (pp. 9-21). Uppsala, 26-29 August, 1992. Uppsala: Association of Applied Linguistics.

Matsuda, P. K. (1999). Composition Studies and ESL Writing: A disciplinary division of labor. *College Composition and Communication, 50,* 699-721.

Nelson, M. (2010). *Andraspråkstalare i arbete: En språkvetenskaplig studie av kommunikation vid ett svenskt storföretag.* Uppsala universitet, Uppsala.

Pecorari, D., Shaw, P., Malmström, H. & Irvine, A. (2011). English Textbooks in Parallel-Language Tertiary Education. *TESOL Quarterly, 45,* 313-333.

Sundberg, G. (2006) Att bedöma and raspråkstexter. In O. Josephson, Å. Af Geijerstam, J. Wiksten Folkeryd, C. Nyström Höög & M. Reichenberg (Eds.), (pp. 102-110). *Textvård: Att läsa, skriva och bedöma texter.* Stockholm: Norstedts,

Shaw, P. & McMillion, A. (2008). Proficiency effects and compensation in advanced second-language reading. *Nordic Journal of English Studies, 7*(3), 123-143.

Silva, T. & Leki, I. (2004). Family matters: The influence of applied linguistics and composition studies on second language writing studies: Past, present, and future. *The Modern Language Journal, 88,* 1-13.

Statistikcentralbyråns (n.d.) Retrieved from http://www.scb.se/sv_/Hitta-statistik/Statistikdatabasen/TabellPresentation/?layout=tableViewLayout1 &rxid=74291870-a0d8-4a11-9e9c-0ab04552c9f9

Chapter 11

Foreign Language Writing in Ukraine: Indefinite Past but Promising Future?

Tatyana Yakhontova

Ivan Franko National University of L'viv

Introduction

Ukraine is a relatively newly independent state. It has distinct cultural traditions and a complicated past marked by various external influences and continuous struggle for independence. In 1989, Ukraine started to develop a democratic society based on the transformations of all spheres of life. Nowadays it is a country generally oriented toward Euro-integration and Westernization of educational policies and standards. This orientation stimulates the interest of Ukrainian educators and researchers in the field of second and foreign language writing which has attracted little attention in the recent past.

The purpose of this paper is to show how pedagogical and scholarly approaches to second language writing, quite new for the Ukrainian context, slowly but steadily pave their way to the education and scholarship of the country. The paper will begin with the explanation of the language situation in Ukraine, followed by the description of its language teaching system, clarification of Ukrainian culture-specific vision of writing in theoretical and applied perspectives, the analysis of new and unique, for the country, pedagogical activities related to teaching English academic writing, a summary of the emerging Ukrainian research in the area of foreign language writing, and, finally, by the outline of appropriate future prospects.

Language Situation in Ukraine

The Ukrainian language is the only official language of the country. It belongs to the group of East Slavic languages (together with Russian and Belarusian) and uses the Cyrillic alphabet derived from the Greek script and named in honor of the two Byzantine Greek brothers, Saints Cyril and Methodius. Ukrainian shares syntactical structures with the Russian language but differs lexically.

Despite the prevalence of the official language, the general language situation in Ukraine is rather complicated. Ukrainian is dominant in the western parts of the country, which, historically, were largely influenced by European culture and managed to preserve a strong national identity and language even being under the rule of Poland (in different periods of history) and the Austro-Hungarian Empire (in the 19th century). In the eastern and southern parts of the country, which were part of the Russian Empire and were essentially russified, the Russian language is mostly spoken. In the center of the country, Russian prevails in the cities; Ukrainian, in the villages. Overall, according to the 2010 data, 65% of the citizens of Ukraine considered Ukrainian as their native language, while 33% identified themselves as native speakers of Russian. There are also speakers of other tongues who live in certain regions of Ukraine and represent national minorities, most prominent of them being Poles, Belarusians, Romanians, Bulgarians and Hungarians.

It is interesting to consider the role of Ukrainian and Russian in the country through the prism of the terms "a first language," "a second language," and "a foreign language." In fact, many residents of the country, especially from mixed families, actively use both languages and perceive them as their first languages. At the same time, for many native speakers of Russian living in the country, Ukrainian is a second language, that is the language "existentially important for the person in question, who needs it in order to be able to live life as a participating citizen in society with all that that entails" (Risager, 2007, p. 70). For Ukrainians living in the east, in the russified territories of the country, Russian performs the role of a second language. However, the residents of the western parts of Ukraine, especially the younger generation who did not study Russian at schools, perceive this language as a foreign one, that is, the language one has to learn with specific aims (Risager, 2007, p. 70). This vision is often politically supported: in numerous Ukrainian mass media, Russian is often called "the language of our northern neighbor" or explicitly referred to as a foreign language.

Ukrainian Foreign Language Education

At secondary schools in Ukraine, the teaching and learning of foreign languages is compulsory. Beginning with the 2013-14 academic year, secondary school students were supposed to study two foreign languages and had to begin to learn them as early as in the first grade. The foreign languages offered at schools are, most often, English, German, French and Spanish. As of 2013, 92% of secondary schools provided courses in English as a "first" foreign language, which is quite understandable in view of its dominant role in the world. The "second" foreign languages learnt are usually German, French, Spanish or Russian, which has recently been added as another option for students who study at schools with Ukrainian as the language of instruction. It should be noted that schools with Russian as the language of instruction as well as schools with instruction in other minority languages (Polish, Romanian, Hungarian, etc.) teach extensive obligatory courses in the Ukrainian language and literature.

On the tertiary level, students usually continue to study their "first" foreign language (in the majority of cases, it is English, but German, French or Spanish courses are offered almost at all universities). The university foreign language course provided by the Bachelor's programs is a short obligatory Language for

Specific Purposes (LSP) course with a special emphasis on professional terminology and translation, which lasts for 1-2 years. Some departments continue to teach LSP courses at the Master's level as well. Doctoral programs offer obligatory courses in foreign languages (it goes without saying that the majority of them are English ones!) with a general focus on the translation of scholarly literature.

There are also numerous specialized departments at Ukrainian universities for students majoring in certain languages and appropriate literatures (e.g., English Philology, Polish Philology or Chinese Philology). The students of these departments take extended language courses and related disciplines often delivered in the language studied (e.g., history of the language in question, its phonetics, lexicology, etc.).

Traditional Ukrainian Approaches to Writing

The theoretical vision of writing and its nature in the Ukrainian cultural context has essentially been influenced by stylistics—the study of style, which "replaced and expanded on the earlier study of elocution in rhetoric" (Wales, 2001, p. 372) in the 20th century. There exist different approaches in this field, but the one adopted in Ukrainian scholarship has been greatly influenced by functional stylistics derived from the classical ideas of the Prague School. Within this methodological paradigm, functional styles are usually considered in opposition to each other; for example, the language of scientific style is viewed as tending to be objective, precise, unemotional and devoid of individuality (in contrast, for instance, to journalistic style marked by high degree of persuasiveness and emotionality). The incorporation into stylistics of some theoretical insights from pragmatics and Hallidayan systemic-functional linguistics as well as the increasing growth, since the beginning of the 1970s, of textlinguistic studies has led to the development of a theoretic-descriptive framework used for investigations of various linguistic features of different types of texts. However, the numerous findings resulting from the considerable body of research in this area have often been presented as theoretical constructs rather than as recommendations applicable to language education and teaching writing (Yakhontova, 2001, p. 401).

This highly theoretical stance seems to correlate with such features of Ukrainian academic discourse as preoccupation with content in writing, a tendency towards a depersonalized style, avoidance of textual organizers, a low degree of formal structuring, and an inclination towards theorizing and generalizations in the humanities (Yakhontova, 2002b, 2002c, 2006).

Furthermore, this theoretical orientation seems to have contributed to the development of the specific, culturally-marked vision of writing as a kind of verbal art that is assumed to be mastered in its three aspects—orthographic, grammatical and stylistic. Much emphasis has been laid upon the so-called "culture of the word" that reflects a striving towards grammatically and stylistically correct written texts which also have to invoke a certain aesthetic impression. The importance of this special attitude towards the effective use of language in writing for the Ukrainian educational context can be, for example, rather vividly illustrated by the two following titles (given here in the English translation): *Culture of the Word* (Ukrainian scholarly journal published on a regular basis by the National Academy of Sciences of Ukraine) and *Dictionary and Handbook of the Culture of the Ukrainian Language* (Hrynchyshyn, Kapeliushnyi & Serbens'ka, 2006). At the same time, the overall structuring of the text, as well as such parameters of written communication as the context of situation, the purpose of the text, or the specifics of the potential audience have been up till now rarely addressed. Not surprisingly, such widespread in English word-combinations as "academic writing," "business writing" or "technical writing" have never had any direct translation equivalents in Ukrainian.

This culture-specific vision seems also to account for the entire absence of writing courses at Ukrainian universities. Ukrainian university curricula have *never* included any subject related to writing and composition, either in the native or in a foreign language. Therefore, Ukrainian students have had to develop their writing abilities by imitating exemplars of writing in areas of study or research interests. Overall, good writing has traditionally been treated in Ukrainian culture not as a *skill* that can be acquired through deliberate training but rather as a *gift*, which may be smaller or greater depending on the level of an individual's intellectual abilities. Therefore, it is a general belief that writing ability could be taught only to a certain extent and writing instruction, consequently, has always been implicit.

Writing in Ukrainian Foreign Language Education: Past Traditions and New Trends

In Ukrainian foreign language education, writing has traditionally been viewed as one of four language skills, together with speaking, listening, and reading. Both listening and writing were implicitly considered less important than speaking and reading, mostly due to the wide application of the grammar-translation method with its tight focus on written texts. However, beginning with the second half of the 1990s, Ukrainian teachers of foreign languages, especially of English, started to switch to a communicative approach and treat their students not as "passive recipients of linguistic information" but "as active and creative learners" (Smotrova, 2009, p. 729).

At secondary schools, most popular genres of foreign language writing include various types of letters and essays. The importance of writing in a foreign language is nowadays officially recognized through the External Independent Knowledge Testing, which replaced, since 2008, traditional entrance exams to Ukrainian universities. The tests in foreign languages have letter or essay writing tasks, which are assessed taking into account not only their grammatical correctness and stylistic appropriateness, but also the strategies of content presentation and the logic of argumentation development.

At universities, foreign language writing has been limited up till recent times to various translations, grammar tests, letters and, infrequently, essays. Sometimes students are asked to write *referats*—extended literature summaries on a certain topic with lists of references at the end. Doctoral students are supposed to write literature summaries and abstracts, while students of specialized language departments (e.g., English or German) usually produce diploma papers (graduation papers on the Bachelor's level) and Master's theses in the languages they major in.

However, the interest in writing, especially in English, is steadily increasing, due to the teachers of English, who, because of their knowledge of the lingua franca, have appeared to be a group of Ukrainian educators most open to innovations and new approaches. Beginning with the end of the 1990s, there can be observed a growing attention to English writing, to possibilities of its teaching in the Ukrainian educational context, and to development of a pedagogically-oriented English or comparative English-Ukrainian writing research. This tendency correlates with the general rise of interest in English and improvement in appropriate teaching practices and learning results. What follows below is an account and analysis of teaching English writing, previously untypical of Ukraine, but nowadays becoming more or less prominent in the educational culture of the country.

Why has English writing attracted the attention of Ukrainian teachers and learners of English? There seems to be a number of reasons. First, this is obviously a result of the influence of the so-called Bologna process which Ukraine joined in May 2005. As is well known in Europe, the purpose of the Bologna process is to establish comparability in the standards and quality of higher education in European countries. The ideology and strategies of this process implementation lay special emphasis on social mobility and transfer of human capital. Therefore, European students and faculty members are encouraged to study and to conduct research for some time at educational institutions located in other countries in Europe, which is only possible if they have a good command of European languages, and, in a majority of cases, of English and writing in English. Second, such circumstances give rise to new personal motives, e.g., desires to study or work abroad, or to participate in world academic communities as equal members, which also requires the development of English writing skills. Third, a deeper reason for acquiring the skills of English written communication arises from the need for changes in the ideology of Ukrainian tertiary education. Throughout its history, it has been based on passive listening to lectures with further memorization of the material and its presentation at oral examinations. Nowadays, the importance of student-centered, research-oriented learning is being realized by many Ukrainian educators, and, therefore, writing, as one of the major ways of building cognitive skills, comes to the fore.

This new, emerging social and educational situation started to take shape at the end of the 1990s, when the elements of English writing were for the first time introduced into the language curricula at some universities and language schools. In 2000, O. Tarnopolsky reported his both negative and positive experiences of introducing an English writing course in a commercial language school in the east of Ukraine (Tarnopolsky, 2000). In 2001, another report, this time from a western Ukrainian university, described and analyzed an academic English writing course delivered to Master's students majoring in sociology and cultural studies. The course was entirely based on a writing textbook for graduate students (Swales & Feak, 1994), aimed at developing the skills of producing research texts in English. The impact of the course was best summarized by one of the students, who mentioned the following in an anonymous survey: "Even if I never become a famous Ukrainian academic writer, but open my private business, I will still need English academic writing for the purpose of good, clear communication with people" (Yakhontova, 2001, p. 404).

Beginning with the new millennium, some Ukrainian university teachers of English have started to teach elements of English academic writing, in most cases within the framework of the general ESP course. These experiences, coming from different Ukrainian universities (e.g., the Ivan Franko National University in L'viv, Kyiv-Mohyla Academy or Petro Mohyla Black Sea State University in Mykolayiv), were discussed at the 1st and 2nd conferences on teaching English academic writing in Ukraine, which were held in 2008 and 2011. In most cases, the experiences were based upon the application of the genre-process approach (mostly with the focus on different types of essay writing), adaptation of the produced abroad textbooks to Ukrainian educational context, and incorporation of writing into other learning activities, for example, educational collaborative projects. As was emphasized at the 2011 conference, the teaching of English academic writing is becoming a "fashionable trend" in Ukrainian higher education. However, in addition to praising their successes, participants of the conferences also shared their concerns related to the lack of motivation on part of both teachers and learners: it has turned out that many teachers of English do not have a desire to teach academic writing as they lack appropriate professional knowledge, while many of their students do not understand why they should learn to write academically. In fact, there have appeared to be only two groups of learners in Ukraine who possess an obvious need and motivation to study English academic writing, the first including the students with a high level of general English knowledge and clear plans to continue their studies abroad, and the second being doctoral students, who realize the importance of publishing in English for their future careers and professional development. As can be seen, the attitudes to learning English academic writing in Ukraine corroborate I. Leki's opinion that the focus of teaching English writing in EFL contexts must not only be on how to teach successfully, but also on why "this should be done in the first place" (Leki, 2001, p. 198).

Realizing that doctoral students are the most interested group of the consumers of English writing teaching in Ukraine, the author of this article developed an English research writing course which has already been delivered (as part of the general course) for 10 years already at the Ivan Franko National University of L'viv. The course is based upon a genre-based approach in J. M. Swales's (1990) spirit, which has proved to be quite efficient in ESL and EFL contexts. Such inherent features of the genre-oriented approach as, for example, the explicit and systematic character of teaching, empowerment of students via access to the patterns of variation in texts, and consciousness-raising in the process of learning writing (Hyland, 2004), were reinforced by the application of an earlier elaborated pedagogical model of teaching academic genres (Yakhontova, 1995a, 1997b). The model has two levels, with the first one devoted to the mastery of genres as normative schemata, and the second dedicated to the development of the skills of their free and creative use. The course has been supported by the first Ukrainian textbook on English academic writing—*English Academic Writing for Students and Researchers* (Yakhontova, 2002a), which become well-known in Ukraine and some neighboring countries.

Gradually, two departments of the Ivan Franko National University of L'viv—the Department of Foreign Languages for Humanities and the Department of Foreign Languages for Sciences—were starting to become more and more concerned with teaching English academic writing. This interest led to an outstanding event for post-Soviet education—establishment of the Center for English Academic Writing (henceforth CEAW). The CEAW, initially supported by the Partnership Program between this Ukrainian institution and the University of Oregon, Eugene (funded by the Bureau of Educational and Cultural Affairs of the United States Department of State) and the administration of the Faculty of Foreign Languages, was founded in 2006. It has its own small premises, a website (www.ceaw.org.ua), basic technical equipment and a small library, but does not receive any permanent funding, relying only on external grant support. Currently, the Center unites about 12 professors of English who dedicate their efforts to voluntary work.

CEAW—The First English Writing Support Structure in Ukraine

The purposes of the CEAW are quite different from those of the writing centers common in the USA as well as in some European countries. While "traditional" writing centers mostly focus on providing tutoring services to students wishing to improve their writing skills, the CEAW emphasizes rather global objectives, which include:

- popularization of teaching and learning English academic writing at Ukrainian universities;

- creating a vibrant community of English writing teachers from the LNU and other Ukrainian universities;
- developing the CEAW as a site of educational innovation and change.

As seen from this list, the CEAW mostly focuses on the dissemination of the idea of learning and teaching English academic writing as a tool for creating new pedagogical approaches and contexts, which seems to be of primary importance for Ukrainian education at the present moment. However, the CEAW also pursues a number of immediate goals, such as the introduction of English academic writing courses into the language curriculum of the Ivan Franko National University of L'viv, development of distance writing courses, organization of short-term training in English academic writing for Ukrainian researchers, elaborating small empirical research projects, and holding national and international conferences.

In accordance with these goals, the activities of the CEAW are realized along a number of lines. First, attention is paid to the preparation of English academic writing and teaching materials. For example, two textbooks with a strong writing focus have already been published (Ivashchyshyn, 2011a; Maksymuk & Dudok, 2006). Second, specialized writing courses, for example, "Writing English essays", "How to write a paper for a degree in English and Linguistics" and "English research writing for doctoral students in sciences" have been developed and delivered at the University under the auspices of the CEAW. Third, some activists of the CEAW are engaged in the elaboration of appropriate distance courses (Kaluzhna, 2009) and language learning computer technologies (Ivashchyshyn, 2011b). Fourth, the CEAW conducted a number of English academic writing training sessions for mature researchers (described in more detail below). Fifth, some of the Center activists conducted small-scale research with the aim of gaining results that would improve the teaching of English writing, for example, tracking the change of students' attitudes in the course of academic writing (Fito, 2013). Finally, the volunteers realized other different projects related to the development of academic literacy in the English language, for example, they organized Internet-conferences for students majoring in applied linguistics, supervised student research work and implemented joint professionally-oriented projects in the course of English for Special Purposes. All these activities not only had a positive effect on drawing the attention of Ukrainian educators to English written academic communication but also helped to build up the community of university teachers interested in pedagogical innovations.

The CEAW also managed to become known outside the borders of Ukraine. Some of its activists are or were members of internationally recognized professional associations such as EATAW (European Association for the Teaching of Academic Writing), EWCA (European Writing Centers' Association) and TESOL (Teaching English to Speakers of Other Languages). The Center volunteers maintain contact with writing specialists throughout the world and actively participate in conferences abroad. International interest in the CEAW and its activities was aroused by the First and Second International Conferences "Teaching English Academic Writing in Ukraine and Elsewhere: Problems and Prospects", organized by the Center in 2008 and 2011.

In 2011-13, the activities of the Center were enlivened by the international project "Literacy Development in the Humanities: Creating Competence Centres for the Enhancement of Reading and Writing Skills as Part of University Teaching (LIDHUM)", funded by the Swiss Science Foundation, in which three activists of the CEAW participated. As the focus of the project was on multiliteracy writing support, the CEAW broadened its scope by conducting the university conference "Role of Writing in the Teaching of Humanities" (L'viv, 2013). This event brought together enthusiasts of teaching writing in foreign and Ukrainian languages, who discussed such vital for Ukrainian education questions as writing as a socio-cognitive activity, the role of writing in the context of the Bologna process, criteria of writing assessment, and the place and tasks of writing centers at universities. Furthermore, a questionnaire was distributed among the University students and faculty members focusing on their genre and writing practices. The results of this survey, which can be viewed as a realization of genre mapping—"a systematic procedure that helps detecting, collecting, defining and understanding genres in a certain professional, academic or cultural field" (Kruse & Chitez, 2012) provided certain insights into genre use in native and foreign languages at a Ukrainian university and allowed comparing them with writing practices at the home institutions of project partners in Romania and Former Yugoslavian Republic of Macedonia (Bekar, Doroholschi, Kruse & Yakhontova, 2015). The initial results of the survey have been reported at the 7th EATAW Conference in 2013.

Teaching English Research Writing to Mature Learners Under the Auspices of the CEAW

It should be emphasized that the CEAW possesses an extremely interesting, if not unique pedagogical experience of teaching writing to an unusual group of learners who are highly motivated to master at least the fundamentals of academic writing in English. They are mature researchers interested in presenting their findings in English, mostly in international peer-reviewed journals. As known to many scholars from non-Anglophone contexts, writing for publication in refereed journals requires specialized skills and knowledge including mastery of English grammar and academic style, the ability to build a persuasive argument, awareness of international norms governing production of research texts and capabilities to psychologically cope with the exasperating experience of repeated submissions (Matalese, 2013).

In an attempt to respond to these urgent needs, a special English academic writing training program focusing on English for Research Publication Purposes has been elaborated by the author of this paper and some CEAW volunteers, and conducted at a number of Ukrainian research institutions and the CEAW beginning in 2004. The training program was supported by a number of non-governmental organizations and grants.

The participants in the training program were researchers of quite different ages (25-60) with an intermediate or upper-intermediate level of English knowledge working in various fields (applied linguistics and mathematics, biology, economics, information technology, medicine, physics and sociology). The training programs were either organized through competitive participation based on application forms and statements of purpose or specially arranged for the staff of certain research and educational institutions—universities and National Academy of Sciences of Ukraine in the cities of L'viv, Ternopil', Kyiv, Poltava, Kharkiv, and Dnipropetrovs'k. There also was one "internationally" co-authored training program, consisting of two parts: the first one dealing with academic research in social sciences, its process and methods (conducted by Yi-Lee Wong, Oxford University), and the second one devoted to English research writing (T. Yakhontova, Ivan Franko National University of L'viv). The training program lasted for 1-2 workdays and included various types of writing activities elaborated with due regard for the East European cultural and educational context. All the participants of the training programs received specially developed handouts in the form of a booklet. After the training, they were asked to fill in an anonymous questionnaire summarizing their feedback.

The training program included the consideration of such issues as strategies of writing in English, cultural differences in writing, English academic style and language, typical structure of the English research paper and conference abstract, ways of avoiding unintentional plagiarism, and communication with reviewers and editors. The application of two theoretical frameworks—a genre-based approach to writing and the notion of intertextuality (Bakhtin, 1986; Fairclough, 1995) contributed to the rapid development of research text construction skills of this specific group of learners. This effect has been vividly enhanced by the use of various templates—stereotypical phrases and certain textual models—offered to participants of the training program during almost all types of activities. These templates successfully provided "accessible ways for academic learners to generate the sections of a research paper, from a 'bottom-up', or inductive perspective; and at the same time to grasp the 'moves', or basic sections of a research paper, from a 'top-down', or deductive perspective" (Broekhoff, 2008, p. 129).

As the trainees indicated in the evaluation forms, participation in such educational events considerably raised their awareness of the norms and conventions of English academic discourse and helped to develop the most important writing skills. This successful experience has also shown that researchers remain the most "grateful," in terms of needs and attitudes, group of English writing learners in Ukraine.

Foreign Language Writing Research: An Emerging Field in Ukraine?

In his article, published in 2000, O. Tarnopolsky wrote about "an almost total absence of research on teaching English writing as a communicative activity" in the Soviet Union (Tarnopolsky, 2000, p. 211). Having analyzed professional literature in the field of English teaching, published in the USSR in 1970-1980, he managed to find only one doctoral dissertation on written communication in English. Following his example, the author of this report searched the database of extended (16-32 page) dissertation self-abstracts (called *avtoreferats*), stored on the website of the largest library in the country—Vernadsky National Library of Ukraine (www.nbuv.gov.ua), beginning in 2001. The database contains more dissertations (than Tarnopolsky found), which explicitly focus on teaching writing in foreign languages and were published within the comparable period of 2001 to the first half of 2012. Their total number of 12 is, however, not impressive, even for Ukraine as a part of the Soviet Union and especially when it is compared to the total number of dissertations (about 200) defended in the field of methodology of teaching foreign languages and foreign language education within the same time period. Out of these 12 dissertations, eight deal with the teaching of English writing, two—with writing in German, one—with French writing, and one—with writing in Ukrainian as a second language. All of these dissertations emphasize the communicative nature of writing and offer teaching methods directed at constructing various types of texts with due regard for their genre conventions, stylistic peculiarities and grammatical features. It is remarkable that at least several of them concentrate not only on the textual characteristics of writing but also suggest how to develop and support students' writing processes through drafting, revising and self-checking, which so far has been quite untypical for the Ukrainian pedagogical context.

Books and volumes on researching and teaching writing published in Ukraine are also scarce, some examples known in the country being O. Tarnopolsky and S. Kozhushko's *Methodology of Teaching English Writing to University Students* and a chapter on a genre-oriented approach to teaching research writing in (Yakhontova, 2009). At the same time, more and more articles devoted to theoretical and applied aspects of writing in foreign languages (primarily English) have started to appear in Ukrainian journals. They can be divided into two groups: the papers which outline and explain to Ukrainian readers western approaches to treating and teaching writing and the papers which focus on the methods of teaching how to compose certain types of texts, based on the consideration of their various extra- and intralinguistic features. The latter usually emphasize the importance of development of various writing competences (sociocultural, grammatical, stylistic), thus combining a general communicative approach with attention to verbal aspects of writing in the spirit of national cultural and educational traditions.

Other types of research related to the field of foreign language writing in Ukrainian scholarship include comparative investigations of Ukrainian discourse versus discourses in other languages (e.g., Dubenko, 2009; Yakhontova, 2002b, 2002c, 2006; Zhabotynska, 2001) and analysis of texts which yields the results potentially applicable in teaching writing in nonnative languages, mostly in research and business spheres (e.g., Yakhontova & Markelova, 2010). The scarcity of this type of research is obviously due to the underdevelopment of applied linguistic studies, which only relatively recently have started to take shape in Ukraine.

It should also be noted that studies of students' writing needs and their composing processes still remain unaddressed (with few exceptions, like the above-mentioned small projects implemented by the CEAW) in Ukrainian scholarship.

Conclusions

As this report has shown, foreign language writing and research was not developed in Ukraine, most probably, due to the interplay of national cultural traditions and social circumstances. Nowadays, however, it has good chances to progress, as new social phenomena, processes and transformations in the country stimulate interest and necessity in writing in nonnative languages, English in the first place. It can be anticipated that this emergence in Ukrainian education and scholarship will further develop based on western approaches. Simultaneously, it will probably preserve the traditional, for this part of the world, focus on linguistic and stylistic aspects of writing that can be viewed in a positive light, as such aspects bear special importance in EFL contexts. Although the interest in English writing will definitely dominate, writing in other European languages also has a chance to attract attention of teachers and researchers, as the concept of multiliteracy, promoted by the "Bologna" process, is shared and supported in Ukraine. Thus, the field of foreign language writing in the country seems to have a rather promising future, even though it still looks to be distant.

References

Bakhtin, M. (1986). *Speech Genres and Other Late Essays*. (V. W. McGee, Trans.). Austin: University of Texas Press.

Bekar, M., Doroholschi, C. I., Kruse, O. & Yakhontova, T. (2015). Educational genres in Eastern Europe: A comparison of the genres in the Humanities departments of three countries. *Journal of Academic Writing*, 5(1): 119-132.

Broekhoff, M. (2008). Templates for academic writing. *Nawa Journal of Language and Communication*, 2(2): 128-139.

Dubenko, O. Y. (2009). *Anglo-amerykanski ta ukrainski naukovi teksty u porivnialno-stylistychnomy aspekti* [British-American and Ukrainian Scholarly Texts in a Comparative Stylistic Aspect]. *Naukovyi Visnyk of Volyn National University*, 16. Lutsk: Volyn University Press, 122-125.

Fairclough, N. (1995). *Critical Discourse Analysis: The Critical Study of Language.* Harlow: Longman.

Fito, T. (2013, June). What can I do when I write? Tracking the change of students' attitudes in the course of L2 academic writing. Paper presented at the 3rd International Conference on Theory and Practice of Foreign Language Teaching: Foreign Language Opportunities in Writing, Łódź.

Hrynchyshyn, D., Kapeliushnyi, A. & Serbens'ka, O. (2006). *Slovnyk-dovinyk z kultury ukrainskoyi movy* [*Dictionary and Handbook of the Culture of the Ukrainian Language*]. Kyiv: Znannia.

Hyland, K. (2004). *Genre and Second Language Writing*. Ann Arbor, MI: University of Michigan Press.

Ivashchyshyn, O. (2011a). *English for Professional Development in Linguistics.* L'viv: LNU.

Ivashchyshyn, O. (2011b, June). Innovative methodology for acquiring language knowledge in a globalized society. Paper presented at the 2nd International Conference: Teaching English Academic Writing in Ukraine and Elsewhere—Problems and Prospects, L'viv.

Kaluzhna, H. (2009, June 30-July 2). Developing an online research paper writing course: Ukrainian experience. Paper presented at the 5th EATAW Conference, Coventry.

Kruse, O. & Chitez, M. (2012). Contrastive genre mapping in academic contexts: An intercultural approach. *Journal of Academic Writing, 2*(1), 59-73. Retrieved from http://e-learning.coventry.ac.uk/ojs/index.php/joaw/article/view/79

Leki, I. (2001). Material, educational, and ideological challenges of teaching EFL writing at the turn of the century. *International Journal of English Studies, 1*(2), 197-209. Universidad de Muecia: Servicio de Publicaciones.

Maksymuk, V. M. & Dudok, R. I. (2006). *English for Ph.D. Students*. L'viv, Astroliabiya.

Matalese, V. (2013). Reporting—the final phase of scientific research—can and should be supported. A case for integrating language professionals into the research setting. *Journal on Research Policy & Evaluation, 1*, 1-13.

Risager, K. (2007). *Language and Culture Pedagogy: From a National to a Transnational Paradigm*. Multilingual Matters: Frankfurt Lodge.

Smotrova, T. (2009). Globalization and English language teaching in Ukraine. *TESOL Quarterly, 43*(4), 727-732.

Swales, J. M. (1990). *Genre Analysis: English in Academic and Research Settings*. New York, NY: Cambridge University Press.

Swales, J. M. & Feak, C. B. (1994). *Academic Writing for Graduate Students: A Course for Nonnative Speakers of English*. Ann Arbor: The University of Michigan Press.

Tarnopolsky, O. (2000). Writing English as a foreign language: A report from Ukraine. *Journal of Second Language Writing, 9*(3), 209-226.

Tarnopolsky, O. B. & Kozhushko, S. P. (2008). *Metodyka navchannia studentiv vyshchykh navchalnykh zakladiv pysma angliiskoyu movoyu* [*Methodology of Teaching English Writing to University Students*]. Vinnytsia: Nova Knyha.

Wales, K. (2001). *A Dictionary of Stylistics* (2nd Ed.). Harlow: Pearson Education.

Yakhontova, T. (1997a). Bakhtin at home and abroad. *A Journal of Composition Theory, 17*(1), 83-94.

Yakhontova, T. (1997b). The signs of a new time: Academic writing in ESP curricula of Ukrainian universities. In A. Duszak (Ed.), *Culture and Styles of Academic Discourse Vol. 104* (pp. 103-112). Berlin: Mouton de Gruyter.

Yakhontova, T. (2001). Textbooks, contexts, and learners. *English for Specific Purposes, 20*(1), 397-415.

Yakhontova, T. (2002a). *English Academic Writing for Students and Researchers.* L'viv: Ivan Franko National UP.

Yakhontova, T. (2002b). "Selling or telling"? The issue of cultural variation in research genres. In J. Flowerdew (Ed.), *Academic Discourse* (pp. 216-232). Harlow: Longman.

Yakhontova, T. (2002c). Titles of conference presentations abstracts: A cross-cultural perspective. In E. Ventola, C. Shalom & S. Thompson (Eds.), *The Language of Conferencing* (pp. 277-300). Frankfurt am Main: Peter Lang.

Yakhontova T. (2006). Cultural and disciplinary variation in academic discourse: The issue of influencing factors. *Journal of English for Academic Purposes, 5*(2), 153-167.

Yakhontova, T. V. (2009). *Lingvistychna Genologiya Naukovoyi Komunikatsii* [*Linguistic Genology of Research Communication*]. L'viv: Ivan Franko National University of L'viv Press.

Yakhontova, T. & Markelova, S. (2010). The genre of the conference handout: Textual features, interpersonal characteristics and peculiarities of interpretation. In R. Loréz-Sanz, P. Mur-Dueñas & E. Lafuente-Millán (Eds.), *Constructing Interpersonality: Multiple Perspectives on Written Academic Genres* (pp. 337-356). Newcastle upon Tyne: Cambridge Scholars Publishing.

Zhabotynska, S. (2001). Author profile in scholarly paper: Anglo-American vs. Ukrainian/Russian. In A. Kertész (Ed.), *Approaches to the Pragmatics of Scientific Discourse* (pp. 73-89). Frankfurt am Main: Peter Lang.

Chapter 12

The Status of Second Language Writing in the United States: Continuing Growth and Change

Tony Silva

Purdue University

Introduction

In this chapter, I would like to talk about the current status of second language (L2) writing in the United States and how the discipline continues to grow and change. This growth and change is evident at all levels of education and in both second and foreign language contexts. Here, however, I will focus primarily on higher education, where most of the work on second language writing has been and continues to be done. Additionally, I will include a list of resources for those interested in finding out more about second language writing in the United States at the end of this chapter.

College Composition in the United States

Relatively speaking, second language writing has become a subject of much interest in the United States, especially over the last 25 years or so. In my view, there are two main reasons for the current popularity of second language writing studies. First, virtually all colleges and universities in the United States require that all undergraduate students take at least one course exclusively devoted to writing, typically in their first year. This is a longstanding tradition in US institutions of higher education. Second, there is a very large and growing population of English language learners in these educational contexts.

English Language Learners in the United States

The current population of English language learners in the United States includes nearly 900,000 international students from throughout the world, and the international student population has been growing at nearly six percent a year over the last five years (Open Doors, 2014). And it is estimated that there are also millions of college level English language learners who are residents or citizens of the United States. Furthermore, in US primary and secondary schools, the population of English language learners is estimated at about five million and is growing rapidly (Office of English Language Acquisition, 2015). It is expected that a substantial number of these students will be entering US colleges and universities in the coming years. All of this suggests that there is a lot of L2 writing instruction being done in institutions of higher education, whether in mainstream writing classes (dominated by native English speakers) or in classes devoted exclusively to English language learners.

The Field of Second Language Writing and its Infrastructure

As the number of English language learners in composition classes has grown, so has the field of second language writing studies. And the field has developed a fairly extensive infrastructure. This infrastructure includes scholarly journals, book series, books, doctoral programs producing L2 writing scholars, dissertations on L2 writing issues, professional conferences where work on L2 writing is presented and discussed, and resources for research on second language writing and writing instruction.

Scholarly Journals

The first journal devoted exclusively to second language writing studies is the *Journal of Second Language Writing,* which began publication in 1992. The *Journal* began as a small niche publication developed and nurtured in the US— in Knoxville, Tennessee; West Lafayette, Indiana; and Norwood, New Jersey to be precise. Now in its twenty-fourth year, it has grown a great deal in terms of number of submissions and articles published as well as in the size of its readership. It has become, to a large degree an international journal, with editorial advisory members from around the globe, with editors from both within and outside the United States, and with a publisher based in Europe. This broadening of scope is also reflected in the *Journal's* recently added subtitle: *An International Journal on Second and Foreign Language Writing and Writing Instruction.* See Silva (2012) for a more detailed account of the *Journal's* founding and development.

There are also a number of US-based journals that, while not exclusively devoted to second language writing, regularly publish articles on it. These include journals focused on ESL and EFL research and instruction (e.g., *TESOL Quarterly, TESOL Journal*), foreign language education (e.g. *Foreign Language Annals, Modern Language Journal), applied linguistics (e.g., Language Learning*), *and composition studies (e.g. Written Communication, Journal of Basic Writing, Teaching English in the Two-Year College, College Composition and Communication, College English,* and *Research in the Teaching of English*).

Book Series

There are currently two US-based book series devoted exclusively to publishing work in second language writing studies. Their descriptions suggest their differences in focus and audience.

One is the *Parlor Press Second Language Writing Series*, which was launched in 2004: I quote from the website:

> This series aims to facilitate the advancement of knowledge in the field of second language writing by publishing scholarly and research based monographs and edited collections that provide significant new insights into central topics and issues in the field. This series seeks submissions that expand, refine, or challenge existing knowledge of the field by using various modes of inquiry such as philosophical, historical, empirical (quantitative and qualitative), and narrative.

Some of the topics addressed by books published in this series include the political and theoretical aspects of the field, genre knowledge, foreign language writing instruction, scientific writing in a second language, and graduate studies in the field.

The other book series devoted exclusively to second language writing studies is the *University of Michigan Series on Teaching Multilingual Writers*, which was launched in 2002. Again I quote from the website:

> The series addresses a variety of issues of interest to L2 writing teachers of all levels in all settings. The Michigan series treats these issues in a focused and illustrative manner.

It is noted that the most important features of books in this series include the thorough treatment of issues, accessibility, and research-based data. Some of the issues addressed by these books include peer response, critical academic writing, controversies in the field, reading and writing connections, genre, teacher-written commentary, speaking and writing connections, technology, assessment, journal writing, intercultural rhetoric, and treatment of error.

Besides Parlor Press and the University of Michigan press, a number of other US-based companies collectively have published many monographs and collections on second language writing. Lawrence Erlbaum Associates (subsequently absorbed Routledge/Taylor & Francis) published the lion's share.

Doctoral Programs

There are more than 150 universities in the United States at which students have produced dissertations on L2 writing studies topics. Since 1963, these universities have produced more than 850 L2 writing focused dissertations. Some of the programs that have produced the largest numbers of these dissertations include the following (in alphabetical order): Arizona State University; Indiana University; Indiana University of Pennsylvania; New York University; Ohio State University; Purdue University; Teachers College, Columbia University; University of Arizona; University of Illinois at Urbana-Champaign; and the University of Texas at Austin.

Professional Organizations

There are currently no US-based professional organizations devoted exclusively to L2 writing studies. However, since the early 1990s, a number of second language writing professionals have successfully infiltrated a couple of large professional organizations in an attempt to raise the profile of L2 writing in these venues. These are the TESOL International Association (TESOL) and the Conference on College Composition and Communication (CCCC).

As a result, TESOL now hosts a vibrant Second Language Writing Interest Section (SLWIS) with more than 2,000 members, a listserve, and a biannual Newsletter—*SLW News*. Furthermore, second language writing professionals have insinuated themselves into almost all of the organizations' major committees and units—including the Board of Directors—and are serving or have served as editors or members of the editorial advisory board of the organization's flagship journal, *TESOL Quarterly*. And at least one second language writing specialist has served a term as the organization's president.

CCCC now has both a Second Language Writing Special Interest Section and a Standing Committee on Second Language Writing. As with TESOL, L2 writing specialists serve or have served on many important committees—including the organization's Executive Committee—and as members of the editorial board of the organization's flagship journal, *College Composition and Communication*. Furthermore, second language professionals in CCCC have produced a very influential position statement, the *CCCC Statement on Second Language Writing and Writers* (first published in 2001 and revised in 2009), which has been endorsed by TESOL.

There are a number of other large US-based professional organizations that, to a greater or lesser extent, take up second language writing issues. These include the American Association for Applied Linguistics (AAAL), the National Council of Teachers of English (NCTE)—which is the parent organization of CCCC—and the American Council of Teachers of Foreign Languages (ACTFL).

Professional Conferences

There is currently only one US-based professional conference devoted exclusively to L2 writing. This is the Symposium on Second Language Writing. The Symposium, which was founded in 1998 in the United States as a biennial conference, has become an annual and international event. To date, it has met in the United States at Purdue University and Arizona State University, in Japan at Nagoya Gakuin University, in Spain at the University of Murcia, in China at Shandong University, and at the Auckland University of Technology in New Zealand.

Another professional forum, The Conference on Contrastive Rhetoric and Written Discourse Analysis, founded in 2004 at Indiana University—Purdue University Indianapolis (IUPUI), has been devoted largely to L2 writing issues. It has met in Indiana at IUPUI, at Ohio State University, at the University of Michigan, and at Georgia State University.

A substantial number of presentations (papers, colloquia, etc.) take place at the annual conference of TESOL—as well as at the annual conferences of all its state and national affiliate organizations (of which there are more than 100, with total membership of more than 47,000 professionals)—and at the CCCC annual conference. In recent years, the international TESOL conference alone has featured more than 50 sessions on L2 writing each year. Fewer, yet an increasing number of presentations on second language writing issues take place at the annual conferences of AAAL, NCTE, and ACTFL.

Resources for Research

There are a number of US-based online resources that index work on second language writing studies. These include the

- *Education Resources Information Center* (ERIC) database developed and maintained by the US Department of Education;
- *Dissertations and Theses Database*, produced by ProQuest—an electronic publisher based in Ann Arbor, Michigan;
- *Linguistics and Language Behavior Abstracts* (LLBA), also produced by ProQuest;
- *WorldCat*—an online catalogue, available free to libraries, that allows access to the collections of 72,000 libraries in 170 countries and territories. It is hosted by the Online Computer Library Center (OCLC) based in Dublin, Ohio; and
- *Comppile*, a bibliographic website focused on writing studies (1939 to present), including second language writing studies. It is produced by composition studies scholars at Texas A&M University, Corpus Christi.

Finally, an annotated bibliography of work in second language writing studies can be found at the end of each issue of the *Journal of Second Language Writing* (from 1993 to the present) in the *Selected Bibliography of Recent Scholarship in Second Language Writing* as well as in yearly reviews of work in

L2 writing studies in *SLW News,* the newsletter of the TESOL Second Language Writing Interest Section.

Trends

I would like to begin to wrap up this chapter with a brief mention of some general trends that are, in my view, in progress in second language writing studies in the United States:

- *Publication*: The numbers of publications on L2 writing are many and continue to increase. This is true of journal articles, the number of journals in which L2 writing focused articles have been published, monographs, collections, and proceedings.

- *Influence from other fields*: L2 writing studies continues to absorb ideas from a number of different fields: formal and functional linguistics, applied linguistics, cognitive and social psychology, rhetoric, composition studies, education, anthropology, sociology, the philosophy of science, and others.

- *Empirical research*: There is continuing movement from a sole focus on the designs and methods of quantitative empirical research to the inclusion of qualitative approaches and designs and designs that incorporate both quantitative and qualitative elements, that is, mixed method studies.

- *Hermeneutic research*: There is increased interest in hermeneutic (non-empirical, interpretive) inquiry, for example, philosophical, historical, and rhetorical studies.

- *Instructional approaches*: In terms of instructional approaches, second language writing continues its movement toward an informed eclectic view, adopting and adapting selected elements from existing approaches and incorporating new theoretical and pedagogical ideas to address second language writing instruction in particular contexts.

- *Infrastructure*: As noted above, second language writing studies has built an infrastructure involving professional journals, book series, conferences, groups within professional organizations, and academic programs in higher education.

For an in-depth look at the influence of other fields on second language writing studies, see Silva & Leki (2004); for an overview and synthesis of research findings on second language writing, see Leki, Cumming & Silva (2008); and for a succinct description of the current state of the field, see Silva (2013).

Conclusion

In conclusion, second language writing studies in the United States is alive, well, growing steadily, and maturing as a discipline. It is also important to note that work being done in second writing studies in the United States is often not carried out by scholars who come from the United States. I base this claim on an exploratory study I did where I looked at all the dissertations on second language writing completed in US universities in 2010. I found that about two thirds of these dissertations were done by individuals from outside the United States. If this pattern holds for publications, students in graduate programs, memberships in professional organizations, and participants in professional conferences—and I think that it may—the status of second language writing studies in the US may also be described as significantly international in scope.

References

Leki, I., Cumming, A. & Silva, T. (Eds.). (2008). *A Synthesis of Research on Second Language Writing in English*. New York, NY: Routledge.

Office of English Language Acquisition. (2014) Reprinted article: Duncan, A & Gil, L.S. (February 19, 2014). English learners an asset for global, multilingual future: Arne Duncan and Libia Gil. *Los Angeles Daily News.* http://www.ncela.us/files/uploads/Eng-Lrn%20OP-ED.pdf

Open Doors/Institute of International Education. (2014). Fast facts. http://www. iie.org/Research-and-Publications/Open-Doors/Data/Fast-Facts. Retrieved July 16, 2015.

Silva, T. (2012). *JSLW@20*: The prequel and the inside story (with several previously unpublished bonus texts). *Journal of Second Language Writing, 21*(3), 187-194.

Silva, T. (2013). Second language writing: Talking points. *Journal of Second Language Writing, 22*(4), 432-434.

Silva, T. & Leki, I. (2004). Family matters: The influence of applied linguistics and composition studies on second language writing studies—past, present, and future. *Modern Language Journal, 88*(1), 1-13.

Resources

The resources listed below are in the order in which they are presented in the text above. The descriptions of these resources are excerpted from their respective websites.

Open Doors. Open Doors, supported by a grant from the Bureau of Educational and Cultural Affairs at the U.S. Department of State, is a comprehensive information resource on international students and scholars studying or teaching at higher education institutions in the United States, and U.S. students studying abroad for academic credit at their home colleges or universities. http://www.iie.org/Research-and-Publications/Open-Doors

Office of English Language Acquisition. The mission of the Office of English Language Acquisition, Language Enhancement, and Academic Achievement for Limited English Proficient Students (OELA) is to provide national leadership to help ensure that English learners and immigrant students attain English proficiency and achieve academically. http://www2.ed.gov/about/offices/list/oela/index.html

Journal of Second Language Writing. The *Journal of Second Language Writing* is devoted to publishing theoretically grounded reports of research and discussions that represent a contribution to current understandings of central issues in second and foreign language writing and writing instruction. http://www.journals.elsevier.com/journal-of-second-language-writing/

TESOL Quarterly. *TESOL Quarterly*, a refereed professional journal, fosters inquiry into English language teaching and learning by providing a forum for TESOL professionals to share their research findings and explore ideas and relationships in the field. http://www.tesol.org/read-and-publish/journals/tesol-quarterly

TESOL Journal. *TESOL Journal* is a refereed, practitioner-oriented electronic journal based on current theory and research in the field of TESOL. *TJ* is a forum for second and foreign language educators at all levels to engage in the ways that research and theorizing can inform, shape, and ground teaching practices and perspectives. http://www.tesol.org/read-and-publish/journals/tesol-journal

Foreign Language Annals. *Foreign Language Annals* is the official refereed journal of the American Council on the Teaching of Foreign Languages (ACTFL) and was first published in 1967. The journal seeks to serve the professional interests of classroom instructors, researchers, and administrators across a range of contexts and is dedicated to the advancement of the teaching and learning of foreign languages, particularly languages other than English. http://www.actfl.org/publications/all/foreign-language-annals

Modern Language Journal. The editorial mission of *The Modern Language Journal* is to publish research and discussion about the learning and teaching of foreign and second languages. The *MLJ* is an international refereed journal that is dedicated to promoting scholarly exchange among researchers and teachers of all modern foreign languages and English as a second language. The journal is particularly committed to publishing high quality work in non-English languages. http://onlinelibrary.wiley.com/journal/10.1111/%28IS SN%291540-4781/homepage/ProductInformation.html

Language Learning. *Language Learning* is a scientific journal dedicated to the understanding of language learning broadly defined. It publishes research articles that systematically apply methods of inquiry from disciplines including psychology, linguistics, cognitive science, educational inquiry, neuroscience, ethnography, sociolinguistics, sociology, and anthropology. http:// onlinelibrary.wiley.com/journal/10.1111/%28ISSN%291467-9922/homepage/ ProductInformation.html

Written Communication. *Written Communication* is an international multidisciplinary journal that publishes theory and research in writing from fields including anthropology, English, education, history, journalism, linguistics, psychology, and rhetoric. https://us.sagepub.com/en-us/nam/ written-communication/journal200767

Journal of Basic Writing. *The Journal of Basic Writing* is a national refereed print journal founded in 1975. Basic writing, a contested term since its initial use in the 1970s, refers to the field concerned with teaching writing to students not yet deemed ready for first-year composition. http://wac.colostate.edu/jbw/

Teaching English in the Two-Year College. *Teaching English in the Two-Year College (TETYC)*, the journal of the Two-Year College English Association (TYCA), is for instructors of English in two-year colleges as well as for teachers of first- and second-year composition in four-year institutions. http://www.ncte.org/ journals/tetyc

College Composition and Communication. *College Composition and Communication* publishes research and scholarship in rhetoric and composition studies that supports college teachers in reflecting on and improving their practices in teaching writing and that reflects the most current scholarship and theory in the field. http://www.ncte.org/cccc/ccc

College English. *College English* is the professional journal for the college scholar-teacher. *CE* publishes articles about literature, rhetoric-composition, critical theory, creative writing theory and pedagogy, linguistics, literacy, reading theory, pedagogy, and professional issues related to the teaching of English. http://www.ncte.org/journals/ce

Research in the Teaching of English. *Research in the Teaching of English (RTE)* is the flagship research journal of the National Council of Teachers of English (NCTE) in the United States. It is a broad-based, multidisciplinary journal composed of original research articles and short scholarly essays on a wide range of topics significant to those concerned with the teaching and learning of languages and literacies around the world, both in and beyond schools and universities. http://www.ncte.org/journals/rte

Parlor Press Second Language Writing Series. Described in the text. http://www.public.asu.edu/~pmatsuda/parlor/index.html

University of Michigan Series on Teaching Multilingual Writers. Described in the text. https://www.press.umich.edu/browse/series/UM129

TESOL International Association. TESOL International Association brings together educators, researchers, administrators, and students to advance the profession of teaching English to speakers of other languages. It has more than 12,000 members representing 156 countries, and more than 100 worldwide affiliates. http://www.tesol.org/

Conference on College Composition and Communication. CCCC supports and promotes the teaching and study of college composition and communication by 1) sponsoring meetings and publishing scholarly materials for the exchange of knowledge about composition, composition pedagogy, and rhetoric; 2)

supporting a wide range of research on composition, communication, and rhetoric; 3) working to enhance the conditions for learning and teaching college composition and to promote professional development; and 4) acting as an advocate for language and literacy education nationally and internationally. http://www.ncte.org/cccc

CCCC Statement on Second Language Writing and Writers. This statement urges writing teachers and writing program administrators to recognize the regular presence of second-language writers in writing classes, to understand their characteristics, and to develop instructional and administrative practices that are sensitive to their linguistic and cultural needs. It also provides a list of guidelines for second-language writers regarding placement, writing assessment, class size, credit-bearing courses, teacher preparation, and teacher support. http://www.ncte.org/cccc/resources/positions/secondlangwriting

The American Association for Applied Linguistics. The American Association for Applied Linguistics (AAAL) is a professional organization of scholars who are interested in and actively contribute to the multi-disciplinary field of applied linguistics. AAAL members promote principled approaches to language-related concerns, including language education, acquisition and loss, bilingualism, discourse analysis, literacy, rhetoric and stylistics, language for special purposes, psycholinguistics, second and foreign language pedagogy, language assessment, and language policy and planning. http://www.aaal.org/

The National Council of Teachers of English. NCTE is devoted to improving the teaching and learning of English and the language arts at all levels of education. The Council promotes the development of literacy, the use of language to construct personal and public worlds and to achieve full participation in society, through the learning and teaching of English and the related arts and sciences of language. http://www.ncte.org/

The American Council on the Teaching of Foreign Languages. ACTFL is dedicated to the improvement and expansion of the teaching and learning of all languages at all levels of instruction. ACTFL is an individual membership organization of more than 12,500 language educators and administrators from elementary through graduate education, as well as government and industry. http://www.actfl.org/

The Symposium on Second Language Writing. The SSLW is an annual international conference that brings together teachers and researchers who work with second- and foreign-language writers to discuss important issues in the field of second language writing. The SSLW aims to facilitate the advancement of knowledge in the field of L2 writing and to build a sense of community among those who are involved in L2 writing research and instruction. http://sslw.asu.edu/

The Conference on Contrastive Rhetoric and Written Discourse Analysis. This conference seeks to integrate current discussions of intercultural competence in language education into intercultural rhetoric and discourse research and application in ESL, EFL, ESP, ELF, and foreign language teaching settings. http://liberalarts.iupui.edu/icic/conference/

The Educational Resources Information Center. The ERIC database is the world's largest source of education information. The database contains more than 1,000,000 abstracts of documents and journal articles on education research and practice. More than 100,000 documents are now available on-line, on-demand. ERIC is a federally-funded project of the U.S. Department of Education, Office of Educational Research and Improvement. http://searcheric.org/readme.htm

Linguistics and Language Behavior Abstracts. LLBA indexes the international literature in linguistics and related disciplines in the language sciences. It covers all aspects of the study of language including phonetics, phonology, morphology, syntax and semantics. http://www.lib.utexas.edu/indexes/titles.php?id=235

ProQuest Dissertations and Theses. ProQuest Dissertations and Theses is the largest single repository of graduate dissertations and theses. It includes 3.8 million works, grows by 100,000 each year, and is international scope, with deposits from universities in 88 countries. http://www.proquest.com/products-services/dissertations/

WorldCat. WorldCat represents a "collective collection" of the world's libraries, built through the contributions of librarians, expanded and enhanced through individual, regional and national programs. It represents the electronic and digital materials most in demand by information seekers, as well as the important, unique items found only in local libraries. http://www.worldcat.org/

Comppile. Comppile has an inventory of publications in writing studies, including post-secondary composition, rhetoric, technical writing, ESL, and discourse analysis. http://comppile.org/

SLW News. *SLW News* provides a forum for the exchange of views, research, and pedagogical practices related to second language writing. This forum creates opportunities for interest section members to advocate for students and other members, to disseminate and promote research on second language writing, and to encourage and support the teaching of writing to ESOL students at all levels. http://www.tesol.org/connect/interest-sections/second-language-writing/slw-news

Chapter 13

The Status of Second Language Writing Studies in Western Europe

Melinda Reichelt
University of Toledo

Introduction

My interest in second language (L2) writing studies in Western Europe dates to the mid-1990s, when I spent a year at the *Gymnasium Kronshagen*, a secondary school outside of Kiel, Germany. While there, I investigated German-language and English-language writing instruction. My goal was to pursue long-term engagement in this context in order to gain an *emic*, or insider's, view of writing instruction at the *gynmasium*. My research contact, a teacher of German and English at this school, knew about the purpose of my research and encouraged me to come. But when I arrived on the scene, I was stymied by the fact that the other English and German teachers at this school told me, "We don't teach writing." Since I had the support of a Fulbright grant to stay in Germany and conduct my dissertation research for one year, I decided to remain there to see what, if anything, I could discover about writing in that context. What I eventually realized was that writing was so integrated into the content of the curriculum that teachers didn't see themselves as teaching writing per se. Instead, they typically used writing as a means of teaching, reinforcing, and testing other content (Reichelt, 1997, 1999, 2005).

This anecdote about my experience illustrates one of the differences between approaches to writing in many places in Europe, on the one hand, and my experiences with writing instruction in the U.S., on the other hand. This difference is that in most of Europe, there is no long-standing tradition of explicit writing instruction in higher education, perhaps because it is assumed that students attending university should already know how to write (See Bräuer, 2012).

For me, the year learning about writing instruction at a secondary school in Germany was just an introduction to L2 writing in Western Europe. Over the course of my career, I have read extensively about this issue and have worked with colleagues in various countries. Since I live and teach in the U.S., I cannot give an insider's account of the development of L2 writing studies in Western Europe. However, my status as an outsider allows me to recognize, in a way that an insider might not be able to, some of the unique and notable features of L2 writing studies in Western Europe. This plenary talk represents my attempt to convey what I see as key characteristics of the development and current status of L2 writing studies in that context. Some of my comments, especially those related to pedagogy, are relevant primarily to continental Western Europe, that is, they may be less pertinent to Great Britain and Ireland, where the situation is a bit different, in part because English is an L1 or a well-established dominant language.

Methodology

In order to investigate trends in L2 writing in Western Europe, I examined the last 10 to 15 years' or so worth of published literature on the topic, starting with works listed in the annotated bibliography published at the end of each issue of the *Journal of Second Language Writing* and eventually progressing to other published sources. In total, I examined about 150 sources on L2 writing in Western Europe. Additionally, I consulted the websites of relevant organizations, including the websites of the European Association of Teachers of Academic Writing (EATAW) and the European Writing Centers Association (EWCA). I also posted questions related to L2 writing studies on the listservs of EATAW and EWCA, and I received very helpful responses from individuals too numerous to acknowledge here, but to whom I am very grateful.

A limitation of my research is that I may have missed some locally-published materials on second language writing that are not indexed in international databases or that are unavailable to me in the U.S.

Contextual and Pedagogical Issues

Through my research, I have identified four factors that have influenced the development of L2 writing studies in Western Europe. These factors shape pedagogical practices and, to some extent, influence which topics are taken up in the research. They include the following: the lack of a long-standing tradition of explicit writing instruction in higher education; the multilingualism of Western Europe; the significant role of English in that context; and the fact that much L2 writing undertaken in Europe is FL writing. Next, I discuss how these factors shape pedagogical practices in Western Europe.

No Long-Standing Tradition of Explicit Writing Instruction in Higher Education

One significant factor that influences the teaching and research on L2 writing in Western Europe is the lack of a long-standing tradition of explicit writing instruction in higher education. As Kearns and Turner (2013) note, much writing instruction in Europe takes place outside traditional departments. In fact, much takes place outside the classroom, in writing centers. Recently, writing centers have proliferated across Western Europe. The impetus has come in part from contact with writing centers in North America (Bräuer, 2002; Bräuer & Girgensohn, 2012); from opportunities that writing specialists have had to network at conferences such as the European Writing Center Association (EWCA) conference, the European Association for the Teaching of Academic Writing (EATAW) conference, and regional conferences (K. Girgensohn, personal communication, August 20, 2013); and recognition that students in Western Europe needed writing support, especially as more students from a range of linguistic and educational backgrounds have begun to participate in larger numbers in higher education (Stassen & Jansen, 2012).

Writing centers in Western Europe vary in their functions and services. Most provide tutoring for papers written in the local L1, for native speakers as well as L2 students (Büker, 2003). Others focus primarily on L2 writers; for example, the writing centers at the University of Lüneberg and the University of Hamburg, both in Germany, focus solely on tutoring L2 writers of German; the writing center at the University of Tübingen in Germany offers tutoring solely for writers of English. Other writing centers operate in multiple languages. For example, the writing center in Freiburg, Germany, offers tutoring in German (both L1 and L2), English, and French (G. Bräuer, personal communication, August 16, 2013). The writing center at Viadrina European University, located in Germany on the Polish border, works primarily in German, but students also bring papers in English and occasionally in French, Spanish, or Polish. All of the tutors know different languages, and some are L2 writers of German themselves. Tutors sometimes switch into other languages when tutoring when discussing a student's text, even if the writing is in German, because it is easier for the student (K. Girgensohn, personal communication, August 20, 2013).

Besides tutoring, some writing centers also provide writing workshops and facilitate writing groups. Beyond this, writing centers in Western Europe may also offer online tutoring, facilitate writing projects with outside partners, provide access to independent learning material, assist faculty with writing, and provide staff development in the teaching of writing (Bräuer, 2012; Deane & Ganobscik-Williams, 2012; Ganobscik-Williams, 2012).

The Multilingualism of Western Europe

Another factor that shapes L2 writing studies in Western Europe is the fact that Western Europe is a multilingual environment, where people regularly need to undertake L2 writing for study or professional purposes. In Western Europe, as discussions of writing have developed, they have included a focus on *all* the languages in which individuals might write. Given the many languages in which writing is undertaken in Western Europe, the field of L2 writing studies there is more inclusive and broad-ranging than it is in many other places, where L2 writing studies has focused primarily on L2 English (Reichelt, in press; Reichelt, Rinnert, Lefkowitz & Schultz, 2012).

The L2 writing undertaken in Western Europe may be in English, another L2, or the locally dominant language, which may be an L2 for any given individual. These languages include, among others, English (Lillis & Curry, 2010; Roca de Larios, Manchón, Murphy & Marín, 2008), French (Bodé, Serres, & Ugen, 2009; Faraco, Barbier & Piolat, 2002; Guillot, 2005; Kuiken & Vedder, 2007, 2008; O'Sullivan & Chambers, 2006, Schindler, 2000), Spanish (Armengol-Castells 2001, Cenoz & Gorter, 2011; Dekhinet, Topping, Duran & Blanch, 2008; de Haan & van Esch, 2005; Niño, 2008), Basque (Cenoz & Gorter, 2011), Italian (Kuiken & Vedder, 2007, 2008), Finnish (Luoma & Tarnanen, 2003), Swedish, (Knutsson, Pargman, Eklundh & Westlund, 2007), German (Bodé, Serres & Ugen, 2009; Frey & Herringer, 2007) and Greek (McDonough & McDonough, 2001).

There is a significant body of literature that outlines approaches to teaching writing in German as a second or foreign language (François, 2004; Lieber & Posset, 1988). This can be attributed in part to the fact that German has historically been a dominant language in Europe and continues to play a significant role in European scholarship; additionally, German-language-dominant countries have a strong tradition of hosting students from abroad, who often must learn to function in German for academic purposes, including learning to write in German.

Krumm, Fandrych, Hufeisen and Riemer (2010) outline varying goals for learners of writing in L2 German, delineating different goals for immigrant learners in German-speaking countries versus goals for learners of German as a foreign language (Starke & Zuchewicz, 2003). This literature also addresses topics such as teaching L2 German creative, literary, and biographical writing (Finke & Thums-Senft, 2008; Schreiter, 2002) as well as helping students of L2 German writing understand German rhetorical conventions (Drewnowska-Vargáné, 1999; Hufeisen, 2002).

Because the audience for this pedagogical literature includes primarily German-speaking teachers of L2 German, most of this literature is published in the German language. It is very rarely cited in the English-language literature on L2 writing, probably because it is linguistically inaccessible to many L2 writing researchers.

The Significant Role of English in This Context

L2 writing studies in Western Europe is also influenced by the fact that English plays a significant role in Western Europe in a variety of realms. These include the workplace, business, science, technology, education, international relations, sports, design and fashion, tourism, media, and entertainment (Berns, Claes, de Bot, Evers, Hasebrink, Huibregtse, Truchot & van der Wijst, 2007). Thus, much of the L2 writing undertaken in Western Europe is done in English. Because of the important role English plays in Western Europe, there is a great deal of interest in teaching students to write in English for specific purposes (ESP) (Hyland, 2007). This includes writing for academic, scientific, or professional purposes. For example, Mungra (2012) describes teaching Italian medical students how to write journal abstracts in English for medical research articles, and Busch-Lauer (1999) discusses teaching ESP writing to medical students in Germany. Gustafsson and Boström (2012) discuss ESP writing instruction in Sweden for engineering students, and Foz-Gil and González-Pueyo (2009) describe their work helping the staff of Spanish small businesses to write correspondence in English.

Much of the L2 Writing Undertaken Is FL Writing Rather than SL Writing

Another factor shaping L2 writing studies is that much of the L2 writing undertaken in Western Europe is foreign language (FL) writing rather than second language (SL) writing. Most of this is in English, but some of it is in other languages (See Kuiken & Vedder, 2007, 2008, for example, on writing in L2 Italian and French, undertaken in the Netherlands.) As Furneaux, Paran and Fairfax (2007) point out, FL instructors, even when teaching writing, may view themselves as language teachers, seeing writing not only as an end in itself, but also as a means of fostering overall acquisition of the target language. In other words, teachers may be interested in what Manchón and Roca de Larios (2011) call the "language learning potential of L2 writing" (p. 181), especially at lower levels of language instruction. Feistauer (2010) argues that writing in the context of language instruction is an important skill in itself, but is also a means of learning the target language. She outlines several goals of L2 writing instruction including communicative-functional writing, personal and creative writing, instrumental writing, and intercultural writing. She describes instrumental writing as writing whose goal is to support the development of other areas, including grammar and vocabulary learning.

L2 Writing-Related Organizations, Conferences, Projects, Journals, and Presses

As a great deal of L2 writing occurs in Western Europe, it is not surprising that an infrastructure exists in support of that endeavor. This includes professional organizations, conferences, journals, and academic presses. Two significant milestones in the development of writing studies in Western Europe include the founding of the European Writing Centers Association (EWCA) in 1989, and the founding of the European Association of Teachers of Academic Writing (EATAW) in 2001. It is important to note that these organizations are devoted to writing in general, not to L2 writing exclusively. In fact, writing specialists in Europe who focus on English may identify more with the community of researchers of English for Academic Purposes rather than seeing themselves primarily as second language writing scholars.

EWCA, is a regional affiliate of the International Writing Center Association (IWCA), formerly the National Writing Center Association. EWCA was the first affiliate of IWCA formed outside the U.S. and currently has about 650 members. According to its website, the EWCA's mission is "to solicit engagement with institutions or individuals interested in the interactive and collaborative work of Writing Centers everywhere" (http://ewca.sabanciuniv. edu/eng/, accessed August 15, 2013). EWCA held its first conference in 2000, and since then has held various conferences and seminars. Its most recent conference was held in July 8-10, 2016 in Łódź, Poland. The EWCA also hosts a listserv. The website for EWCA is http://ewca.sabanciuniv.edu/eng/.

EATAW has approximately 600 members. EATAW held its first conference in 2001, and held its most recent conference, its eighth, in June 2015 in Tallinn, Estonia. EATAW aims to connect teachers and scholars of academic writing; to raise awareness, organize continuing education, and foster research about teaching academic writing in various languages in Europe; to define and secure standards for teaching, tutoring, and research; and to connect teaching academic writing with related fields (http://www.eataw.eu/constitution.html, accessed July 4, 2013).[1] National affiliates of EATAW include *Forum Schreiben* (http://www.forumschreiben.ch), the Swiss affiliate, the *Gesellschaft für Wissenschaftliches Schreiben (GewissS)* (http://www.gewisss.at), the Austrian affiliate, and *Gesellschaft für Schreibdidaktik und Schreibforschung* (www. schreibdidaktik.de.), the German affiliate.

EATAW hosts a listserv and also publishes the *Journal of Academic Writing*. This journal "focuses on the teaching, tutoring, researching, administration and development of academic writing in higher education in Europe" (http://

---

1 The homepage for EATAW can be accessed via the following URL: http://www.eataw.eu/.

e-learning.coventry.ac.uk, accessed July 12, 2013). The *Journal of Academic Writing* publishes articles about writing in Ll as well as L2. Closely affiliated with the *Journal of Academic Writing* is the database WritingPRO: Knowledge Center for Writing Process Research (http://www.writingpro.eu/). The purpose of the database is to provide a means of sharing and developing expertise in all types of writing process research.

Other professional organizations related to writing also exist, including, the writing SIG (Special Interest Group) of EARLI, the European Association of Research on Learning and Instruction. According to the EARLI website, "SIG Writing aims to provide a forum for exchange of ideas about writing and promoting research collaboration between writing researchers from different countries as well as from different disciplines" (http://www.earli.org/special_interest_groups/writing, accessed July 4, 2013). The EARLI SIG Writing holds a conference every two years; the last one was held in July 2016 in Liverpool, UK. The EARLI SIG Writing publishes the *Journal of Writing Research*, which aims to publish inquiry from a broad range of disciplines that focuses on writing in first, second, and other languages.

Another relevant professional organization is Prowitec, an interdisciplinary forum founded in 1993 whose goals include fostering professionally-related communication and text production, with a focus on continuing education and industry and technology. It is based in Aachen, Germany, and its website is in German (http://www.prowitec.rwth-aachen.de/).

Thus, a number of organizations, several of which support conferences and/or journals, provide writing specialists in Western Europe a means of connecting with others in the field. Additionally, the Symposium on Second Language Writing, which rotates its venue from place to place around the globe, took place in Murcia, Spain, in summer 2010.

The writing project Lidhum involves cooperative research between four European universities in Macedonia, Ukraine, Switzerland, and Romania. Its goal is to gain an understanding of the writing context in the participating universities and to foster writing research and teaching.[1]

Several additional journals and presses based in Western Europe publish work related to L2 writing, most of which focuses on both L1 and L2 writing. Besides the previously-mentioned *Journal of Academic Writing* and *Journal of Writing Research*, the on-line journal *Zeitschrift Schreiben*, also known as the *European Journal of Writing*, publishes some work on L2 writing. This journal is aimed at readers in schools and higher education, mostly in German-speaking countries. It publishes work about writing in general, work that sometimes encompasses writing in L2 English since much academic writing done by students pursuing higher degrees is done in English. The international journal *System*, published by Elsevier, was founded in Sweden and focuses on applications of technology and applied linguistics to L2 teaching, especially L2 English, (http://www.journals. elsevier.com/system/, accessed July 13, 2013). It regularly publishes articles about L2 writing.

In terms of books, Cambridge University Press publishes volumes related to L2 writing. Kluwer, based in Dordrecht, the Netherlands, publishes a series entitled "Studies in Writing," edited by Gert Rijlaarsdam. The series focuses on writing in general, including but not limited to L2 writing.

Trends in L2 Writing Research

In my examination of about 150 sources on L2 writing in Western Europe, I have identified several lines of research, ones which focus on the following topics: text analysis; writers' processes and strategies; language-learning and error; assessment; publishing in English; and computer-assisted language learning (CALL).

---

1 Lidhum's homepage can be accessed through the following URL: http://www.ceaw.org.ua/lidhum.html.

Text Analysis

A significant body of research stemming from Western Europe focuses on text analysis. Some of this work investigates the features of professional texts, which supports the pedagogical interest in teaching writing for academic, scientific, or professional purposes. For example, Connor, Davis and de Ruycker (1995) compared job application letters written in L2 English by Flemish speakers with those written in L1 English, and Connor and Mauranen (1999) analyzed grant proposals written in English by Finnish speakers.

Most of the text analysis research, however, focuses on texts written by students. This work uses analysis of texts written by L2 learners to attempt to uncover information about a broad range of topics. For example, Kuiken & Vedder (2002) analyze texts written collaboratively by three groups of students, Dutch L2 learners of French, Italian, and English. They investigated the effect of group interaction on the grammatical and lexical quality of the texts, finding no positive effect. Kuiken and Vedder (2008) analyzed the writing of Dutch students writing in L2 Italian or French, in response to two tasks of differing complexity. The cognitively more demanding task yielded more linguistically accurate writing, but there were no differences on measures of syntactic complexity or lexical variety. Other analyses of student texts have focused on topics such as textual borrowing (Pecorari, 2003, 2005; Petrić, 2012), age-related differences (Torras & Celaya, 2001), coherence (Arfé & Boscolo, 2006), lexical issues (Agustín Lach, 2011; Ädel & Erman, 2013; Olsen, 1999), writing development (de Haan & van Esch, 2005), L1 influence (Maxwell-Reid, 2011), narrative features (van Beijsterveldt & van Hell, 2009), rhetorical positioning (Vergaro, 2011), and negation (Herriman, 2009).

Writers' Processes and Strategies

While the above researchers have focused on written products, many researchers in Western Europe have investigated students' writing processes.

For example, Armengol-Castells (2001) found that students' planning behavior was consistent across three languages: L1 Catalan, L2 Spanish, and L2 English. As part of "The Murcia L2 Writing Project," Manchón, Murphy and Roca de Larios (1997, 2000) and Roca de Larios, Murphy and Manchón (2008) investigated the activities of Spanish students of English when rescanning and assessing their texts in order to move forward in their writing. The researchers found variations depending on task type, proficiency level, language used for rescanning text, and the writer's approach to task completion. Victori (1997, 1999) and Faraco, Barbier & Piolat (2002) also investigated writers' strategies. Additionally, researchers have investigated revision (Kehagia & Cox, 1997; Lindgren, Miller & Sullivan, 2008; Porte, 1996; Stevenson, Schoonen & de Glopper, 2006), L1 use during L2 writing (Manchón, Murphy & Roca, 2007; Murphy & Roca de Larios, 2010; van Weijen, van den Bergh, Rijlaarsdam & Sanders, 2009), and allocation of time during the writing process (Roca de Larios, Manchón & Murphy, 2006; Roca de Larios, Manchón, Murphy & Marín, 2008; Roca de Larios, Marín & Murphy, 2001). Roca de Larios and Murphy (2001) argue for a socio-cognitive interpretation of L2 writing processes; they suggest that process research should take into consideration not only cognitive aspects of the composing process, but also contextual and social factors that affect writing.

Language-Learning and Error

Other researchers in Western Europe have focused on the language-learning aspect of writing. Manchón & Roca de Larios (2011) report on EFL learners' perceptions of "the language learning potential of L2 writing" (p. 181); they note that this potential was a motivating and guiding factor in students' writing activities. Santos, López-Serrano & Manchón (2010) draw a connection between error correction and language learning. These researchers compared the effects of two types of corrective feedback—error correction versus reformulation—on noticing and uptake. They found that error correction induced more uptake than reformulation, and they discuss the implications for the language-learning potential of corrective feedback. Along similar lines, van Beuningen, de Jong & Kuiken investigated the effect of direct versus indirect feedback (2008) and of comprehensive error correction (2012).

Many of the researchers who focus on error correction reference the error correction debate begun by Truscott (1996), who posited that error correction is ineffective and should be abandoned. Bruton (2009a, 2010) offers an alternative analysis of previous findings on the topic, and offers suggestions for improved research design. Bruton (2009b) argues that the focus of the error correction debate has been too narrow because communicative writing includes discourse features beyond grammar. In fact, in Bruton (2007), he reports students' gains in vocabulary after completing a translational writing activity, noting that a focus on errors alone does not account for language gains that are the result of writing instruction. Other researchers investigate error issues from a different perspective. Furneaux, Paran & Fairfax (2007) investigated the roles teachers assume in providing feedback, and Porte (1999) examined faculty toleration of error.

Assessment

As Leki (2001) points out, students who learn to write in L2 are almost always tested in writing as well. This is often the case in Western Europe, and researchers have thus focused on various aspects of assessment of L2 writing. Some have focused on self assessment (Luoma & Tarnanen, 2003; Sullivan & Lindgren, 2002) or automated assessment (Frey & Herringer, 2007), while others have focused on development of writing tests (Shaw & Weir, 2007). Several researchers have investigated how scoring scales or rubrics can be used within writing instruction, to improve student writing and help students prepare for specific tests such as the IELTS (Green, 2005, 2006), Cambridge ESOL tests (Hawkey & Barker, 2004), and assessments based on the *Common European Framework of Reference for Languages* (Neff-van Aertsler, 2013).

Publishing in English

Given the dominant role of English in Europe and in academia, it is not surprising that research is devoted to the phenomenon of non-native English speakers publishing in English (Lillis & Curry, 2010). Authors have investigated various aspects of this issue, including how texts written by non-native English speakers are shaped and edited for publication (Burrough-Boenisch, 2003; Yli-Jokipii & Jorgensen, 2004), scholars' attitudes toward publishing in English (Ferguson, Pérez-Llantada, & Plo, 2011), and issues of access and inequality related to the need to publish in English (Curry & Lillis, 2004, 2010; Lillis, Magyar & Robinson-Pant, 2010).

Computer-Assisted Language Learning (CALL)

Researchers in Western Europe have also investigated Computer-Assisted Language Learning (CALL) in L2 writing. Some researchers have focused on the use of various technological tools in writing, including the use of word-processing in revision (Kehagia & Cox, 1997; Lindgren, 2008; Stevenson, Schoonen & de Glopper, 2006), corpus consultation (Chambers, 2010; O'Sullivan, 2010; O'Sullivan & Chmabers, 2006), and the use of grammar, spelling, and style checkers (Knutsson, Pargman, Eklundh & Westlund, 2007; O'Regan, 2010). Other researchers investigating CALL have explored the effects of interactive writing within the context of the Internet, including chat rooms and forums (Foucher, 2010), collaborative writing for Wikipedia (Ollivier, 2010), and online tutoring (Dekhinet, Topping, Duran & Blanch, 2008).

Conclusion

L2 writing specialists in Western Europe work under a unique set of circumstances. As Kearns & Turner (2013) point out, the context for teaching writing in Europe is quite different from that of North America, for example, with most writing instruction in Europe "situated, in most cases, outside traditional departments, [and] tasked with teaching specialized professional and/or disciplinary writing" (conference abstract). Although Kearns & Turner are describing the state of writing instruction in general in Europe, their contentions hold true for L2 writing instruction in Western Europe. L2 writing specialists have faced their unique challenges by developing pedagogical and research approaches that are suitable to their specific environment, and by creating or joining local organizations that foster connections and communication among themselves and the worldwide community of L2 writing specialists. It is my prediction that interest in L2 writing will continue to grow in Western Europe, and that the field of L2 writing studies will increasingly benefit from theory, research, and pedagogical ideas from this context.

Acknowledgments

I am very grateful to the organizers and student assistants for the Symposium on Second Language Writing. Special thanks also go to the following individuals who helped me in my research: Gerd Bräuer, Angela Chambers, Christiane Donahue, Inge Eijkhout, Katrin Girgensohn, Helmut Gruber, Judith Kearns, Karin Lach, Daniel Spielmann, Judith Kearns, and Brian Turner. Thanks also to Łukasz Salski for introducing me to the European Writing Centers Association, which has significantly shaped my understanding of L2 writing studies in Europe—and has broadened my conception of what writing centers can do and be.

References

Ädel, A. & Erman, B. (2012). Recurrent word combinations in academic writing by native and non-native speakers of English: A lexical bundles approach. *English for Specific Purposes, 31,* 81-92.

Agustín Lach, M. P. (2011). *Lexical Errors and Accuracy in Foreign Language Writing.* Bristol, Buffalo: Multilingual Matters.

Arfé, B. & Boscolo, P. (2006). Causal coherence in deaf and hearing students' written narratives. *Discourse Processes, 42,* 271-300.

Armengol-Castells, L. (2001). Text-generating strategies of three multilingual writers: A protocol-based study. *Language Awareness, 10,* 91-106.

Berns, M., Claes, M.-T., de Bot, K., Evers, R., Hasebrink, U., Huibregtse, I., Truchot, C. & van der Wijst, P. (2007). English in Europe. In M. Berns, K. de Bot & U. Hasebrink (Eds.), *In the Presence of English: Media and European Youth (pp. 15-42).* Springer.

Bodé, S., Serres, J. & Ugen, S. (2009). Similarities and differences of Luxembourgish and Romanophone 12 year olds' spelling strategies in German and French. *Written Language & Literacy, 12,* 82-96.

Bräuer, G. (2002). Drawing connections across education: The Freiburg writing center model. *Language and Learning Across the Disciplines, 5,* 61-80.

Bräuer, G. (2012). Academic literacy development. In C. Thaiss, G. Bräuer, P. Carlino, L. Ganobscik-Williams & A. Sinha (Eds.), *Writing Programs Worldwide: Profiles of Academic Writing in Many Places* (pp. 467-484). Fort Collins, CO: The WAC Clearinghouse and Parlor Press.

Bräuer, G. & Ganobscik-Williams, L. (2012). Literacy development projects initiating institutional change. In C. Thaiss, G. Bräuer, P. Carlino, L. Ganobscik-Williams & A. Sinha (Eds.), *Writing Programs Worldwide: Profiles of Academic Writing in Many Places* (pp. 225-238). Fort Collins, CO: The WAC Clearinghouse and Parlor Press.

Bruton, A. (2007). Vocabulary learning from dictionary referencing and language feedback in EFL translational writing. *Language Teaching Research, 11,* 413-431.

Bruton, A. (2009a). Designing research into the effects of grammar correction in L2 writing: Not so straightforward. *Journal of Second Language Writing, 18,* 136-140.

Bruton, A. (2009b). Improving accuracy is not the only reason for writing, and even if it were. *System, 37,* 600-613.

Bruton, A. (2010). Another reply to Truscott on error correction: Improved situated designs over statistics. *System, 38,* 491-498.

Büker, S. (2003). Teaching academic writing to international students: Individual tutoring as a supplement to workshops. In Björk, L., Bräuer, G., Rienecker, L. & P. Jörgenson (Eds.), *Teaching Academic Writing in European Higher Education* (pp. 41-57). Dordrecht: Kluwer.

Burrough-Boenisch, J. (2003). Shapers of published NNS research articles. *Journal of Second Language Writing, 12,* 223-243.

Busch-Lauer, I. (1999). Fremdsprachige Schreibkompetenz: Erfahrungen bei der Ausbildung von Medizinstudenten. In Kruse, O., Jakobs, E.-M. & Ruhmann, G. (Eds.), *Schlüsselkompetenz Schreiben* (pp. 249-268). Neuwied: Luchterhand Verlag.

Cenoz, J. & Gorter, D. (2011). Focus on multilingualism: A study of trilingual writing. *Modern Language Journal, 95,* 356-369.

Chambers, A. (2010). L'apprentissage de l'écriture en langue seconde á l'aide d'un corpus spécialisé. *Revue Française de Linguistique Appliqué, 15,* 9-20.

Connor, U., Davis, K. & de Rycker, T. (1995). Correctness and clarity in applying for overseas jobs: A cross-cultural analysis of U.S. and Flemish applications. *Text, 15,* 457-475.

Connor, U. & Mauranen, A. (1999). Linguistic analysis of grant proposals: European Union research grants. *English for Specific Purposes, 18,* 47-62.

Curry, M. & Lillis, T. (2004). Multilingual scholars and the imperative to publish in English: negotiating interests, demands, and rewards. *TESOL Quarterly, 38,* 661-688.

Curry, M. & Lillis, T. (2010). Academic research networks: Accessing resources for English-medium publishing. *English for Specific Purposes, 29,* 281-295.

de Haan, P. & van Esch, K. (2005). The development of writing in English and Spanish as foreign languages. *Assessing Writing, 10,* 100-116.

Deane, M. & Ganobscik-Williams, L. (2012). Providing a hub for writing development: A profile of the centre for academic writing (CAW), Coventry University, England. In C. Thaiss, G. Bräuer, P. Carlino, L.

Ganobscik-Williams & A. Sinha (Eds.), *Writing Programs Worldwide: Profiles of Academic Writing in Many Places* (pp. 189-201). Fort Collins, CO: The WAC Clearinghouse and Parlor Press.

Dekhinet, R., Topping, K., Duran, D. & Blanch, S. (2008). Let me learn with my peers online! Foreign language learning through reciprocal peer tutoring. *Innovate: Journal of Online Education, 4.* Retrieved from http://www.innovateonline.info

Drewnowska-Vargáné, E. (1999). Textlinguistik für Germanistikstudenten im nichtdeutschsprachigen Raum—im besonderen Hinblick auf Textrezeption und Textproduktion. *Deutsch als Fremdsprache, 36,* 35-40.

Faraco, M., Barbier, M. & Piolat, A. (2002). A comparison between notetaking in L1 and L2 by undergraduate students. In S. Ransdell & M. Barbier (Eds.), *New Directions for Research in L2 Writing* (pp. 145-167). Dordrecht, The Netherlands: Kluwer.

Feistauer, R. (2010). Schreibdidaktik. In Barkowski, H. & Krumm-H.-J. (Eds.), *Fachlexicon deutsch als Fremd- und Zweitsprache* (pp. 283-284). Tübingen, Basel: A Francke Verlag.

Ferguson, G., Pérez-Llantada, C. & Plo, R. (2011). English as an international language of scientific publication: A study of attitudes. *World Englishes, 30,* 41-59.

Finke, E. & Thums-Senft, B. (2008). *Begegnung in Texten. Kreativ-Biographisches Schreiben in der interkulturellen Bildung und im Unterricht Deutsch als Fremdsprache oder Zweitsprache.* Stuttgart: Schmetterling.

Foucher, A.-L. (2010). Clavardage, forum et macro-tâche pour l'apprentissage du FLE: quelle(s) articulation(s) possible(s) pour quells apports? *Revue Française de Linguistique Appliqué, 15,* 155-172.

Foz-Gil, C. & González-Pueyo, I. (2009). Helping Spanish SMEs staff to develop their competence in writing business letters. *International Journal of English Studies, 9,* 43-61.

François, A. (2004). Wissenschaftliches Schreiben in der Fremdsprache Deutsch: Am Beispiel von Abschluss Arbeiten französischer Studierender. Doctoral Dissertation, University of Siegen, Germany.

Frey, E. & Heringer, H. (2007). Automatische Bewertung schriftlicher Lernerproduktionen. *Linguistische Berichte, 211,* 319-335.

Furneaux, C., Paran, A. & Fairfax, B. (2007). Teacher stance as reflected in feedback on student writing: An empirical study of secondary school teachers in five countries. *IRAL, 45,* 69-94.

Ganobscik-Williams, L. (2012). Reflecting on what can be gained from comparing models of academic writing provision. In C. Thaiss, G. Bräuer, P. Carlino, L. Ganobscik-Williams & A. Sinha (Eds.), *Writing Programs Worldwide: Profiles of Academic Writing in Many Places* (pp. 499-511). Fort Collins, CO: The WAC Clearinghouse and Parlor Press.

Green, A. (2005). EAP study recommendations and score gains on the IELTS Academic Writing test. *Assessing Writing, 10,* 44-60.

Green, A. (2006). Washback to the learner: Learner and teacher perspectives on the IELTS preparation course expectations and outcomes. *Assessing Writing, 11,* 113-134.

Guillot, M.-N. (2005). Il y a des gens qui disent que . . . "there are people who say that . . . " Beyond grammatical accuracy in FL learners' writing: Issues of non-nativeness. *International Review of Applied Linguistics, 43,* 109-128.

Gustafsson, M. (2011). Academic literacies approach for facilitating language for specific purposes. *Ibérica 2,* 101-122.

Gustafsson, M. & Boström, T. (2012). Multi-disciplinary, multi-lingual engineering education writing development: A writing programme perspective. In C. Thaiss, G. Bräuer, P. Carlino, L. Ganobscik-Williams & A. Sinha (Eds.), *Writing Programs Worldwide: Profiles of Academic Writing in Many Places* (pp. 377-388). Fort Collins, CO: The WAC Clearinghouse and Parlor Press.

Hawkey, R. & Barker, F. (2004). Developing a common scale for the assessment of writing. *Assessing Writing, 9,* 122-159.

Herriman, J. (2009). Don't get me wrong! Negation in argumentative writing by Swedish and British students and professional writers. *Nordic Journal of English Studies, 8,* 117-140.

Hufeisen, B. (2002). *Ein deutsches Referat is kein englischsprachiges Essay: Theoretische und praktische Überlegungen zu einem verbesserten textsortenbezogenem Shreibunterricht in der Fremdsprache Deutsch an der Universität.* Innsbruck: Wien: Studienverlag.

Hyland, K. (2007). Genre pedagogy: Language, literacy, and L2 writing instruction. *Journal of Second Language Writing, 16,* 148-164.

Kearns, J. & Turner, B. (June, 2013). Practices and perspectives: A further analysis of EATAW conference discourse. Unpublished paper presented at the European Association of Teachers of Academic Writing Conference, Budapest, Hungary.

Kehagia,, O. & Cox, M. (1997). Revision changes when using wordprocessors in an English as a foreign language context. *Computer Assisted Language Learning, 10,* 239-253.

Knutsson, O., Pargman, T., Eklundh, K. & Westlund, S. (2007). Designing and developing a language environment for second language writers. *Computers & Education, 49,* 1122-1146.

Krumm, H.-J., Fandrych, C., Hufeisen, B. & Riemer, C. (2010). *Deutsch als Fremd- und Zweitsprache.* Berlin, New York: De Gruyten Mouton.

Kuiken, F. & Vedder, I. (2002). Collaborative writing in L2: The effect of group interaction on text quality. In S. Ransdell & M. Barbier (Eds.), *New Directions for Research in L2 Writing* (pp. 169-188). Dordrecht: Kluwer.

Kuiken, F. & Vedder, I. (2007). Task complexity and measures of linguistic performance in L2 writing. *IRAL, 45,* 261-284.

Kuiken, F. & Vedder, I. (2008). Cognitive task complexity and written output in Italian and French as a Foreign Language. *Journal of Second Language Writing, 17,* 48-60.

Leki, I. (2001). Material, educational, and ideological challenges of teaching EFL writing at the turn of the century. *International Journal of English Studies, 1,* 197-209.

Li, J. & Shmitt, N. (2009). The acquisition of lexical phrases in academic writing: A longitudinal case study. *Journal of Second Language Writing, 18,* 85-102.

Lieber, M. & Posset, J. (1988). *Texte schreiben im Germanistik-Studium.* München: iudicium verlag.

Lillis, T. & Curry, M. (2010). *Academic Writing in a Global Context.* London: Routledge.

Lillis, T., Magyar, A. & Robinson-Pant, A. (2010). An international journal's attempt to address inequalities in academic publishing: Developing a writing for publication programme. *Compare: A Journal of Comparative and International Education, 40,* 781-800.

Lindgren, E., Miller, K. S. & Sullivan, K. (2008). Development of fluency and revision in L1 and L2 writing in Swedish high school years eight and nine. *ITL International Journal of Applied Linguistics, 156,* 133-152.

Lindgren, E. & Sullivan, K. (2003). Stimulated recall as a trigger for increasing noticing and language awareness in the L2 writing classroom: A cast study of two young female writers. *Language Awareness, 12,* 172-186.

Luoma, S. & Tarnanen, M. (2003). Creating a self-rating instrument for second language writing: From idea to implementation. *Language Testing, 20,* 440-465.

Manchón, R., Murphy, L. & Roca de Larios, J. (2007). Lexical retrieval processes and strategies in second language writing: A synthesis of empirical research. *International Journal of English Studies, 7,* 149-174.

Manchón, R. & Roca de Larios, J. (2007). Writing-to-learn in instructed language learning contexts. In E. Alcón Soler and M. P. Safont Jordà (Eds.), *Intercultural Language Use and Language Learning* (pp. 101-121). Dordrecht, The Netherlands: Springer.

Manchón, R. & Roca de Larios, J. (2011). Writing to learn in FL contexts: Exploring learners' perceptions of the language learning potential of L2 Writing. In R. Manchón (Ed.), *Learning-to-write and Writing-to-learn in an Additional Language* (pp. 181-208). Amsterdam, Philadelphia: John Benjamins.

Manchón Ruiz, R., Roca de Larios, J. & Murphy, L. (1997). Backward operations in L2 writing: A tentative classification. *Learning and Instruction, 10,* 36-52.

Manchón, R., Roca de Larios, J. & Murphy, L. (2000). An approximation to the study of backtracking in L2 writing. *Learning and Instruction, 10,* 13-35.

Maxwell-Reid, C. (2011). The challenges of contrastive discourse analysis: Reflecting on a study into the influence of English on students' written Spanish on a bilingual education program in Spain. *Written Communication, 28,* 417-435.

McDonough, J. & McDonough, S. (2001). Composing in a foreign language: An insider-outsider perspective. *Language Awareness, 10,* 233-247.

Mungra, P. (2010). Teaching writing of scientific abstracts in English: CLIL methodology in an integrated English and Medicine course. *Ibérica, 20,* 151-166.

Neff-van Aertsler, J. (2013). Contextualizing EFL argumentation writing practices within the *Common European Framework* descriptors. *Journal of Second Language Writing, 22,* 198-209.

Niño, A. (2008). Evaluating the use of machine translation post-editing in the foreign language class. *Computer Assisted Language Learning, 21,* 29-49.

Ollivier, C. (2010). Ecriture collaborative en ligne: Une approche interactionnelle de la production écrite pour des apprenants acteurs sociaux et motivés. *Revue Française de Linguistique Appliqué, 15,* 121-137.

Olsen, S. (1999). Errors and compensatory strategies: A study of grammar and vocabulary in texts written by Norwegian learners of English. *System, 27,* 191-205.

O'Regan, B. (2010). From spell, grammar and style checkers to writing aid for English and French as a foreign language: Challenges and opportunities. *Revue Française de Linguistique Appliqué, 15,* 67-84.

O'Sullivan, Í. (2010). Using corpora to enhance learners' academic writing skills in French. *Revue Française de Linguistique Appliqué, 15,* 21-35.

O'Sullivan, Í. & Chambers, A. (2006). Learners' writing skills in French: Corpus consultation and learner evaluation. *Journal of Second Language Writing, 15,* 49-68.

Pecorari, D. (2003). Good and original: Plagiarism and patchwriting in academic second language writing. *Journal of Second Language Writing, 12,* 317-345.

Pecorari, D. (2006). Visible and occluded citation features in postgraduate second-language writing. *English for Specific Purposes, 25,* 4-29.

Petrić, B. (2012). Legitimate textual borrowing: Direct quotation in L2 student writing. *Journal of Second Language Writing, 21,* 102-117.

Porte, G. (1996). When writing fails: How academic context and past learning experiences shape revision. *System, 24,* 107-116.

Porte, G. (1999). Where to draw the red line: Error toleration of native and non-native EFL faculty. *Foreign Language Annals, 32,* 426-434.

Reichelt, M. (1997). L2 writing instruction at the German "Gymnasium": A 13th-grade English class writes the "Abitur". *Journal of Second Language Writing, 6,* 265-291.

Reichelt, M. (1999). A cross-cultural perspective on writing curricula. *International Education, 29,* 16-42.

Reichelt, M. (2005). WAC practices at the secondary level in Germany. *The WAC Journal, 16,* 89-100.

Reichelt, M. (in press). L2 Writing in Languages Other than English. Accepted for publication in the *Handbook of L2 writing.*

Reichelt, M., Rinnert, C., Lefkowitz, N. & Schultz, J. M. (2012). Key issues in FL writing. *Foreign Language Annals, 45,* 22-41.

Roca de Larios, J., Manchón, R. & Murphy, L. (2006). Generating text in native and foreign language writing: A temporal analysis of problem-solving formulation processes. *Modern Language Journal, 90,* 100-114.

Roca de Larios, J., Manchón, R., Murphy, L. & Marín, J. (2008). The foreign language writer's strategic behaviour in the allocation of time to writing processes. *Journal of Second Language Writing, 17,* 30-47.

Roca de Larios, J., Marín, J. & Murphy, L. (2001). A temporal analysis of formulation processes in L1 and L2 writing. *Language Learning, 51,* 497-538.

Roca de Larios, J. & Murphy, L. (2001). Steps toward a socio-cognitive interpretation of second language composition processes. *International Journal of English Studies, 2,* 25-45.

Roca de Larios, J., Murphy, L. & Manchón, R. (1999). The use of restructuring strategies in EFL writing: A study of Spanish learners of English as a foreign language. *Journal of Second Language Writing, 8,* 13-44.

Santos, M., López-Serrano, S. & Manchón, R. (2010). The differential effect of two types of direct feedback written corrective feedback on noticing and uptake: Reformulation vs. error correction. *International Journal of English Studies, 10,* 131-154.

Schindler, K. (2000). Gemeinsames Schreiben in der Fremdsprache: Muster, Kreativität, und das Glück des Autors. *Dlottodidactica 28,* 161-184.

Schreiter, I. (2002). *Screibversuche. Kreatives Schreiben bei Lernen des Deutschen als Fremdsprache.* München: iudicium.

Shaw, D. & Weir, C. (2007). *Examining Writing: Research and Practice in Assessing Second Language Writing.* Cambridge: Cambridge University Press.

Starke, G. & Zuchewicz, T. (2003). *Wissentschaftliches Schreiben im Studium von Deutsch als Fremsprache.* Frankfurt am Main: Peter Lang.

Stassen, I. & Jansen, C. (2012). The development of an academic writing centre in the Netherlands. In C. Thaiss, G. Bräuer, P. Carlino, L. Ganobscik-Williams & A. Sinha (ED). *Writing Programs Worldwide: Profiles of Academic Writing in Many Places* (pp. 293-300). Fort Collins, CO: The WAC Clearinghouse and Parlor Press.

Stevenson, M., Schoonen, R. & de Glopper, K. (2006). Revising in two languages: A multi-dimensional comparison of online writing revisions in L1 and FL. *Journal of Second Language Writing, 15,* 201-223.

Sullivan, K. & Lindgren, E. (2002). Self-assessment in autonomous computer-aided second language writing. *ELT Journal, 56,* 258-266.

Torras, M. R. & Celaya, M. L. (2001). Age-related differences in the development of written production. An empirical study of EFL school learners. *International Journal of English Studies, 1,* 103-126.

Truscott, J. (1996). The case against grammar correction in L2 writing classes. *Language Learning, 46,* 327-369.

van Beijsterveldt, L. & van Hell, J. (2013). Evaluative expression in deaf children's written narratives. *International Journal of Language & Communication Disorders, 44,* 675-692.

van Beuningen, C., de Jong, N. & Kuiken, F. (2008). The effect of direct and indirect corrective feedback on L2 learners' written accuracy. *ITL International Journal of Applied Linguistics, 156,* 279-296.

van Beuningen, C., de Jong, N. & Kuiken, F.(2012). Evidence on the effectiveness of comprehensive error correction in second language writing. *Language Learning, 62,* 1-41.

van Weijen, D., van den Bergh, H., Rijlaarsdam, G. & Sanders, T. (2009). L1 use during L2 writing: An empirical study of a complex phenomenon. *Journal of Second Language Writing, 18,* 235-250.

Vergaro, C. (2011). Shades of impersonality: Rhetorical positioning in the academic writing of Italian students of English. *Linguistics and Education, 22,* 118-132.

Victori Blaya, M. (1997). EFL composing skills and strategies: Four case studies. *RESLA, 12,* 163-184.

Victori, M. (1999). An analysis of writing knowledge in EFL composing: A case study of two effective and two less effective writers. *System, 27,* 537-555.

Yli-Jokipii, H. & Jorgensen, P. (2004). Academic journalese for the Internet: A study of native English-speaking editors' changes to texts written by Danish and Finnish professionals. *Journal of English for Academic Purposes, 3,* 341-359.